BEYOND HOPE

LETTING GO OF A WORLD IN COLLAPSE

DEB OZARKO

FOREWORD BY LOUISE LEBRUN

Published by: Deb Ozarko Publishing, debozarko.com
Cover and book design: Deb Ozarko
Printed by: CreateSpace, an Amazon.com company

Cover Image: Throughout the centuries, the hummingbird has become a spiritual symbol of note. Floating weightless in the air, she reminds us of the Soul, unencumbered by the density of our humanity. In some South American indigenous cultures, she is the symbol of resurrection. Her wings flutter in the shape of the infinity symbol. An appropriate metaphor for the content of this book. Beyond hope, lies eternity.

ISBN 978-0-9949845-5-5

Available from Amazon.com and other online stores.

To the courageous few who know that "it's over" does not apply to the Soul.

Contents

Foreword   2

Author's Note   9

Introduction   11

PART 1: ASLEEP:
The "Eyes Wide Open" Decimation of Earth and Soul   19

The Evolution of Knowing   20

The Big Lie   32

The American Dream   46

The Culture of Addiction   55

Breeding Ourselves into Oblivion   67

The Blessed Curse of Technology   87

Powerlessness Power   100

The Myth of a New Story   113

It's Over   128

The Fuck-it Point   142

PART 2: AWAKENING:
Living Fully, Loving Hard and Letting Go   151

Planetary Hospice   152

The Power of Grief   159

In Praise of Mortality   173

Return to Essence   183

The Paradox of Awakening   196

Being is More than Enough   218

Beyond Hope   234

Redefining Meaning   243

Activated Presence   254

Endnotes   265

Where to Go from Here   271

Gratitude   274

About the Author   275

Foreword

By Louise LeBrun

As I sit here—waiting to hear from my son and daughter-in-law if it's a boy or a girl—I feel the double-edged potential of this moment in time: is climate collapse to be our ending, or will it be what it takes to propel us to become more than we had ever thought imaginable for ourselves as a species? Perhaps our grandchildren would like to know.

Before we can begin a new conversation, we must be willing to move beyond the one we are in. Sometimes, that release demands a provocation that cannot be readily dismissed. We have to open our hand and release what it holds before there is room to reach out for something else. Something different. Something that is not shaped and molded by that which is already so firmly embraced. Far too often, the consequence for stubbornly and mindlessly holding firm and allowing fear to lead is to have that which our death-grip grasps so tightly, be eventually pried—one finger at a time—from our cold, dead hand. In these tumultuous times, letting go will not be an incremental journey. It is already demanding abrupt change from within us. This is the only response that can counteract the abrupt change of all that is unfolding around us.

Over many decades, I have come to trust a few simple precepts that shape the essentials of how I choose to live:

- Despite conflicting perceptions and judgments, there is always genius in what presents that will move me forward. Dare I look for it?
- In the face of what feels like evidence to the contrary, I know that

I am whole, I am unique and I am essential to my world—and so are you. Will I trust it?

- Contrary to (often brutal) opposing dogma, I know that I am a living godforce expressing through the tissue of the body, into a physical world. Will I choose from it?

It is through these lenses that I choose to consider my choices at this complex, pivotal and deeply defying time in our shared reality. Sooner rather than later, we will all have to choose—mindfully or otherwise—perhaps even coming to discover that choosing not to choose is indeed, a telling choice of its own that will shape our lives.

As much as I am blessed to call Deb Ozarko my friend, I am also old enough and wise enough to recognize a visionary and boundless LeaderSelf when my life is touched by one. In Deb, the ability to embrace clarity of both mind and being makes it possible for her to move beyond personal fears and dare to name what is presenting in full flow. Such is the road she travels, not for any reason other than her essential nature demands this level of commitment to her own inner truth, for its own sake.

This new offering from Deb is a profound act of love; a deep and intimate truth-telling that transcends social convention and seeks to lay bare the depth of respect, personal integrity and generosity of Spirit she holds for herself and others. Beyond a simple litany of all that is in collapse, Deb's perspective compels us to awaken to something beyond our abilities to tell stories about what is happening 'out there' and begin to turn the formidable power of our attention to what is happening 'in here' … inside, where we live. Inside, where we are already whole, unique and essential to our world. There, is where the power lies—just waiting for us to claim it.

In her latest work, Deb lays down the sword. The desire to do battle has fallen away, leaving visible the powerful embrace of a new and very different potential. Gone is the need to press against … the need to rise up against anything … given the recognition that it is all us. The surrender comes in being freed of the need to deny or wait or hope. What presents is the potential for a new direction—one that is driven by the moment of an inner truth rather than the voracious appetite of the next pressing story of an outer one. Only one of these will create a gateway for a different world.

Deb's book leaves no stone unturned in terms of what has been, what is and what might become. The continuum of 'reality' is well-traveled, with breadcrumbs left along the way for us—the readers—to carve out our own deeply personal and intimate path. It is impossible to read Deb's thoughts and not find ourselves on any given page; roiling inside ourselves at the stark realities and truths that she dares speak out loud—directly, without apology and in full voice. The essential first step is that we own what we already know and in so doing, free ourselves of the lingering cowardice that keeps us curled up in a ball in the darkest corners of our own mind … terrified to turn on the light that we might recognize who we have been. Yet, it is only in doing so that we will also be able to see who we might become.

This book, from beginning to end, is itself the offering of a process for change: significant and in-the-moment change, that can make way for a very different experience of Self that leads to a different experience of living in the moment … and of living our own lives.

Deb's gift through the pages of this creation presses us to consider that most difficult and avoid-at-all-costs question: "How do I choose to die? What does it mean for me to die? And how might I consider a mindful death as a new invitation to Life?"

Although some things are harder to absorb than others, it does not make them any less imperative or true. Perhaps more than anything else, Deb's book makes it impossible for us to ignore the degree to which our reality is shaped by what we are willing to entertain.

Our motto seems to be: if I close my eyes, it will no longer be there. Sadly, once past age three, we are left with a very different and indelible truth: not looking at it does not mitigate its impact on the context of my existence.

Impending collapse has increased the density and intensity of The Call to a far greater expression of our Being than that which we have been encouraged to allow. It is now more ragged and raw; it induces terror, and it is also pivotal and impossible to ignore. Eventually, we will all have to face our mortality. The question becomes: how will we choose to do that? Will there be Grace? Will there be the recognition of a higher order of expression of Being? Will we dare to face into it rather than run from it? Deb's book lays out before us a compelling journey of potential—and one that, if we choose it, can bring freedom at a time when bondage has become our nearest and dearest friend.

I know that I see through different eyes. My world has always been about process; about going beyond the content to notice the invisible frameworks that allow the content to continue to exist. What is the process that makes it possible for us to go forward from here? Telling the story over and over keeps us stuck in our fear and helplessness. What does it take for us to move out of our own fear? We have to do that for ourselves—no one else can do it for us.

We need to move away from telling the story (of the planet, our histories, our wounds, our excuses, etc.) and move toward becoming the unfolding story we desire—the one that will become the legacy we choose for those that will follow: our children, their children and beyond.

We are culturally conditioned—intergenerationally and via the process of parenting—to be incapable of acting on our own. We are pressed into service at an early age; socialized and entrained into our inability to oppose authority in any timely, immediate and significant way. We keep waiting for something outside of us to notice … to fix it … to make it better. It is not going to happen.

My personal belief? As I ponder the arrival of my first Grandchild, I know that I cannot allow myself to fall into despair on the cusp of the arrival of this new and precious godforce. I trust that there is genius in all of it and I know that without an even deeper trust in internal referencing, I will struggle to find my way through what is already reshaping reality. I think our greatest challenge, in this moment for all of us, is to discover how to become the version of our Selves that will allow us to hold two diametrically opposing truths (climate collapse and potential) in our reality, at the same time, without having to jettison one; without making one or the other wrong or impossible. We must discover now, within ourselves, how to become both willing and able to free ourselves of the deep and vast limitation of a binary system of thinking (good/bad, right/wrong) and expand into our innate ability to know and trust the intelligence of it all.

Yes, these times do require that we pay attention. Yes, these times do require that we be able to see and calibrate for and within the big picture; to connect the dots and trust what is revealed that we may make wise choices for ourselves and the people we love. And yes, these times do also require that we have an equally deep and abiding trust in our capacity for living in the moment we're in; and in finding the great joy that is always present.

We no longer have the luxury of time to lie to ourselves or each other. We can no longer defer or delay taking the long, hard look at who we have become. The greatest gift that accelerated climate change offers lies in the density and intensity of its press for us to notice how intimate it all is—and how it is about us as a force of collective consciousness that defines and shapes our very existence. It can be a propellant. It can move us into our own evolution in a non-incremental, non-linear way. As much as I have absolutely no idea what the outcome will be, I know one thing for sure: we will indeed, evolve!

We will become more than what we already are. And through it all the planet will simply do what She needs to do, without even a whisper of a thought of our wellbeing.

As strange as it may sound and in the midst of all that is to come, I think our greatest responsibility towards our children is to teach them to know joy. To find it within themselves and to honor their moments of delight. These are the moments that will shape who they become and will redefine the way they go about choosing and shaping the quality of their lives. In this will be found their ability to be conscious and aware; their ability to live in and for the organic 'now' rather than surrendering the seed of this creation to some intellectually defined outcome that may never come.

Our greatest challenge is not climate. Our most significant challenge is to become greater than who we have been that has allowed us to produce this outcome that now challenges our very existence. Impending climate collapse is not the problem—it is the compelling invitation to our own evolution that can no longer be ignored. The problem lies in the deepest, most intimate and closely guarded aspects of our Being: our internal and unexpressed truths. Courage and cowardice. Terror and the still point of peace. Exhaustion and surrender. Daring and compliance. Rage and release. And these are but a few of the many that await discovery and the full embrace of our willingness to engage.

Governments and politics are not designed to press us forward into our own greatness. They are designed to attend to low level, immediate problems, and fixes designed to appease and silence. It's up to us, outside of these systems, to choose a path for ourselves and support each other in exploring the mad and the messy, and not be so mesmerized and paralyzed by the many, many things that are beyond our control. What is within our control is our own evolution and the truth of it is: nothing is going to change until we evolve. It is a fool's game to be lulled into compliance by taking inventory and perpetual calibration of all that is already not working and is not going to take us where we need to go. Beyond a waste of our time, it is a waste of our lives.

In her deeply authentic and compelling way, Deb shares with us the path she has chosen for herself, "My life is a reflection of the level of commitment to my own evolution. ... I've let go of the world, and in this, despair is no longer a dominant factor in my life. Seeing the world through the eyes of the Soul detaches me from the illusion the masses believe to be real. It's not my story. It's not my choice. It's not my reality. In my reality, I choose life."

As Deb's words resonate, stop ... and consider for yourself what your path might be.

Educate yourself—and change your own mind. Do not leave such a life-determining moment to anyone else!

Think for yourself—chart your own course. We are fooling ourselves to think that waiting to follow is the easier path to a better future.

Choose meaningfully for yourself—create your own reality. Know that the legacy of this reality will shape the future of your children's children.

Live fully—now and from this one moment to the next. The example of your Life will be the encouragement for the people you love.

LOUISE LeBRUN
Founder of the WEL-Systems® Institute and Gramma-to-Be

Author's Note

Throughout this book, you will notice repetitive references to the human allegiance to the Big Lie, and the external repercussions of this unwavering devotion: from addiction, distraction, powerlessness, delusion, and denial; to overpopulation, rampant obesity, racism, sexism, homophobia, and speciesism; to wildfires, droughts, superstorms, epic floods, and Arctic meltdown. This repetition is deliberate. The only way to penetrate the profoundly conditioned intellect is through repetition, as this is what it knows best. Of course, even repetition is without guarantees when the intellect refuses to see beyond its conditioned rigidity. Ultimately, my words will either ring familiar, or not. So be it.

I also do not claim to have answers to the fatal predicament we are now living in. I do, however, know my own ongoing journey of Self evolution, and the urgency for reclamation of the Soul in these dire times. Through the combination of repetitive references to the brutal consequences of a collective allegiance to the Big Lie, and the raw revelations of my personal journey away from it, space is created for the reader to discover within their own Selves a way home, back to the Soul.

Introduction

"Many people, especially ignorant people, want to punish you for speaking the truth, for being correct, for being you. Never apologize for being correct, or for being years ahead of your time. If you're right and you know it, speak your mind. Speak your mind. Even if you are a minority of one, the truth is still the truth."

– GANDHI

This book began as something very different than what you now hold in your hands. Originally conceived as a testament to the "beautiful new world" my heart still believed was possible, the working title for this masterpiece was, *Revolution 3.0*.

Revolution 3.0 would be the ultimate transformation in consciousness that inspired the reclamation of wholeness leading us back to the very essence of who we are: the interconnected, non-separate Soul. It would be a heart-driven revolution that roused the collective from the coma of disconnect that has destroyed all that is sacred in our world. *Revolution 3.0* would inspire an epic awakening, activating what deep ecologist, Joanna Macy calls, "The Great Turning": a life-sustaining, Soul-inspired, utopian Earth that made manifest the words of John Lennon's beautiful song, "Imagine."

I duped myself.

In the last few years, it's become increasingly clear that the beautiful world of my imagination has always been nothing more than an elusive dream. With a collective of 7.6 billion (as of this writing) and growing exponentially, each child birthed to this world is enslaved by the cultural conditioning of those who preceded them. Because of a rigid allegiance to the story driving the endless perpetuation of this cultural programming, there is no way out. Every human bred to this world is born into an industrialized civilization that conditions them to be separate, and to therefore negate life through the commoditization and consumption of animals, Earth and the Soul. There is no way to stop an epidemic of madness when the global mind has so willingly embraced it.

The rapid acceleration of violent events around the globe: the uprising of religious fundamentalism, xenophobia, homophobia, speciesism, misogyny, societal breakdown, mass animal die-offs, the unparalleled disintegration of the cryosphere, and the rapid decay of our very biosphere; it all weighs heavy on my mind and heart. There is no denying that we are living through what scientists are calling, the 6th Great Extinction Event. These are indeed unprecedented times.

For the past few years, persistent premonitions of total ocean collapse have haunted me. These portents consistently present with two words: "It's over." The result is a dramatic about-face for this book.

We are living in a time of planetary hospice.

Regarding the message I'm now implored from within to share, I was recently criticized by someone who said to me, "that is some heavy stuff." I believe it's only "heavy" when denial is the primary modus operandi in life.

What's heavy is the voracious consumption of trillions of sentient land and aquatic beings for their flesh, maternal and menstrual secretions—every single year.

What's heavy is the persistent technological distraction that rules, and ruins our lives.

What's heavy is the frivolous obsession with narcissistic celebrity culture and blatant indifference about the plight of the planet.

What's heavy is the economic stratification of society into rich and poor.

What's heavy are wars against terror, wars against drugs, wars against cancer, wars against animals, wars against each other, and the war against Earth and Soul.

What's heavy is rampant overpopulation, starvation, poverty, homelessness, mass shootings, racism, xenophobia, transphobia, homophobia, speciesism, and generalized hate.

What's heavy is the widespread epidemic of depression, obesity, fear, anxiety, addiction, stress, and mental illness.

What's heavy is the uprising of sexism, misogyny, objectification, rape, and violence toward all that is feminine.

What's heavy is fracking, oil spills, plasticized oceans, overfishing, aquatic dead zones, mountain-top removal, tar sands, mining, smog-filled air, clearcut forests, wetland development, nuclear waste, polluted rivers, lakes, streams, and oceans: ecocide.

What's heavy is the numbing of our capacity to care because of our addictions to alcohol, pharmaceuticals, reality tv, pornography, gambling, social media, shopping, and conspicuous consumption.

What's heavy is the meltdown of the Arctic, raging floods, wildfires, droughts, superstorms, hurricanes, rain bombs, algae blooms, Medicanes, earthquakes, bomb cyclones, and our wholly fucked-up Earth climate.

What's heavy is the vortex of space garbage spinning around Earth, and continent-sized garbage patches choking the seas.

What's heavy is the arrogance that prevents us from owning our role in this mission of ruthless omnicide.

We've created it. We've ignored it. We've denied it. Earth is writhing in pain, and she's fed up. We are now experiencing the dramatic repercussions and getting precisely the cultural, civilizational, and ecological breakdowns we've created. The laws of the universe are inexorable. For every action, there is a reaction.

Action: Rape of Earth. Reaction: Runaway biosphere decay.

For every cause, there is an effect.

Cause: Human separation. Effect: Extinction of life.

We are caught between a rock and a hard place.

Karma dictates. We are so fucked.

Separating from, and destroying an intricate web of life while denying the dire reality of our collective choices is what's really, really heavy.

There is no more "don't worry, be happy, everything will be ok" world anymore.

It's over.

There is no Revolution 3.0. There never was. There never could be.

The words that follow speak to painful truths. At times, they are outright scathing.

I make no apologies for the disillusionment, betrayal, and disgust I feel for my species. I also make no excuses for giving a damn, and for loving life as much as I do.

The bottom line is that I don't write for comfort. I don't write to make friends. I don't write to preserve the status quo.

I write to rattle cages until the locks fall off. I write to demolish old paradigms. I write to give voice to the voiceless: animals, Earth, and the Soul. I write to make hearts bleed with grief, and heal from Self reclamation. I write to shock, anger, irritate, and destroy the ignorance of antiquated belief systems. I write to bring light to the critical conversations that are swept under the rug and spotlight the cracks in our consciousness that have separated us from life.

I write to puncture the bloated, arrogant, profoundly conditioned ego.

Michael Beckwith once said, "A bad day for the ego is a good day for the Soul." If my words irritate, ruffle, anger, and get under your skin, I've touched your Soul.

I write from the heart for the heart.

I am the irritating pattern interrupt that rattles your core and reminds you of the sacredness of life.

The words that follow channel my inner Kali: goddess of death, destroyer of the illusion of the separate self, and best friend to the Soul. To embrace the energies of Kali is to embrace the destruction of human conditioning for an expansion in consciousness. That is Kali's ultimate intention. Kali the destroyer demands our attention so that—whether we like it or not—we are transformed.

And so the words that follow are meant to provoke, agitate and shake the very foundation of cultural programming that holds the Soul hostage. I write without apology for the courageous few who are willing to claim their most profound truth by remembering who and what they are, even in—especially in—a world that is falling apart.

The words that follow shine a spotlight on the collective shadow so it no longer lurks in the moldy, dank darkness of the heavily programmed human mind. This is not a book about saving, fixing or changing the world. It's much too late for that. This is a book about radical personal evolution for the sake of Earth and the Soul—right now.

This book speaks unsparingly to painful truths. It's written for those who are no longer willing to deny what they already know in their hearts: that we have reached the end of the line. It's a book written for the warriors of truth who are ready to reclaim the Soul, let go of our broken world, and put love and compassion into action for no other reason than because that is the deepest truth of who they are.

When I write about the dire predicament we are now living in, I use the language of "our" and "we" throughout this book. I realize the implications of these sweeping generalizations. Because of our collective enslavement into a lifeless civilization that has negated the Soul, however, we are in this together. Like it or not, we are all plugged-in to a collective consciousness that is hell-bent on ruin. And so fire and flood, drought and deluge, displacement and death, are the extreme natural responses to the extremely unnatural conditions we have created.

At a time when there was not the scientific, technological or cultural separation from the Soul we now know, came prophecies of war, social unrest, cultural collapse, and ecological devastation. Every spiritual tradition spoke of the dire times we now find ourselves living in. By opening the lens of our awareness this truth becomes clear, and we can no longer rationalize the irrational, or deny the undeniable. It is upon us now.

I realize that warnings of "collapse," "end times," "apocalypse," and the "end of civilization" are often viewed as fringe, "doomer" or alarmist, but I also believe that on some level, we are all feeling it. To the naked eye, things may still look relatively "normal" as business-as-usual plods along, but lurking below the surface, many of us know something very different.

The Greek definition of apocalypse is "revelation," or "a lifting of the veil." As the truth of our Soul separation becomes more apparent with widespread breakdown, a collective uprising of resistance, fear, violence, and denial accompanies this revelation. Those who stand the most to lose in our harsh world are growing increasingly oppressive with their military-like rule. Cultivating a stable inner sanctuary is of great importance in these unprecedented times. The Soul is—and always has been—the only source of peace and power, regardless of how desperate things may become.

For the few who understand this on a visceral level, they will also recognize the urgency for their accelerated evolution. This urgency prompts an awakening to the only thing that can liberate the Soul from the confines of our conditioned humanity: acceptance.

This is not a book about science, history or philosophy. It's a book about letting go. Letting go of the need to define an outcome. Letting go of the fear of uncertainty. Letting go of false hope for an illusory future. Letting go of the dream for a collective awakening. Letting go of the stories of what may or may not be. Letting go of what once defined meaning. Letting go of the fear of mortality. Letting go of what we've been conditioned to believe ourselves to be. Letting go of our broken, dysfunctional world.

In most books that expose the horrors of our world there is often a final chapter that states, "if we can collectively pull ourselves together and do "Y," we can save ourselves *from ourselves*, and "X" will not happen." But words drenched in hopium succeed in only lulling us back to sleep. The implication is that somebody, somewhere, is somehow dealing with this monstrous mess and we need only make a few small adjustments in our personal lives to save our sinking ship. And of course, the worst stuff will never happen in our lifetime.

The reality is that time has run out. We are well past global warming, climate change and even anthropogenic climate disruption. We are in an irreversible state of runaway biosphere decay with no way back to what once was. And so I write this book with no hope-filled final chapter to lull anyone back to sleep. There is no to-do list filled with quick steps, painless fixes, and simple solutions. There is no strategic plan to perpetuate the belief in a happy ending anymore. The line in the sand has been drawn.

It's over.

This is a book written for those who are no longer willing to deny the reality of our broken, dying world. It's a book of painful truths. It's the book I've been hungering to read my entire life. A book free of lies, magical thinking, denial, and hopium. It is a book I could never find because I was meant to write it.

This book is not for the faint of heart. It highlights everything wrong with the culturally conditioned human, and how by separating ourselves from the natural world and the Soul, we have become our own executioners.

My purpose with this book is not to convince you of the apocalyptic times we are now living in, or of the biosphere collapse currently underway, or of what you already know inside yourself. The fact that this book is in your hands is indicative of a truth that already lives within. My purpose for this book is to highlight the inauthenticity of who and what we've allowed ourselves to become so that in these final times, we can awaken to, and embrace all of who and what we've always been meant to be. At the very least, let's make our final ride enlightening, compassionate, and caring. Let's at least *become* as a result of what now is.

In the end, my hope for those who heed these words is not to soften the blow by couching it in passive language, but to inspire presence, passion, and compassion, for no other reason than because that is the calling of the Soul—the most profound truth of what we are. Ultimately, my greatest desire for this book is to break the cycle of samsara once and for all so that we never incarnate among such lunacy again.

NOTE: When I reference "the Soul," I refer to the energetic, non-physical whole of what we are as life-force expressing through matter in a physical world. The Soul knows no separation: from animals, birds, fish, plants, trees, races, ages, genders, etc.

IMPORTANT: When delving into the depths of this book, it is important to remember one thing: breathe.

The power of breath is the gateway to truth and transformation.

PART 1: ASLEEP

The "Eyes Wide Open" Decimation of
Earth and Soul

The Evolution of Knowing

"Let me tell you why you're here. You're here because you know something. What you know, you can't explain. But you feel it. You felt it your entire life. That there's something wrong with the world. You don't know what it is, but its there. Like a splinter in your mind, driving you mad."

– Morpheus, character in the movie, *The Matrix*

I entered the world on a chilly autumn evening in November 1963. I was born at the Grace Hospital in Ottawa, Canada. My entrance was not without drama. In the ultimate irony, the umbilical cord of life became the umbilical cord of near-death. Within moments of strangulation, and by the grace of the Soul, I drew my first breath.

Grace: a word that has defined my life, and a word I'm increasingly learning to embrace in these uncertain, tumultuous times.

Since my rousing emergence into this world, I've had a passionate love for Earth—for Gaea. I've consciously participated in the healing of Earth through ongoing activism, as well as mindful personal choices and actions. Although I'm hardly perfect, I have a tireless hunger for living as close to my essence as possible. With this in mind, I'm always willing to examine the conditioning that leads to inconsistencies in my life. I realized early on that this is the only way to express the infinite, immaterial, interconnected truth of *what* I am in a world of physical matter: the Soul.

Accompanying my love for Earth is a heightened awareness that allows me to feel and see what most people refuse.

My life has been defined by a "knowing". I live with an amplified sensitivity to energy which implores me to insulate from the claustrophobic nature of human civilization, and liberate myself in the expansiveness of nature. My "knowing" is directly connected to Earth.

I've never fit in, and quite frankly, I've never bothered either. Instinctively, I knew that "fitting" was not only wrong, it was destructive to the Soul.

Since childhood, I've known that something was amiss with our world. I had no words for it, but the feelings in my body and heart were unmistakable: Something was very, very wrong.

From early on, I couldn't understand why people hated Earth so much. How they could mindlessly toss garbage into rivers, lakes, streams, oceans, forests, parks, and meadows. I couldn't understand why people were so disconnected from such breathtaking beauty.

I could never understand the ease with which people destroyed mosses, ferns, fungi, trees, and entire forests. How they could swing their axes, drive their chainsaws and bulldozers, and saturate Earth with their poisons and pesticides with such blatant indifference. Did they not know how these mindless actions impacted the natural world; and the insects, birds, and animals who called these places home? As a young child, I knew these actions to be wrong. Were the adults who engaged in these destructive behaviors not supposed to be smarter than me?

I was confused about why so many people were fearful, indifferent or uncaring toward animals. Even more confusing was why most animals were "food," others were pests, and a select few were pets.

I wanted to know who made up the rules that pigs, chickens, turkeys, lambs, and cows were edible; but dogs, cats, hamsters, robins,
sparrows, and budgies were not. Nobody would tell me why, nor did
they seem to want to explore the answers for themselves. More importantly, I wanted to know why people believed in the stories of edible animals versus inedible animals, and humans versus nature in the
first place.

Why did men like my father, uncles, teachers, and male school
friends believe that "manliness" was defined by the consumption of
copious quantities of dead animal flesh? Who taught them this silly
tale? And why were they naive enough to believe it?

I could never understand why people yelled at each other, fought
with each other and said mean things behind their backs. Why was it
so hard for humans to be honest with each other and just get along?

I couldn't understand why people didn't care about what mattered, and why they felt so righteous in their entitlement to be
so indifferent.

Why was there so much fear? Why did people need borders, walls,
fences, property, bolts, locks, keys, alarms, rules, regulations, "mine"
and "yours"? I grew out of the "mine/yours" mindset early on. Why
did adults confine themselves to such infantile thoughts?

Why were stupid things important, and important things stupid?

Why? Why? Why? The persistent questions of a curious young
mind who did not suffer fools gladly.

Nothing about this world made any sense to me. I could not understand why humans were so fearful of the truth.

Something within me has always felt completely at odds with, and
out of resonance with the rest of the world. Intuitively I knew that
how I was being taught to live, and who I was being trained to be in
this world, was flawed. I refused to conform. I would not comply. I
had to know why.

The red pill of truth has always been my medicine of choice. As a child, my father labeled me, "smart ass" because I challenged everything, including the petty jealousies he projected on my mother. He despised this.

I've consistently been able to see what others can't see, hear what others tune out, feel what others negate, and express in ways that bring discomfort to the minds of the deeply conditioned. A relentless hunger for truth has always driven my life. From early on, I was able to see through the illusion of the "reality" that defines our fucked-up world.

By the tender age of seven, I knew—with steadfast conviction—that I would never bring a child into this world. In an act of youthful defiance, I boldly declared this deep truth to my father. He insisted I document this declaration to show me in later years, the error of my beliefs. With pencil and paper in hand, I complied. "I WILL NEVER HAVE CHILDREN," I brazenly wrote in my childlike scrawl (he kindly helped with the spelling). My love for Earth trumped all. Instinctively, I already knew the burden of humanity on Earth. I knew that every child born to the world was a recipe for ecological disaster. Even if I were to change my mind for some foolish reason, I knew the odds were slim that I could rear an enlightened child in an unenlightened world. The weight of the collective consciousness was too heavy for all but the strongest of hearts and minds. I could not—and would not—add to the burden of Earth with another mouth to feed, another consumptive mindset ... another human being conditioned into—and seduced by—the ugly monster I've come to know as the paradigm of separation.

I had an innate resistance to dogma. Although we were not a religious family, I threw inconsolable tantrums on the few occasions I was forced to experience Sunday school. I despised the conformity of Brownies (the precursor to Girl Guides) and made my mother's life a living hell until she conceded that it was not meant to be. Groupthink was a terribly wrong thing for my wild spirit.

I abruptly ended the consumption of animal flesh at the age of 12. In my heart, there was no silencing the haunting cries of the ghosts in our destructive human machine. I could no longer stomach the dismembered, rotting corpses of living beings who wanted no more than me: respect, equality, freedom, and life. My father fought me. I won. Because of his authoritative manner, I learned early on how to fight for truth by speaking out, and standing up for what I knew in my heart to be right.

I abandoned university when restrictions were placed on my freedom to study what moved my spirit. The rigidity of a standardized line of thought conflicted with my need for fluidity and independence. So I let it all go, bought a backpack and a one-way ticket to Europe and immersed myself in the school of life.

My European travels were not about museums, galleries, and culture; they were about savoring the beautiful wild landscapes of Gaea. The Swiss, Austrian and Italian Alps; the Bavarian forests; the lush, rolling hills of Great Britain; the French countryside; and the pristine Mediterranean beaches of Spain, Portugal, France, and Greece.

I traveled the Caribbean, crewing on sailboats and becoming one with the ocean I loved so dearly. I had no interest in what others my age held in regard: restaurants, bars, and nightclubs. I preferred swimming in the crystal clear waters of an ocean still teeming with life, and sleeping under the stars in the open cockpit of a gently rocking sailboat.

For much of my youth, I was radically different. In my heightened sensitivity, I saw, felt and experienced what the masses could not. I cared about life in a lifeless world. I cared about compassion in an indifferent world. I cared about truth in a world of deception. I pondered life in ways that few could comprehend. I lived in an alternate reality, surrounded by a civilization in denial.

I sometimes wondered if I was not of this world ... an alien perhaps. My grandparents seemed to know better. Their profound love for animals and the natural world nourished mine. Through their loving guidance, I realized that my differences were my strengths. In a world that coveted the highly conditioned intellect, my allegiance was to the Soul. They made it clear to me that this was the way to truly *live*.

I have always felt safer in the natural world than in cities and suburbs, far removed from the noise, busyness, anxiety, impatience, fear, and judgment of humanity. Into the nurturing safety of the trees, wind, rain, ferns, mosses, mushrooms, and the animal kingdom I so dearly love. Nature and animals never pretend to be other than what they authentically are. They never lie.

My outdoor adventures have brought remarkable experiences with animals, insects, birds and sea creatures of many different kinds. I've never felt superior or held fear or malice in my heart. I've only known reverence. I firmly believe that my choice to remain connected to Earth has allowed for this sacred, unspoken trust.

For most of my life, I've moved against the dominant flow of consciousness. While the collective has mindlessly chosen to zig, I've preferred to zag. It's a lonely place to stand and one that doesn't garner much support, but it has shown me the important things in life: equality, integrity, respect, autonomy, simplicity, compassion, presence, and truth. I've often wondered why this was so hard for so many to understand.

It wasn't until my early 20's that I discovered the answer. I became aware of a collective psychosis of which I seemed to have immunity— a psychosis deeply rooted in the belief of human superiority over animals, the natural world, and the Soul.

In so many ways I've struggled with the myth of human superiority. I've longed to live in a world that feels more, cares more and loves more. I confess to holding a lifelong disdain for the toxic civilization deemed "real"; a world that has separated the masses from life, love, and truth.

For much of my life, I was ashamed to be a member of a species steeped in such hatred for the sacred. I wondered why a species so unconscious to itself was gifted such a beautiful planet to destroy. It baffled me how humans could defy the laws of nature for so long and get away with it. I wondered why the few who loved Earth so profoundly were forced to co-exist with the inculcated masses who didn't give a damn.

Even though it seemed that everyone around me was hell-bent on destroying life, I couldn't live as if life didn't matter—even if I was the last one standing who cared.

I became an activist for animals and Earth. As I began exploring more of the truths so skillfully hidden from view, I was enraged. Behind the culturally accepted lies was a bloody, horrific sight. I wanted for everyone to see what I could see; know what I knew, and feel what I felt. I wanted to shout from the rooftops for everyone to wake up and stop the madness! Where I could so clearly see what was blatantly wrong, few others could. Even fewer cared. They were too entranced by the illusion.

Humans are a prolific species with no natural predators and a voracious appetite for consumption at every level: mentally, emotionally and physically. In my birth year of 1963, 3.2 billion humans were gobbling up Earth. In the short 50 plus years of my lifetime, we've more than doubled ourselves, with over 7.6 billion humans rapidly devouring what remains of the planet. Our global crises have escalated in direct proportion to our runaway population growth. Collective awakening has always been our only salvation as a species, but this has proven to be an impossible task with the explosion of culturally programmed humans now infecting the planet.

When I finally allowed myself to see the truth of this bleak reality, I was disheartened. In 2010 however, I had a paradigm shift that revealed to me the unifying power of personal evolution for the greater whole of life.

The pivotal death of my mother in that year and the painful dark night of the Soul that followed, inspired a profound hunger to know myself as Soul embodied. The deeper I delved into my evolution, the clearer my inner vision became, and the more I felt myself letting go of the material world.

I began to see the writing on the wall: our world, our biosphere, our planet is in a massive state of collapse.

Admittedly, collapse has been in my consciousness for much of my life. I've always known something was terribly wrong with a species that so flippantly—and so callously—normalized the abnormal to preserve an inert, unyielding and destructive status quo. I knew this could never end well.

When I look back on my life, I see the undercurrent of knowing that has been with me since my earliest years. This "knowing" has never left me. As I grew older, however, it receded into the background of my consciousness so I could do my part to "save the world," and live some semblance of a "normal" life. But in the autumn of 2014, I was struck with repetitive premonitions about ocean collapse that made it entirely clear to me that we've crossed the line. Two words accompanied these warnings: It's over.

There were many times in my childhood when I remember sobbing to my mother in gut-wrenching despair, "I just want to live long enough to see the healing of Earth." Little did I know the profound truth of these painful words.

I've known about these times of collective demise all along. With my recent startling remembrance, all remnants of resistance dissolved and I finally accepted a reality that I've worked my entire life to change.

I confess that as I share my story, I observe myself resisting the desire to self-edit to not cause despair. As much as my inner truth is painful to absorb, it does no good for me to edit myself for fear of the ridicule and judgment that dominates our world. In speaking my truth, I allow space for those who are no longer willing to silence their own truth about these profound times. I now know that I'm far from alone.

As the destruction, violence, and decimation of the sacred continues unabated, the world becomes increasingly foreign to me. I often feel like I'm living in an elaborate science fiction movie where I know, and a handful of others know, yet the masses are so stupified by the illusion of the dominant reality that they're incapable of seeing beyond the trivialities of their conditioned minds. I now live on a different timeline; an aggressive timeline that continually accelerates as I allow myself to move deeper into acceptance of what I already know is.

As I move through my fifth decade of life on this Earth, I find myself feeling increasingly alone. Despite the pain of personal loss, it's not the deaths of family and friends that incites my sorrow. It's the heartbreaking aloneness that comes from the obliteration of birds, fish, wildlife, forests, mountains, and life in the ocean. It comes from men with their high-powered rifles, crossbows and fish hooks destroying the sacred for self-serving bloodlust, "trophies" and "sport." It comes from plasticized oceans, fishing farms, and massive nautical fleets that indiscriminately annihilate life. It comes from the absence of biodiversity and birdsongs decimated by men with their chainsaws, bulldozers, explosives, machines, highways, and trucks. It comes from the feedlots, battery cages, gestation crates, veal crates, and slaughterhouses that explode with suffering and blood. It comes from endless wars, smokestacks, nuclear waste, oil spills, tar sands, and dirty transport ships that bring us an endless array of throwaway trinkets to feed our addictive, psychotic ways.

Soon there will be nothing left but us, the most destructive species ever known. The damage we engender is eating us alive, no matter who we are, what we do, or where we live.

Contrary to indoctrinated belief, we are not more valuable than any other living being. In fact, it's quite the opposite. No earthworms and we perish. No bees and we are gone. No trees and we suffocate. No living ocean and we fry. Biologist Jonas Salk summarized it well: "If all the insects were to disappear from the earth, within 50 years all life on earth would end. If all human beings disappeared from the earth, within 50 years all forms of life would flourish." What a profoundly tragic statement.

Whatever the future may bring, in my heart I know that life will prevail. In the billions of years of her existence, and in the expanse of her great wisdom, Earth has healed from several extinction events that have preceded our own. I believe the scars of humanity will persist for several million, perhaps billions of years to come. My allegiance, however, is to the healing power of Gaea. In this, I have faith.

Authenticity requires that I give voice to my truth. Whether you agree or disagree with me is unimportant. If you are courageous enough to be reading this book, I know we can both agree that we are living in unprecedented times.

Throughout this book, I do not paint a false picture of myself as a lover of humanity. My greatest pain and heartbreak has always been at the hands of my species. I do, however, paint a picture of myself as a lover of the Soul—the interconnected, infinite, non-separate aspect of what we all are: human and non-human alike.

I don't write this book to offer false hope or a trail of despair. I write it to shine a light on a civilization gone wrong, and what we've allowed ourselves to become as a result. This book offers reminders that reach into the heart of who we are so that we may choose to think, behave and act in alignment with what we have always been meant to be.

As the Great Dying unfolds before us, I refuse to be a silent witness. From global social unrest to nuclear annihilation, to pollution soiling every inch of the planet (and beyond), to mass animal and plant extinction, to runaway biosphere decay; many powerful forces are converging to create unprecedented chaos and breakdown. For the longest time, Earth changes have been incremental. But incremental becomes exponential at disorienting speed when rot overtakes the foundation. With our deluded mindset of superiority, we have reached a point where we are now eating our tail. In eating our tail, we eventually disappear.

Ultimately the choice to awaken is highly personal, which means there are no guarantees. The greatest power in choosing is in knowing that we have choice in the first place. Ironically, we've had it all along. Choosing from the Soul is the ultimate act of revolution in our collapsing, dying world.

These are deeply spiritual times.

I've done everything I can to serve a better world with the desperate hope that I would live to see the more beautiful world my heart once believed was possible. It was a lovely dream.

There is no new world. It's over.

We are living in significant times as the biosphere collapses at dizzying speed, and we hurtle toward the dystopian world that was once only the theme of science fiction movies. As tragic as this is, it can also be a profound time for awakening to the Soul.

Holding this in my consciousness, my devotion to living awake and present is unwavering. Few on this planet are willing to be sacrificed by Gaea, for Gaea. I am one. This is the path of the Soul warrior. This is the path to liberation.

The Big Lie

"A lie is a lie even if everyone believes it. The truth is the truth even if nobody believes it."

– David Stevens

We are born into an elaborate Lie.

Long before we can shape our world, the world has firmly shaped us. What we are shaped to become, is no accident. Almost everything we are taught to believe originates from the Lie. We are shaped by our parents, who were shaped by the very same Lie as the generations who preceded them. How far back this fable goes is anyone's guess. The details have been cunningly edited to support those who benefit most from the ongoing perpetuation of the long-standing Lie.

Although our arrival into the world is arbitrary, the world that receives us is not. We are born into the expectations of our culturally programmed parents. In most cases, a single thought is the prompt for our emergence. Rarely is this thought conscious, however. More often than not, it is powered by a dominant, yet covert cultural expectation to self-replicate and carry forth the Lie.

The lives that we lead, the beliefs, values, and attitudes we hold, and the identity of who we are shaped to become, are founded by those labeled, "mom" and "dad." Who they are is who we are. Our starting point in life is one of helplessness and total reliance on external forces over which we have no control.

We have evolved to pay close attention to our parents and absorb everything they feed us for the first few years of our lives: physically, mentally and emotionally. By our very nature we are trusting and apt to be less skeptical than we should be. We tend to accept the foundational assumptions of the culture we are born into without dispute. The key to evolution and progress in any civilization, however, is to ask questions. But questions are threatening to a worldview reliant on groupthink for its sustenance.

Dominant forces within a Soul-destroying civilization have engineered the context in which we are born. The environment we grow up in paints a version of reality that influences the beliefs we carry forth for the entirety of our lives. So wholly do we learn to identify with these mental constructs, that we detach from our very essence within the first few years of life. We are not born free. In fact, in taking our freedom for granted, we extinguish all possibility of ever attaining it.

We have bought into a dangerous story; a misperception of truth that perpetuates a collective consciousness that blindly violates, degrades and destroys the web of life that sustains existence on Earth.

Adolf Hitler designed a propaganda technique called "The Big Lie." The source of the Big Lie technique is found in a passage extracted from James Murphy's translation of Hitler's autobiography, *Mein Kampf*. It reads:

> … In the Big Lie there is always a certain force of credibility; because the broad masses of a nation are always more easily corrupted in the deeper strata of their emotional nature than consciously or voluntarily; and thus in the primitive simplicity of their minds they more readily fall victims to the Big Lie than the small lie, since they themselves often tell small lies in little matters but would be ashamed to resort to large-scale falsehoods. It would never come into their heads to fabricate colossal untruths, and they would not believe that others could have the impudence to distort the truth so infamously. Even though

the facts which prove this to be so may be brought clearly to their minds, they will still doubt and waver and will continue to think that there may be some other explanation. For the grossly impudent Lie always leaves traces behind it, even after it has been nailed down, a fact which is known to all expert liars in this world and to all who conspire together in the art of lying.[1]

Hitler went on to say, "Make the Lie big, make it simple, keep saying it, and eventually, they will believe it."[2]

A colossal untruth is the basis for the elaborate Lie we are born into: that we—species homo sapien sapiens—are superior to, and therefore separate from, the laws of nature that bind all things living to an intricate web of life on a complex, living organism, within an ever-evolving universe. We have separated from the Soul. This Big Lie is a most insane and destructive fallacy.

Humans are a complex, multi-faceted species. The consciousness that motivates us is a dichotomy of material, mortal, conditioned, separate self; and immaterial, immortal, intuitive, non-separate Soul. The aspect of consciousness we choose to nurture molds our character, and ultimately determines our destiny.

Collectively, we are engineered by all cultural systems to think in only one direction: separation. The result is a world that reinforces our alienation, denial, entitlement, fear, apathy, despair, arrogance, and ignorance by hapless design. Ubiquitous amnesia drives the story we believe to be real, suppressing our consciousness and preventing the remembrance of the whole of who and what we authentically are.

In this great forgetting, we have morphed into a 7.6 billion strong collective operating outside the laws of nature, pillaging a complex living organism; stagnant in our consciousness, in an ever-evolving universe. The imperious inertia of this mass identity portends a short-term future for our species.

Dogma is the process for managing large collectives. Every system and institution in our civilization is under its influence. From the dogma of gender, parenting, appearance, and education; to the dogma of profession, religion, health, economics, law, media, medicine, and culture. The rules for functioning and behaving like a "normal" citizen within the Lie of our dominant civilization pummel the psyche from every direction. Because we willingly comply with the dogma of each of these systems and institutions, we've built a story around them and call it, "truth." This consensual "reality" traps us in unconscious behaviors, reckless actions, and an ignorant, arrogance that knows no bounds.

Everything about our civilization was designed to dumb us down and polarize us to sustain an inert status quo. With the rigid mindset of separation, the masses are compliant with an unwavering allegiance to a destructive, Soul destroying machine. Believing this purgatory to be real, they blindly proceed—against overwhelming evidence of cultural collapse and ecocide—with business-as-usual. Because compliance is so highly rewarded, the Big Lie remains firmly intact.

In this collective ignorance, we are now so enmeshed in the Big Lie that we know nothing else. When a story is told long enough, it becomes real to its recipients. For generations, the Big Lie has grown, morphed and expanded into an enormous monster with a life-force of its own—a dysfunctional illusion that has entirely devoured the human psyche. In our comatose haze, we've abandoned our role as participants within the web of life, and are now captive to our separation sickness. In the delirium of this deathly illness, we've traded in the sacred web of life for a dystopian web of lies.

The story of separation has enormous inertia. It spins its web around the mind and pulls it relentlessly toward consumption, indifference, and powerlessness. To resist it is to suffer the wrath of the dominant collective who have been programmed to normalize the abnormal by denigrating the sacred. Fear of truth is the driver of this unconscious behavior. The Soul is the most feared truth of all.

In the delusion of our separation, the mutated human psyche has devolved us into a uniquely violent species. By far, humans are the most violent animal on the planet. We are the supreme predator in the air, the water and on land. We kill mercilessly, with nary a thought. In the 20th century alone, we slaughtered more than 200 million of our own kind[3]. And while other predators rarely kill us, we kill them—and every other living being—on an unfathomable scale.

According to the website, Animal Equality, "Over 56 billion farmed animals are killed every year by humans. These shocking figures do not even include fish and other sea creatures whose deaths are so great they are only measured in tonnes."[4]

The numbers become exponential when we factor in the millions of animals killed every year in shelters, research labs, and animal-slavery enterprises such as circuses, rodeos, zoos, and marine parks; as well as fur farms, trapping, and those animals labeled "nuisance", "pests" and "game" to be slaughtered, poached and hunted.

A widespread meme exists that states, "If humans were slaughtered at the same rate animals are, our species would be extinct in less than two weeks." Our cruel indifference toward animals and each other with our thoughts, beliefs, behaviors, choices, and actions means we all have blood on our hands.

The state of the world in which we live is indicative of the fact that our violent, separated nature has prevailed. It comes as no surprise when we are mindlessly fed heaping portions of violence from early on. Violence infects our history. Our games are violent; our entertainment is violent, our sports are violent, our books are violent, our news is violent, our heroes are violent; even our gods are violent. This incessant violence desensitizes us and puts us into an emotional-psychological state that makes it impossible to relate to the natural world and each other. The most insidious form of violence, however, lurks at the end of our forks multiple times daily as we consume the dismembered, rotting corpses, ovulations, and maternal secretions of helpless, sentient beings. In separating ourselves from life, we willingly consume all the suffering, terror, and violence that brings this profound misery to our plates.

By the time we grow into full "adulteration," we are so contaminated—physically, mentally and emotionally—that we accept violence as the norm. Consider how violence—from judgment, blame and shame; to incarceration, slaughter, and war—is the "go-to" solution for every problem in our world. Peace on Earth is as foreign a concept as traveling to alternate space dimensions.

Humanity's capacity to envision and invent new ways to destroy life appear boundless. There are no limits to our cruelty toward animals, Earth and each other. The separated mind always prefers familiarity and desire, over truth and compassion. It will even defend its familiar, desirable actions using rationale and reason, regardless of how cruel and insane they may be.

Our dominant narrative worships money over life, power over compassion, competition over cooperation, hubris over humility, war over peace, and fear over love.

It wasn't always this way. For much of our existence, we were like other animals operating seamlessly within the web of life, not removed from the natural order. Something changed along the way that separated us from the web of life—and the Soul—however.

There are many stories about how, when and why we chose to adopt the Big Lie and forget who and what we are, but this book is not about speculative history. It's about the epic Lie that brings us to the place we now stand, squarely facing the near-term end of life on Earth.

Louise Leakey summarized it well in her 2008 TEDx talk, *A Dig for Humanity's Origins*, "...The question now is, 'Who are we?' We're certainly a polluting, wasteful, aggressive species with a few nice things thrown in perhaps, but for the most part we're not particularly pleasant at all. We have a much larger brain than our ape ancestors. Is this a good evolutionary adaptation or is it going to lead us to be the shortest-lived hominid species on planet Earth?"[5]

Our fear of reclaiming the Soul perpetuates our ongoing war against Earth. Our refusal to evolve beyond our conditioning is our refusal to awaken to what we authentically are. Remaining captive to the antiquated belief systems of our parents and preceding generations, is what brings us to the critical place we stand today.

Separation is a learned identity. It is taught to us by our parents, relatives, friends, schools, churches, media, politics, health-care system, corporations, and every other cultural institution. Through the teachings of our fallen civilization, we are altered by corruption and greed. Whenever we make anything outside of ourselves more important than the Soul, we are bound to separation. The very institutions that hold us captive to separation all suffer from the same fatal affliction: they have pursued power and growth to the point of insanity, and have made money, consumption, and destruction more valuable than life.

We are now living in what scientists call, the Anthropocene epoch—the age of humans—or the era of human-centric planetary destruction.

Australian professor of Public Ethics, Clive Hamilton articulates this destructive era in his article, *The Great Climate Silence*, where he states:

> After 200,000 years of modern humans on a 4.6 billion-year-old Earth, we have arrived at a new point in history: the Anthropocene. The change has come upon us with disorienting speed. It is the kind of shift that typically takes two or three or four generations to sink in.

Our best scientists tell us insistently that a calamity is unfolding, that the life-support systems of the Earth are being damaged in ways that threaten our survival. Yet in the face of these facts, we carry on as usual.

Most citizens ignore or downplay the warnings; many of our intellectuals indulge in wishful thinking; and some influential voices declare that nothing at all is happening, that the scientists are deceiving us. Yet the evidence tells us that so powerful have humans become, that we have entered this new and dangerous geological epoch, which is defined by the fact that the human imprint on the global environment has now become so large and active that it rivals some of the great forces of nature in its impact on the functioning of the Earth system.[6]

According to the story we've been told, modern humans have been around for some 300,000 years (according to recent studies), or less than .01% of Earth's timeline. In this small sliver of time, we have left an unfathomable impact on the planet. Our impact has been most significant in the 200 years of our industrialized civilization, where we have violently disrupted 4.6 billion years of natural history on planet Earth. We've placed ourselves so ruthlessly at the center of things that we no longer see the beauty of life, but only how we can profit from it in ways that serve our selfish desires. Everything around us suffers from our existence. We leave massive footprints everywhere we go. The more our desires grow, the more complex our destructive technologies become. No matter what we do, our dominant civilization is destroying the natural world around it. We spit out polluting materials in all directions: into the air, the soil, the rivers, streams, lakes, and ocean. In the hubris of this separation madness, we seem to believe that we can carry on with our frenzy of growth and consumption without consequence.

The prevailing human mindset is not one that supports life. Rather, it is meticulously trained to defend the Big Lie and the lifeless civilization spawned from it. This delusional outlook paints a dismal future for life on Earth.

Most humans have checked out of the reality of this grim truth in favor of the "realities" they live through their televisions and portable devices. The dominant culture distracts our attention by reinforcing the misconceptions that money will make us happy, drugs will keep us healthy, weapons will keep us safe, looks will bring us success, and endless information—regardless of its source—will up the ante on our smarts. Majority consciousness dictates the power of these fallacies. Our separation is boundless in its disconnect from life.

We've separated ourselves from the entire natural world. We clearcut, frack, blow up, mine, pollute, poison, rape, and pillage Earth as if her capacity for abuse can be indefinitely sustained.

We've separated ourselves from the non-human animal kingdom. We enslave, cage, domesticate, rape, hunt, breed, poach, exploit, torture, trap, imprison, skin, and slaughter with reckless abandon as we declare to ourselves our moral superiority.

We've separated ourselves from our physical bodies. We suppress, oppress, overfeed, starve, distrust, drug, cosmetically alter, disfigure, dismember, medicate, numb, and silence the great wisdom within.

We have both the technology and the understanding of how to use it to destroy our entire world with the push of a single button.

With our hubristic sense of superiority, we've altered the course of the most sacred gift of all: life. Cloning, genetic engineering, artificial intelligence, geoengineering and other such Franken-creations threaten the very fabric of existence. As Jeff Goldblum said in the movie, *Jurassic Park*, "Scientists were so preoccupied with whether they could, that they didn't stop to think if they should."

With an arrogant sense of entitlement, we ransack the sea and put back plastic, sewage, oil, and an endless stream of garbage. As Gaea cries for mercy, we denude her forests, blow up her mountains, develop her coastlines, alter her creations, poison her air, soil, and water, and blindly reproduce ourselves with no thought for the future. Who do we think we are? What have we allowed ourselves to become? How can we possibly believe we can continue this way without massive repercussions for life on Earth?

Earth is filled with trash. The oceans are filled with trash. Outer space is filled with trash. Our bodies are filled with trash. Our minds are filled with trash. Our contempt for the sacred knows no limits.

The web of life is unraveling before our eyes, and the masses are too blind to see. We've become cynical, jaded and apathetic to the overwhelming chaos of our world, so much so that we simply tune it out.

We now find ourselves on a runaway train hurtling wildly down the tracks, barely holding its course; powered by a Big Lie that fuels the avaricious consumption that eats at the very heart, flesh, and blood of the planet. As the failing train hurtles wildly on, we are quickly reaching the end of the line.

In the sickness of our separation, we have become so lost in the hall of mirrors that we have lost our sanity and given away the Soul to systems of exploitation and manipulation; institutions of deceit and domination; and structures of delusion and disconnection. The civilization we have created for our very survival is killing us.

Our civilization does not, and will never care about life. It was created to replicate a virus that can only be destroyed by itself. It was designed for self-perpetuating growth, expansion, and consumption at all costs—including the destruction of its very host. Its only intelligence is its own survival. Appealing to the "better nature" of our civilization is futile because it has no conscience. There is no reasoning with it. There is no fixing it. There is no changing it. The inner work of self-evolution is the only way to stop feeding it. But self-evolution is painful, so the masses don't bother.

We are so much more than what we've allowed ourselves to become, yet denied the connection and meaning that nourishes what we authentically are, we've grown small, stunted and invasive in the poisoned soil of our dominant civilization. The problems of our world are more profound than the crises of our altered planet, endless wars, rapacious consumption, human supremacy, judgment, fear, racism, sexism, ageism, ableism, heterosexism, speciesism, and so on. The most significant crisis on Earth is the crisis in consciousness that closes our hearts and holds our minds firmly in the grip of separation.

Are we authentically predatory? Competitive by nature? Are we the selfish, materialistic, utilitarian, violent, fear-filled, domineering, arrogant breeders with an insatiable libido and addiction to consumption that we've allowed ourselves to become? If that's who we are, we've been doomed from the very beginning.

Despite overwhelming evidence pointing in that direction, I don't believe this to be so. Our inflated sense of self-importance has flatlined our consciousness and distorted our perception of who and what we are. In the hubris of this demented identity, we've designed a one-way world of take, take, take. But the isolation that accompanies this worldview is a heavy burden to bear. We are aching for authentic relationships—commencing with our Selves. Seeping through our separation is the quiet voice of the atrophied Soul pleading for liberation.

On a deep, primal level, we know that we are connected to—not separate from—the web of life. Our animal bodies formed by Earth itself, desire and require authentic relationship to the world: to the water, air, and soil. To the animals, birds, trees, plants, and fellow humans that comprise the complex living system in which we were born.

Most of us have no sense of community where we can feel safe. In our civilization, there are so many systems in place to prevent us from connecting to what matters most: integrity, equality, respect, unity, compassion, life, and truth. Our consumptive civilization thrives on this disconnect because it's easy to sell stuff to people who are lost to their Selves. The endless sea of advertisements, billboards, stores, and shopping malls are filled with bandages for the wounds from our Soul-separation.

When our minds are captive to the Big Lie, we lose our relational nature and feel compelled to control everything around us. In the grip of this fear, we forget that mutual, reciprocal relationships are possible, believing instead that all relationships are based on hierarchy, power, competition, and domination. When we look at our civilization, this is undoubtedly the case. This belief only serves to perpetuate our fears, however, so we become too frightened to relate to our neighbors, the forests, the oceans, and non-human animals, for instance. This fear is the very root of our separation. It enslaves us in the superiority complex that drives us to dominate, exploit, commoditize, hate, and destroy.

When we look to nature in its unaltered state, we see the triumph of diversity, and the celebration of uniqueness. We see the intricate interconnection of each plant and animal species and how they symbiotically support each other in life-affirming ways. This relational interconnection is the sacred in action. It is truth made manifest.

Every species on the planet has evolved into existence over the 4.6 billion year history of Earth. It has taken the entire history of planetary evolution to bring forth the diversity and complexity of our biosphere. This incredible story is utterly awe-inspiring. But in the sickness of our collective separation, we have single-handedly catalyzed, the 6th Great Extinction Event.

Species come and go, but in mass extinction events, species vanish in droves. At this time, we are losing thousands of species annually by our own hand—perhaps far more than we are able to discover. Ironically, most humans are unable to think of themselves at the level of a species. But that is precisely what we are: just another species. Despite our delusions of grandeur, we are not immune from our own self-destruction. Despite the overwhelming denial from those who project animus on the harbingers of this somber truth, the incontrovertible evidence for our imminent demise is becoming increasingly clear.

In their blog post, *Climate Change: Saving the Planet, Saving Ourselves*, Richard Gale and Dr. Gary Null wrote:

> The Earth's history is a long story of numerous species birthing, evolving and eventually going extinct. There is no manifest destiny for our species. There is no divine promise that humanity may not in the future follow in the footsteps of the dinosaurs. Our lives are not transcendent to Nature nor the multitude of other natural forces, animals, plants, microbes and other life forms and molecules upon which our existence depends."[7]

What is it that prevents us from looking into the mirror—into the Soul—and asking ourselves, why? What is it that prevents us from sitting with the pain of what we have done to create this sickening reality? What is it that binds us to the narrow, short-sighted worldview that compels us to destroy our only home? Why are we so fearful of the Soul?

Homo sapien sapiens has evolved to become the destroyer of all. It is evident that this species will not rest until every millimeter of the planet has been decimated. There has never been a species in the last 65 million years that has been so destructive—and one that is so utterly blind to its destructive nature.

We are not only living through a cultural and ecological crisis; we are experiencing a story crisis. There is something terribly wrong with the way we understand who and what we are, and our relationship with Earth. The accelerated breakdown of our civilization and our biosphere is making this painfully clear. We are being forced to awaken from the Big Lie and look deeper within.

There is a Hindu story that goes as follows:

Once upon a time, humans had the power of the god force. But they behaved so badly the gods decided to remove this great privilege. Once removed, they had the daunting task of concealing this great power so it could not be readily found. Because of its sacred nature, it was only to be recovered by those who remembered who and what they are.

One god said, "Let's put it at the bottom of the deepest part of the ocean. They will never find it there." But the other gods disagreed. They knew that one day, humans would reach the bottom of the ocean and therefore discover it.

Another god said, "Let's put it in the far reaches of the skies. They will never find it there." Once again, the other gods disagreed. They knew that one day, humans would learn to fly and would, therefore, discover it.

And then Brahma, Hindu god of Creation said, "I know where to hide it. Let's put it inside the human heart because they will never think to look within."

The gods enthusiastically agreed, and the power of the god force was placed deep inside the heart of every human being.

So to free ourselves from the Big Lie, we need only look within to discover the truth that has been with us all along. It is in this expanded awareness that we liberate the Soul to lead us through these increasingly daunting times.

The American Dream

"None are more hopelessly enslaved than those who falsely believe they are free."

– GOETHE

Embedded within the Big Lie are outdated beliefs, narcissistic dreams, toxic myths, and distorted illusions. The ethos that drives the consumptive nature of our world was inflamed by "The American Dream." Seemingly benign in its inception in 1931 by James Truslow Adams in his book, *The Epic of America*:

> The American Dream is that dream of a land in which life should be better and richer and fuller for everyone, with opportunity for each according to ability or achievement. It is a difficult dream for the European upper classes to interpret adequately, and too many of us ourselves have grown weary and mistrustful of it. It is not a dream of motor cars and high wages merely, but a dream of social order in which each man and each woman shall be able to attain to the fullest stature of which they are innately capable, and be recognized by others for what they are, regardless of the fortuitous circumstances of birth or position.[8]

It was a dream for a better way of life; a dream since perverted into a pursuit of "happiness" through prosperity, success, fame, and the acquisition of material things. Like all things pursued outside of ourselves, however, the sense of meaning we sincerely desire, remains perpetually elusive. And so we work, chase, seek, and consume to no avail, always feeling more empty in the end.

In 80 short years, the American Dream has become the most dev-astating global nightmare to infect the minds of humanity. "Freedom" through material prosperity and self-serving "success" has caused global oppression, rampant greed, incessant consumption, social iso-lation, and widespread malaise. We are anything but happy or free. In our relentless pursuit of happiness, we have self-mutated; morphing into an invasive species, choking out life and paving the way for our own demise. Our culture of greed has separated us from everything that matters. With over 7.6 billion homo sapien sapiens inhabiting planet Earth, we should feel anything but alone, but the widespread epidemic of depression, anxiety, hostility, and isolation shows the ex-tent of our spiritual bankruptcy. We've lost our capacity to care.

We willingly offer our minds, our health, and our power to an-tiquated patriarchal institutions (education, religion, the medical/pharmaceutical complex, government, law, the economy, and sci-ence); while entrusting our global problems to political puppets whose interest in the common good inexorably dissolves in the face of corporate interests.

That's not the end of it though. The collapsing outer world is a direct reflection of our collective inner world. It's evident on a more personal level that we've lost our inherent ability to discern fact from fiction.

Let's dissect this a little further.

As a species, we no longer know how to care for our bodies. Six-pack abs, tight buns, shapely thighs, and fat-busting hacks are the paragon of wellness, as the fitness-meets-porn industry would have the gullible masses believe. Contrast this with the metaphoric couch potato growing sicker and fatter as life passes by in lonely anonym-ity, and warped extremes poison the collective mindset. Civilization has taught us that the body is something to ostentatiously flaunt, or venomously loathe. Either way, we've disconnected from ourselves in ways that permit the carte blanche objectification of all bodies, regardless of race, gender, or species. The body as an object bodes well for no living being.

We are the only species on the planet that has lost its intuitive ability to properly nourish itself. The corporate monoliths feed us unfathomable animal cruelty, pesticides, genetically modified organisms, processed junk, fast "food," confusion, and lies. Add to this a multi-billion dollar diet industry skilled in the art of hypnotic manipulation, and the gullible masses eagerly jump on the "latest and greatest" weight loss trend—even if it means identifying as a modern day cave dweller.

Mainstream media has created the kingdom of fear. It poisons the mind by sensationalizing the minutia of all the world's pain. It is the most potent tool for manipulating the minds of the gullible masses. It shapes beliefs and attitudes and defines what is acceptable to sustain the inert qualities of the status quo. As stated in the film, *Waking Life*:

> Society has a vested interest in considerable losses and catastrophes. Wars, famines, floods, fires, and quakes meet well-defined needs. Man wants chaos. In fact, he must have it. Depression, strife, riots, murder. All this dread. Humans are irresistibly drawn to that almost orgiastic state created out of death and destruction. Humans revel in it. The media tries to put a sad face on these things, painting them up as human tragedies. But we all know, the function of the media has never been to eliminate the evils of the world. Their job is to persuade us to accept those evils and get used to living with them. The powers that be want us to be passive observers. And they haven't given us any other options, outside of the occasional, purely symbolic, participatory act of 'voting.' 'Do you want the puppet on the right or the puppet on the left?' It's all there to control you: two

sides of the same coin. Two management teams bidding for the CEO job of Slavery, Incorporated.[9]

With our mindless allegiance to mainstream media, we now have wars on terror, wars on drugs, wars on cancer, wars on poverty, wars on germs, and wars on each another. Wars create fear. Fear creates compliance. Numb the minds of the masses by running them on the treadmill of fear, and compliance is a sure win for the profiteers of this madness.

Celebrity culture distracts us from our own lives by deifying narcissism, wealth and fame. Because of its omnipresence, it is an idea that permeates the psyche without resistance. Riding shotgun with mainstream media, the rich and famous are given the appearance of great significance. This serves well to highlight the belief in our own insignificance. The vacuous nature of celebrity culture has contributed to an increasingly degraded collective consciousness. In the emptiness of our perceived insignificance, we care more about who's sleeping with whom, who's wearing what, and who's plagued with cellulite, than we do about our own health and well-being or the critical condition of the planet.

The global explosion in human population now burdens the planet beyond capacity. Gaea is groaning and sagging under the weight of humanity. Unless raised by the enlightened (who would likely be wise enough not to breed), the ignorance of separation rapidly devours every child born to the world.

Our cult of self(ie)-expression has spawned colossal monuments to vacuity, entitlement, and mediocrity; worthy monuments to a generation who venerate narcissism without remorse, and "autonomy" without equipping people to think for themselves.

Technology has nullified all possibilities for inner peace. The perpetual state of impatient distraction, under the guise of "busy", is accompanied by an arrogant sense of self-importance. We now have so many devices to escape the Soul that we have become hopelessly lost in the purgatory of "progress." Our minds have been iFried into obscurity. Technology may have given us everything we thought we wanted, but it has stripped us of all we truly need.

The New Age self-improvement movement preys on our low self-worth with empty promises for our spiritual salvation. "For the right price, you too can become an enlightened, self-confident, and sexy gazillionaire!", blare the seductive marketing headlines. The endless stream of books, programs, seminars, online courses, and workshops have reaped material bliss for the gurus of abundance, but they've done little to return us to wholeness. We can manifest, attract, and affirm with the devotion of hope in our minds, while lack lingers on in our hearts. We've mastered the talk, but the walk still fills us with pain.

Like a devious pusher, the advertising industry hypes the mindless consumption of unnecessary "stuff" to feed addictive behaviors that create insecurity, unhappiness, debt, and planetary destruction. Botox swollen movie stars, rakish music idols, steroid-enhanced athletes, and airbrushed supermodels seduce us into emulating their "perfection" by buying into their high-paid messaging. The Siren songs of false promises leave us feeling inadequate, however, driving a perpetual desire for the "infinite more." With our profoundly ingrained scarcity consciousness, we are driven to want more, more, and still more, as we relentlessly chase after the latest and greatest shiny new toy. The strategic planning of obsolescence has created the selfish culture of iWantMoreRightNow. In the madness of our consumptive fury, our spirits have been stripped of their significance. We've become the zombie apocalypse we so deeply fear.

While the American Dream merrily chugs along, the medical-pharmaceutical complex salivates in the wings, ready to medicate the anxiety born from the appearance we will never have, the food that poisons our bodies, the fear that never leaves, the depression that feeds our inertia, the self-worth we will never claim, the technology that numbs our minds, and the consumption that destroys the Soul.

The dawn of the American Dream birthed an era of narcissism that now knows no bounds. Commencing with Baby Boomers—a generation (in generalized terms) of shallow-minded, short-sighted, self-absorbed, bloviating, financially affluent, know-it-all's who now run, and have ruined the world—the consciousness of every subsequent generation spawned from this age of entitlement has appreciably degraded. A Guardian article titled, *A Generation of Sociopaths review—How Trump and other Baby Boomers Ruined the World* states, "(from failing infrastructure, education, and healthcare, to climate change) ... the Boomers have bequeathed their children a mess of daunting proportions. (They) have made sure that they themselves will live long and prosper, but only at the expense of their offspring.[10]

Embraced enthusiastically by Boomers, the American Dream has been exceedingly successful at expanding the hellish abyss of separation. The normalization of obesity, arrogance, greed, and rabid consumption has created a bottomless chasm of emptiness that most are unaware they're even trapped even in. The documentary, *Racing Extinction*, summarized it perfectly, "It is quite possible that the Baby Boomer generation is the most (negatively) impactful generation this planet has ever seen."[11] (Personal note: I concur. Being a "tail-end" Boomer myself, I've lived in the eye of the storm, bearing witness to the real-time degradation of consciousness that has created the hellish societal and Earth conditions now upon us.)

From Boomers to Gen X, Millenials and beyond, there's not a generation since that has chosen to awaken from the smothering coma of cultural conditioning that holds the Dream and the Lie of separation intact.

As long as we have a cultural narrative that suppresses the essence of who we are—compassion, kindness, integrity, authenticity, and connection—in favor of negative human traits such as greed, selfishness, entitlement, arrogance, and fear, we will always exist in opposition to ourselves and each another. Opposition breeds separation and ensures that we are exploitable by the cultural entities who prey upon these negative characteristics. Today's "American Dream" is one that celebrates, aggravates, and stimulates the ugliest qualities of humanity. By inculcating these characteristics and rewarding them financially, and with "success," power and fame, we've been seduced into a cultural hysteria that causes us to mindlessly destroy ourselves, the planet, and each other.

The American dream of today is an artificial, corporate-fueled "reality" complete with denuded landscapes, billboards, cities, high-rises, highways, SUV's, cheap oil, suburbia, shopping malls, big-box stores, plastic, meat, dairy, eggs, pornography, GMO's, fast "food", reality tv, iPhones, celebrity culture, and money, money, money. Like our industrialized civilization, the American dream has no conscience. At great expense to our bodies, minds, and Souls, bigger, better and cheaper are the standard benchmarks for consumer decisions in the American Dream. Critical thought, integrity, and morality are absent.

The American Dream is hell on Earth celebrated as growth, progress, and success. We've been culturally altered: from citizens to consumers. The tragic irony is that globalization has allowed the American Dream to infect billions of minds around the world. Brands such as McDonald's, Coke, and Nike are more recognizable than the faces of our own neighbors. There is no place on the planet—including the far reaches of space—that our plasticized creations do not pollute. There are more people now than ever before who readily sell their Souls for empty promises of success, riches, and fame. Are we in the dominant civilization, with our spiritually impoverished ways, as privileged as we believe ourselves to be; or is this yet another mental construct that implies our consumptive habits are better than everything else?

We've become complacent in a flawed mindset, and we live in the shadow of an exhausting orgy of addiction to success, money, fame, and power. The American Dream has corroded our consciousness and made us more miserable in the end. It has clearly shown us the bankruptcy of our ways. Still, we persist in doing nothing about it. The cultural narrative of the American Dream is deeply embedded within the Big Lie. We call this "normal." I call it insane.

Human behaviors, shaped by generations of culturally indoctrinated habits, rituals, traditions, and beliefs have overwhelming inertia. Molded by the dogma of our conditioning, everything good, feeling, compassionate, caring, and virtuous about the essence of our true nature is silenced. We may believe that we are in control of our own greater destiny, but the deeper truth of who and what we are remains elusive as long as we search outside of ourselves for what will always live within.

This prompts the questions:

What if our beliefs about more are what make us feel less?

What if our beliefs about abundance are what trap us in scarcity?

What if our beliefs about self-worth are what make us feel insignificant?

What if our beliefs about health are what makes us sick?

What if our beliefs about food are what harm our bodies?

What if our beliefs about love are what prevent us from loving?

What if our beliefs about relationships are what perpetuate loneliness?

What if our beliefs about emotions are what prevent us from feeling?

What if our beliefs about knowledge are what prevent us from wisdom?

What if our beliefs about success are what trap us in mediocrity?

What if our beliefs about intimacy are what feed our isolation?

What if our beliefs about dying are what prevent us from living?

What if our fear of pain is what traps us in anguish?

What if all we believe to be true is a lie?

What if all we've been taught to believe about ourselves is the biggest lie of all?

As the Dream has provided evermore stuff for us to consume under the guise of "convenience," we've become more infantile. We are now less able to think for, and provide for ourselves than ever before. We've become willfully ignorant in our allegiance to the groupthink of our dominant civilization. In our deliberate disempowerment, we take our cues from everyone around us, regardless of how demented they may be. In the degraded state of consciousness that now prevails, we have proven the American Dream to be unsustainable. Because it is built on a foundation of faulty assumptions that cannot be reformed, the fundamental laws of life have been broken, and the consequences are ramping up in intensity.

There is no such thing as infinite consumption on a finite planet. There is no such thing as a fair and just economy with equality for all when run by a billionaire elite. There is no such thing as freedom and democracy when owned by corporate interests. There is no such thing as happiness, when always in pursuit. The Dream is dying, and as the Dream dies, those who wish to defend it band together in a psychosis of denial, rage, arrogance, and madness. We can clearly see the expression of this folly through the uprising in fundamentalism, white supremacy, misogyny, and the oppressive power of those who "lead" us.

As the world becomes increasingly hostile, the Dream grows increasingly grim. Between the Lie and the Dream, few know what is real anymore. It is this very confusion that holds it all intact.

The Culture of Addiction

"It isn't that they cannot find the solution. It is that they cannot see the problem."

– G.K. CHESTERTON

Collectively, our hearts and minds have been cloaked in the shroud of illusion separating us from all that matters. Enslaved by the Big Lie, the minds of the masses have been hijacked by hand-me-down belief systems that fuel scarcity fears and addictive behaviors. We are desperate for permission to be who and what we authentically are, but we fear a most pernicious form of violence: judgment. The pervasive nature of this vicious mindset prevents authentic expression by silencing our voices and depressing the Soul. We no longer feel safe: in our heads, in our hearts, and in the world.

We're birthed to the world a cog in the wheel to feed a civilization that separates us from everything sacred. No one escapes with their authentic life. Our dominant society has set us up to fail so that we never realize the essence of who we are. We've been cheated, not out of intended malice, but from generations of ignorance rooted in an inviolable cultural trance. We've been programmed to normalize the abnormal to preserve a dangerous status quo.

We are a collective of walking wounded. Infantile adults inflicting incomprehensible emotional abuse on each other, trying to gain some semblance of control over our inauthentic lives. Our culture of distraction will do anything to prevent us from feeling empowered enough to change our ways so we can be who we authentically are.

Emptiness saturates our civilization. Consumption and materialism are prominent symptoms of this disastrous condition. More accurately, they're pitiful attempts to cope with unbearable feelings of barrenness.

We've become a civilization of conscious addicts conforming to outdated belief systems, mass media, technological trends, antiquated stories, compulsive habits, low self-worth, self-destructive behaviors, and excessive consumption; neurotically searching for distractions to ease the longing in our hearts to be so much more than what we've allowed ourselves to become.

We've been taught to think rather than feel. Programmed by a civilization that demoralizes us, our beliefs are designed to support its destructive ways. We've been trained into fake humility, self-loathing and in always feeling inadequate. Our dominant civilization keeps us hooked on fantasies that seduce us into interminable consumption. We rarely think of anything pure, beautiful, and meaningful anymore. It's appalling what we've allowed ourselves to become.

We're inculcated into an engineered paradigm that leaves us feeling anxious, exhausted, distracted, selfish, depressed, and willing to consume anything and everything. Existing in a haze of unease, we eat, drink, surf, smoke, game, text, tweet, gamble, excuse, and buy our way out of pain that never leaves. A hit of distraction and we're in the clear. Civilization rules. No questions asked.

The prevailing mindset today is one of addiction. We stuff our feelings to feed the machine. When discomfort creeps into consciousness, we've learned well how to numb it, rather than feel it. The blue pill of illusion beats the rabbit hole of truth any day because once we know, we cannot un-know. With truth comes consciousness. With consciousness comes responsibility. With responsibility comes what the sleeping masses dread: awakening. And so it goes on and on, samsara—maya—the endless cycle of life, suffering, death, and rebirth, caused by the ignorance of illusion and the subsequent denial of truth.

Many institutions and industries such as media, politics, religion, corporations, education, and the medical/pharmaceutical complex have a vested interest in how we think, feel, behave, and act. An addicted society is a compliant society. A compliant society is a selfish society. A selfish society is a fearful society. A fearful society is a profitable society. Addiction is fear made manifest. Fear is the enemy of truth and the glue that binds humanity to the Big Lie.

In his international bestseller, *The Tibetan Book of Living and Dying*, Soygal Rinpoche, writes:

> Sometimes I think that the greatest achievement of modern culture is its brilliant selling of samsara and its barren distractions. Modern society seems to be a celebration of all the things that lead away from the truth, make truth hard to live for, and discourage people from even believing that it exists. And to think that all this springs from a civilization that claims to adore life, but actually starves it of any real meaning; that endlessly speaks of making people "happy," but in fact blocks their way to the source of real joy.
>
> This modern samsara feeds off the anxiety and depression that it fosters and trains us all in, and carefully nurtures with a consumer machine that needs to keep us greedy to keep going. Samsara is highly organized, versatile, and sophisticated; it assaults us from every angle with its propaganda and creates an almost impregnable environment of addiction around us. The more we try to escape, the more we seem to fall into the traps it is so ingenious at setting for us.
>
> Obsessed, then, with false hopes, dreams, and ambitions, which promise happiness but lead only to misery, we are like people crawling through an endless desert, dying of thirst. And

all that this samsara holds out for us to drink is a cup of salt water, designed to make us even thirstier.[12]

Today's society fosters so much self-loathing that we're ashamed of everything real about ourselves: our bodies, our gender, our feelings, our sexual orientation, our needs, our sense of meaning, our creativity, our compassion … our essence. We may say that we value freedom, but when it comes to our addictions, we've chosen our enslavement. We're addicted to the illusion. We're addicted to the Lie.

So many people are depressed, anxious, stressed-out, and lonely. Collectively, we find ourselves moving at a breathless pace, trying to keep up with the ceaseless machine of our civilization and the inauthentic conditioning that holds it intact.

To tolerate the intolerable in our world: the jobs we hate, the conversations that bore us, the relationships that bleed us, the unending destruction and violence, the pain in our hearts, our own self-loathing; we ingest "stuff" to quiet the body from the chaos and turmoil because we just can't stand it anymore. Because the body will not be silenced, the cocktail of drugs for the ailments of our modern world must be continually increased. The truth is, there's no way around what we bury, ignore or deny because it always finds a release valve somehow, somewhere. We can delude ourselves by believing our depression, anxiety, rage, hypertension, heart disease, skin problems, tumors, aches, pains, and cancers are anomalies, but we'd be better off getting honest with ourselves. The more we deny, medicate, numb, and ignore the messaging of the Soul, the louder and more painful it becomes. In our fervent commitment to the Big Lie, our strategies of anesthesia know no limits. Entire industries have emerged to ensure that the senses are dulled and distracted, and problems that don't even exist are invented so that "solutions" can be marketed and sold to remedy our self-deception.

Addiction is so pervasive in today's world that it has been perversely normalized. We're addicted to concepts, strategies, ideas, trends, and behaviors. Gluten-free anyone? We're addicted to our iPhones, computers, tv shows, diet and exercise programs. We're addicted to our anxiety, pain, fatigue, impatience, and unease. We're addicted to our thoughts, beliefs, memories, and stories.

We're addicted to "busy," filling our lives with noise and activity, however meaningless and trivial, to ensure we can never access the truth within. We've become a civilization that is addicted to addiction—a population of automatons desperately attached to a separate way of being. We're addicted to a way of life that is killing us.

From *The Tibetan Book of Living and Dying*, Soygal Rinpoche once again writes, "We are fragmented into so many different aspects. We don't know who we really are, or what aspects of ourselves we should identify with or believe in. So many contradictory voices, dictates, and feelings fight for control over our inner lives that we find ourselves scattered everywhere, in all directions, leaving nobody at home."[13]

We're are so addicted to looking outside of ourselves for everything in life that we've become lost to ourselves. This illusion may be "normal," but because it's based on a Lie, it can never be real.

In *The Tibetan Book of Living and Dying*, Soygal Rinpoche writes about the unconscious, living corpses the masses have become in today's civilization of separation and addiction. He writes:

> Most of us do live like that (unconscious, living corpses); we live according to a pre-ordained plan. We spend our youth being educated. Then we find a job, and meet someone, marry, and have children. We buy a house, try to make a success of our business, aim for dreams like a country house or a second car. We go away on holiday with our friends. We plan for retirement. The biggest dilemmas some of us ever have to face are where to take our next holiday or whom to invite at Christ-

mas. Our lives are monotonous, petty, and repetitive, wasted in the pursuit of the trivial, because we seem to know nothing of the better.

> And so our lives drift on, unless a serious illness or disaster shakes us out of our stupor.[14]

Illnesses and disasters can be profound catalysts for awakening, but they are without guarantees. One would think the ominous threats of runaway biosphere decay, cultural collapse, or imminent extinction would be motivation for awakening, but a mind infected by the Big Lie is hard-wired for dissonance and denial. So we do nothing. Dissonance and denial are intimate bedfellows. They seduce each other, coddle each other, inflate each other, and lie to each other. We're well trained in finding comfort in this strange partnership, no matter how much inner turmoil it may cause. Our addiction to inertia trumps all.

When we're still able to get what we want, and while things still seem relatively stable in our world, there's no will or desire to change our ways. We may be aware of the severity of our global problems on the periphery, but the problems often seem to be somewhere else, far from view. So we cram our lives with compulsive, frivolous activities to distract ourselves from the real issues confronting our broken, dying world.

Seeping through our mental haze, however, we all seem fraught, flattened by the helplessness of our domestication; lurching from one new horror to another wondering, will it ever stop? Can it ever stop? Does sanity exist anymore? Did it ever?

The civilization we live in models our creations: asylums, cages, prisons. With resignation so profound in our world, it seems there's little left to do but make the asylum, cage or prison as comfortable as possible. So we numb ourselves to make it through the monotony of each new, inauthentic day.

The impetus for our numbing is the sustenance of sameness and comfort. In our numbness, there's no room to face the reality of a dying planet; of trillions of brutally slaughtered animals; of the poisoning of our bodies, and of our imminent extinction. It will not be the collective who takes on this terrible reality. It can only happen on an individual basis. To step into this truth means feeling the anguish of our dying world and accepting the isolation of caring in a world that prefers stasis above all else.

At its simplest, addiction is attachment. Attachment arises from the denial of truth fueled by the mind's habitual tendency toward distraction from the Soul. Addiction/attachment is one of the most significant roots of separation, and the cause of many of today's personal and global problems.

Attachment can plague us to varying degrees. A fine line exists between habit and addiction, and habits can quickly morph into addictions. A typical indicator of addiction is two simple words— "I can't."

We often perceive addiction as extreme behavior. Personified as the angry drunk, the strung-out junkie, the compulsive gambler, the sex addict; what we fail to realize is how pervasive addiction can be on the sliding scale of "I can't." We selectively label what isn't socially acceptable as addiction, but here's the rub, if "I can't" has a grip on the psyche, addiction is present.

On the sliding scale of "I can't," here are a few typical examples:

"I can't give up my iPhone."

"I can't give up Facebook, Twitter, Instagram, etc."

"I can't give up my coffee."

"I can't give up my cheese, yogurt, sour cream, eggs, (name any animal secretion)."

"I can't give up my chicken, fish, steak, bacon, (name the rotting flesh of any animal species)."

"I can't give up my Coke, Pepsi, Big Mac, Whopper, Slurpees, (name a junk 'food')."

"I can't stop watching the news or (name a television show)."

"I can't leave my job because (name an excuse)."

"I can't stop smoking, taking Tylenol, drinking Red Bull, eating donuts, etc."

"I can't run that fast, walk that far, write that well ... blah, blah, blah". (Addiction to self-limiting beliefs).

"I can't; I can't, I can't ..."

When we peek under the hood of "I can't," we see the rationalized (rational lies) resistance of "I won't" that accompanies the fear of change. Franklin D. Roosevelt once said, "There are many ways of going forward but only one way of standing still."

It's such a strange world.

Along with addiction comes a plethora of ingeniously packaged defense mechanisms designed to deflect the truth. Denial is cunning in its manifestation and wears the many masks of excusing, rationalizing, intellectualizing, blaming, justifying, minimizing, joking, agreeing, threatening, generalizing, and projecting.

It's important to note that denial differs from lying. Those who lie know what is right, but choose to speak or act falsely. In denial, however, the lines are cognitively blurred between truth and fiction. The result is an absolute belief in one's self-deception.

On a much deeper level, many people sense their deep-rooted unease by hopelessly grasping for fallacious solutions outside of themselves. But using the outer world to change our inner world only makes matters worse by taking us further from the Soul. As a collective, our addiction to external distraction is the most common affliction in the modern world of today.

Technology is the most seductive externally-sourced addiction

in its fast-paced, ever-changing, quick-fix gratification. We no longer know patience, compassion, empathy, presence, or how to listen
to one another anymore. Our attention often spans as long as the
latest tweet.

Our addiction to "entertainment" is an odd paradox. Actors and
actresses are paid absurd amounts of money to play fictitious characters to entertain people who are lost to who they are. Our obsession
with the pretend lives of these characters shows the ridiculous lengths
we go to distract ourselves, from our Selves.

Our addiction to sameness ensures the culture of conformity. We
fear the depth of our most authentic essence. We fear the Soul. Conformity removes us from the sacred. It traps us in the paradigm of
scared. Scared is the sacred within, forgotten.

The most ubiquitous addiction imposed on the collective psyche
is the violent belief system that normalizes the consumption of animal flesh and secretions. In the deluded belief of our human supremacy, we destroy animals en masse as we grasp at false "truths" derived
from our arrogance. To complicate matters, addiction to these "foods"
alters brain chemistry and renders the mind incapable of the critical
thought required to remember our connection to all life. We've become mentally addicted to a cruelty-based belief system, and physi-
ologically addicted to the consumption-based effects that accompany
it. The machine reaps such outrageous profit from this psycho/physi-
ological addiction that it goes to great lengths to ensure its survival.
Is it any wonder why the violence inherent in this barbaric industry is
cloaked in such impenetrable secrecy.

We fear death, yet we consume death. We desire peace, yet
we ingest violence and suffering in every meal, never realizing the
incongruity of it all.

Because of our flippant willingness to accept such destructive beliefs, we've become a force for merciless violence, wreaking planetary

havoc from our ferocious appetite for the flesh of suffered corpses. From the moment of its unnatural conception, every animal bred to the world to satiate this bloody belief system is cursed with a miserable life and a brutal death sentence. As long as the illusion of human supremacy remains intact, there's no incentive to question our beliefs.

Gratuitous violence can be found in every dollar spent to feed the machine. "Do it again. Kill for me so I can feed my addiction" is the message conveyed as we dole out our cash for the shrink-wrapped, sanitized body parts of the brutalized corpses that line the grocery store shelves. Grass-fed, free-range, wild-caught, local, organic; no matter how we phrase it, feel-good labels warp the mind but not the truth. Slaughter is murder, end of story. Every dollar spent is a reflection of what we choose to believe; a vote for how we wish to see the world. This vote, as insignificant as we may perceive it to be, is of critical importance. It's a vote we can personally leverage to create mass destruction, or remembrance of our place within the web of life. This is the power of free will. As Thomas Edison so wisely stated, "Until we stop harming all other living beings, we are still savages." To be conscious or not—that is the ultimate question.

In his 2010 talk titled *Eating for Peace: Mindful Consumption*, venerable Zen Master Thich Nhat Hanh said:

> By eating animals, we share the responsibility of climate change, the destruction of our forests, and the poisoning of our air and water. When we eat the flesh, eggs, and milk of animals, because these substances are made from the suffering of other people and beings and of our mother Earth, it is as if we are eating our own flesh and blood. Every day 40,000 children die in the world for lack of food. We who overeat in the West, who are feeding grains to animals to make meat, are eating the flesh of these children.

Mindful eating can help maintain compassion within our heart. A person without compassion cannot be happy, cannot relate to other human beings and other living beings. And eating the flesh of our own son is what is going on in the world because we do not practice mindful eating.

Every one of us can transform himself or herself into a Bodhisattva doing the work of awakening. Because only awakening can help us to stop the course we are taking, the course of destruction.[15]

What have we become to demand the destruction of so much life because of the rigid beliefs that trap us in such violent addictions? Are we really the biped carrion eaters we've chosen to be?

Gandhi once said, "The greatness of a nation and its moral progress can be judged by the way its animals are treated." His words speak to a profound truth about the quality of our relationship with non-human animals that mirrors where we are in our collective evolution.

Despite our unconscious, violent choices, why is it that many of us still innately gravitate toward animals and nature? The answer is simple: because no matter what we do to them, they never forget their role within the web of life. They are not separate. They are essence embodied. They were never indoctrinated into the Big Lie. They only become part of the Big Lie when we impose our separation-based belief systems on them. It's only then that they become the tragic victims of our addiction to the Big Lie.

I used to believe it was the walls of slaughterhouses that needed to be demolished to live in a peaceful, compassionate world. I've since realized it is the wall around our hearts that must be destroyed before we are ever to live peacefully within ourselves. As long as we believe in our superiority over all, it will never matter how many walls of oppression are demolished. In the delusion of our separation, we will always build others to replace them.

The human heart can express limitless compassion. We are a species designed for compassion. In the depth of our essence, we are compassionate. Anything less is the Lie we've accepted to separate us from life. The reason we do what we do to those we perceive as "other," is because we are asleep at the wheel. We are the only species on the planet who doesn't know who and what we are because we've bought into the illusion of separation. If we were to remember what we are, we would never be able to treat ourselves and others the way we do: through our thoughts, choices, behaviors, or actions.

We have the choice to live the Lie or not. We are the ones who created it. We are the ones who can un-create it. Just as we've chosen ignorance, so too can we choose truth. It means detoxing from our addiction to the mad civilization in which we live—a journey that is not for the faint of heart.

When the drug of choice is removed, be it food, shopping, gambling, porn, Netflix, pharmaceuticals, alcohol, television, Facebook, Twitter, news, compulsive email checking, texting, or any of the endless distractions in our world, we are often left feeling anxious and empty, realizing the wound we've created for the Soul. Facing this emptiness is key to our freedom. Until we do, we remain captive to our destructive patterns of distraction and avoidance.

After centuries of mass distraction, it appears as though we are desperate to bottom out. It's almost as if we want to hit bottom so hard, there is no possibility for survival. So many of us are desperate for this nightmare to end. What many don't realize is that the death they seek is a cultural death; one that has the potential to spawn an awakening that allows for liberation from the binding addictions of an outdated, broken world.

Breeding Ourselves Into Oblivion

"I want to share a revelation I've had during my time here. It came to me when I tried to classify your species and I realized that you're not actually mammals. Every mammal on this planet instinctively develops an equilibrium with the surrounding environment. But you humans do not. You move to an area and you multiply and multiply until every natural resource is consumed. The only way you can survive is to spread to another area. There is another organism on this planet that follows the same pattern. Do you know what it is? A virus. Human beings are a disease. A cancer of this planet."

– CHARACTER, A. SMITH FROM THE MOVIE, *THE MATRIX*

Breeding, Parenting, Overpopulation: The Conversation We're Too Afraid to Have

The views that follow will likely not be popular, as I am heavily outnumbered by the Goliath of anthropocentric breeders in a separation steeped world. In contrast, my views are Gaeacentric, emerging from an expansive perspective connected to the greater whole of life, and viewed through the eyes of the Soul. Gaeacentricism runs against everything we've been conditioned to believe in the fallacy of our anthropocentrism. In the words of Indian philosopher, Jiddu Krishnamurti, however, "It is no measure of health to be well adjusted to a profoundly sick society." As such, I choose to be outspoken in my bold exposé of a grave problem that is rapidly destroying life on Earth.

Rather than dance around the issue with faux politesse, I'll say it straight: children are killing us, and we in turn, are killing them.

Humans are an unprecedented force in nature. Like a prolific virus, we are everywhere, pervasive in our dominant existence. There is hardly a place on Earth—on land, in water, in the air, and even in space—that has not been altered by humanity. Earth is infected by humans. Ironically, one of the most taboo topics in our broken world is that of human breeding, and the subsequent overpopulation crisis that threatens the immediate habitability of the planet.

With over 7.6 billion humans and growing aggressively, our problems are now so significant and complicated they can no longer be solved, regardless of what we do or do not do. For decades, we've known about the burden of our consumption on Earth, yet in our conditioned arrogance, we've chosen to consume more recklessly instead. Our consumption has risen exponentially in tandem with our frenzied obsession to self-replicate. More humans equal more consumers. It's a self-reinforcing feedback loop with dire consequences. The outcome of our insatiable compulsion to breed, and therefore consume, is increased hostility as we encroach on the space of each other, and all those who call Earth home.

One needs only to skirt the edges of the topic of human breeding to understand how deeply entrenched our obscene sense of entitlement is, and how quickly it morphs into denial at the peril of Earth. Politesse saturates the topic of human breeding, so we avoid it at all costs. The unspoken reality is that every child birthed into our desecrated world is akin to a tumor on our terminally ill planet. Children are not benign. With our insatiable desire to breed, we are killing the very planet we paradoxically wish to leave for our children.

Every innocent life-force born to this world is enslaved; mutated by the Big Lie and groomed to become another human supremacist with a single purpose: consumption—of ideas, beliefs, patterns, history, dogma, technology, and stuff. Parenting is the primary delivery mechanism for indoctrination into the mindset of separation. Conditioned by the programming of their parents, and of the parents who preceded them, every new child is born into generations of mental, emotional and spiritual captivity with belief systems that starve the Soul. Every aspect of our civilization perpetuates these damaging belief systems. Separation is programmed into the mind at an early age so it remains firmly held in place throughout life. Like St. Francis Xavier once said, "Give me a child until he is seven, and I will give you the man."

Children arrive in our world with an innate sensitivity and connection to the sacred, traits that are unwelcome in our desensitized, life-hating world. Author, Harvey Diamond once said, "You put a baby in a crib with an apple and a rabbit. If it eats the rabbit and plays with the apple, I'll buy you a new car." This simple quote shows that separation is not innate. It is taught. Children are inherently compassionate and know their interconnected nature. Through the shaming, ridicule, judgment, punishment, and silencing by parents, friends, teachers, and authority figures, this intrinsic sensitivity is quickly suppressed for purposes of self-preservation. Bullying by children already damaged by their parents ensures that inborn sensitivity rarely sees the light of day. Children learn early on that it's not safe to be authentic, compassionate, sensitive, and caring.

In his blog post, *Killing the Biosphere to Fast-track Human Extinction*, researcher Robert J. Burrowes writes:

> I have been researching why human beings are violent since 1966, and the evidence has convinced me that the origin of all human violence is the violence inflicted by adults on children under the guise of what sociologists call 'socialization.' This violence takes many forms—what I call 'visible', 'invisible' and 'utterly invisible' violence—and it creates enormously damaged

individuals who then personally inflict violence on themselves, those around them (including their own children), non-human species, and the Earth, while creating, participating in, defending and/or benefiting from structures of violence and exploitation.

Hence, in my view, the evidence is overwhelming that if we want to end human violence, whether inflicted on ourselves, others or the Earth, then the central feature of our strategy must be to end adult violence against children. (In my blog post), 'My Promise to Children', I claim that this must be 'the central feature of our strategy' for the simple reason that each damaged child grows up to become a willing and active perpetrator of violence when, if they were not so damaged, they would be powerful agents of peace, justice, and sustainability committed to resisting violence and exploitation in all contexts until it is eliminated.

This profound evolutionary inheritance—to be an individual of integrity who consciously chooses and lives out their own unique, powerful and nonviolent life path—has been denied to virtually all of us because humans endlessly terrorize their children into mindless obedience and social conformity, leaving them powerless to access and live out their conscience.

And this makes it very easy for elites: By then using a combination of our existing fear, indoctrination (via the education system, corporate media and religion) and intimidation (via the police, legal and prison systems), sometimes sweetened with a few toys and trinkets, national elites maintain social control and maximize corporate profits by coercing the rest of us to waste our lives doing meaningless work, in denial of our Self-hood, in the corporate-controlled economy.[16]

Our dominant civilization conditions us to fragment our innately compassionate nature, and thus close our hearts. A closed heart is an untouchable mind. An untouchable mind is an ignorant mind. An ignorant mind is a separated mind.

Alienation from the natural world is instilled into the minds of children early on. Infants become consumers by being raised in a consumer-driven society. Consumer-conditioned parents then teach them that it's not only normal to be anthropocentric, it's natural.

In an anthropocentric worldview, self-replicating is a cultural expectation dripping with self-righteous entitlement. In a Gaeacentric worldview, however, bringing another human onto a sick and bloated planet, sagging under the weight of humanity, is a profoundly selfish act. It is not the enlightened who breed; it is the culturally entitled who breed.

People who envision breeding a child often forget (and ignore) that they are creating an entirely new human being who will rapidly grow into a voracious consumer for most of its life. We may believe it is our "right" to self-replicate, but it is in this ignorance that we negate our moral obligation to a habitable planet.

Breeding and parenting are two of the most significant sacred cows in our global civilization. In the words of author, Louise LeBrun:

> Parenting is the conduit for our intergenerational insanity. It is the most damaging process that enslaves us into someone else's mind. It is detrimental at the best of times and vicious and destructive in its worst expressions.
>
> We are a species that cannibalizes its young. We give birth to these little creatures and then we rip the Soul out of them by making them functional to do the work of the civilization. We typically do not teach them how to be their own person.

We teach them how to function as a person somebody else is going to want.[17]

Every child is a byproduct of their parents, and the subsequent wounds imposed by generations of hand-me-down belief systems. We are parented by wounded children, who were parented by wounded children, and on and on it goes. Broken parenting has been with us for so long, we know of nothing else. Wounded children now teach us, police us, doctor us, inform us, and govern us.

When humans breed, they replicate themselves: their biases, fears, limitations, anxieties, shame, judgments, old beliefs, and dysfunctional patterns. A deeply rooted cultural program exists that eliminates the question of morality that should accompany the decision to have a child.

In her *Engaging and Awakening Others* cd program, Louise LeBrun says it well:

> Many women are not parents by choice. It's historical. It's intergenerational. It's expected. But it's not by choice. Imagine if the only children in the world were born to the people who *really* wanted them—not just thought they wanted them. It would be a different world. We'd have a lot fewer children and there would be meaning in their lives. But we don't treat our children as people. We treat our children as responsibilities, as concerns, as obligations, as problems; not as people. If you stop to think about how you treat your kids, if you treated your friends like that, they wouldn't be your friends for very long.[18]

When we look closely (and honestly) at the parenting process, it's a conduit for the intergenerational construct of choosing mindlessly. The parenting process is replicated in every aspect of our civilization: in the church environment, which dictates how we parent. In the educational environment, where teachers become surrogate parents. In the corporate environment, where bosses become "parents" to the "children" they employ. In the political environment, where politicians become parents to the citizens they "lead." And in the medical profession, where doctors become parents to the patients they treat. We are conditioned at an early age to renounce the truth of our own experience, only to become adults who don't even know there is any other way. And so we become the four-year-old in the body of a 40-year-old, still acting and choosing like that of a four-year-old. There is nothing in place in our civilization to encourage the emotional maturity that accompanies personal evolution.

Good parenting in our civilization is measured by the degree to which parents enforce compliance on their children: be well-behaved, speak when allowed, be quiet otherwise, and when speaking, only say what parents approve of to prevent embarrassment. In other words, children should be seen and not heard. It's about ensuring that children demonstrate "respect" for all those in positions of "authority." Parenting is about control. In most cases, parents never allow children to discover the deep truth of who they authentically are. Instead, they define who their children are meant to be based on their own beliefs, perceptions, attitudes, wounds, fears, and patterned behaviors. Losing one's Self happens quickly within the parenting process.

In her blog post, *Children and Potential*, Louise LeBrun writes:

> …As parents, we so strongly identify ourselves by who our children have become. Are my kids well-behaved, doing well in school, holding down summer jobs, etc.? Then I'm a good parent. Are my kids failing in school—or worse yet, dropping out? Are they doing drugs, or loafing around the house all summer? Then I must be a bad parent.
>
> See how that works? My children become the mirror that reflects back to me my level of success in having

"shaped" them "appropriately"; and subsequently, the measure of my value as a person. Is it any wonder so many of us press hard for our children to become who we want them to become, rather than who they know themselves to be drawn to becoming?[19]

Children are not taught *how* to think. They are taught *what* to think, and how to conform to the rules and dogma of the systems that comprise our civilization.

Many people buy into the notion that children are the bright lights of the future, yet each new generation is groomed by the compounded conditioning and dogma of the past. Our past is scarred by war, racism, sexism, speciesism, heterosexism, consumption, slaughter, cruelty, homophobia, misogyny, violence, and environmental desecration. The fact is, we cannot teach our children what we ourselves are unable and unwilling to live. In being taught to shape the future from the past, we're ensured nothing but increasingly desperate problems that can only lead to one outcome: breakdown.

While we may dream about our children as the saviors of the future, we control them, silence them, humiliate them, shame them, abandon them, yell at them, yank them around, beat them, and tell them they're stupid, lazy, and won't amount to anything; or we do the same in reverse. We press them into the relentless pursuit of excellence in academics, sports, music, or art. We are not sustainable as a species. We have not taught our children how to be sustainable by living as integral members of an intricate web of life because we don't live this way ourselves.

In Neale Donald Walsh's book, *Conversations with God*, he writes:

> No one is more ill-equipped to raise children than young parents. And no one knows this, by the way, better than young parents.

Most parents come to the job of parenting with very little life experience. They're hardly finished being parented themselves. They're still looking for answers, still searching for clues.

They haven't even discovered themselves yet, and they're trying to guide and nurture discovery in others even more vulnerable than they. They haven't even defined themselves, and they're thrust into the act of defining others. They are still trying to get over how badly they have been mis-defined by their parents.

They haven't even discovered yet *Who They Are*, and they're trying to tell you who you are. And the pressure is so great for them to get it right—yet they can't even get their own lives "right". So they get the whole thing wrong—their lives, and the lives of their children.

If they're lucky, the damage to their children won't be too great. The offspring will overcome it—but not before passing some on to their offspring.

Most of you gain the wisdom, the patience, the understanding, and the love to be wonderful parents after your parenting years are over.

A good many humans—perhaps most—are not truly capable of raising children when they are capable of having them.[20]

He goes on to write:

Your younger years were never meant to be for truth-teaching, but for truth-gathering. How can you teach children a truth you haven't yet gathered?

You can't, of course. So you'll wind up telling them the only truth you know—the truth of others. Your father's, your mother's, your culture's, your religion's. Anything, everything, but your own truth. You are still searching for that.

And you will be searching, and experimenting, and finding, and failing, and forming and reforming your truth, your idea about yourself, until you are half a century on this planet, or near to it.[21]

Most children in our modern world grow up in abusive, divorced, broken, or dysfunctional households. There is nothing outside of parental programming that gives a child a vote. Trauma abounds. Our parents shape us, and unless we awaken from—and evolve beyond— the conditioning they imposed upon us, we replicate what we are taught and impose it on our own children. This ensures the everlasting longevity of the Big Lie.

In most cases, the trauma of childhood commences with our industrialized birth into a sterile medical setting: pharmaceutical pain suppressants, bright lights, cold metal instruments, latex gloves, facial coverings, etc. Newborns leave the warmth and safety of the womb to be mutilated by circumcision if male, or culturally demoted if female. There is nothing natural about our entrance into an unnatural world.

Within the first year of life, children have already been fed a steady diet of antiquated belief systems, plastic, animal suffering, and technological distraction. The norm these days is to give a young child an iPad and speak in irregular intervals from that point forward. In their early years, children are shuffled off to daycare to ease the burden on sleep-deprived parents with scarcity fears that bind them to meaningless jobs. Parents abdicate responsibility for their children by blindly handing them off to authoritative strangers employed by profit-driven cultural institutions. Absentee parenting is the norm. Few families parent with intent anymore. Between the encumbrance of parenting, and the introduction of culturally conditioned thought, childhood innocence is quickly degraded.

Ultimately, self-replication is about extending the lineage of the culture and preparing worker drones to perpetuate the Big Lie. Children are not taught how to create meaningful lives for themselves; they are taught how to map to lives that conform to culturally imposed gender roles that slot perfectly into our industrialized civilization.

We need only look at our teenagers and young adults to see how we have collectively failed our children. Gun violence, bullying, suicide, teenage pregnancy, sexual assault, campus rapes, cutting and self-harm, Attention Deficit Disorder, obesity, bulimia, anorexia, low self-esteem, distorted body image, substance abuse, addiction, depression, anxiety, stress, repressed rage, and a plethora of other self-worth issues infect the minds of young adults early on. Our youth are exceedingly troubled in today's world, and the root can always be traced back to parenting. When young adults no longer find the family love they so desperately need, they either act out or seek it elsewhere. Young people of today have been sold a plethora of bad ideas. Every system—with emphasis on the family system—is failing them. Not only is it selfish to breed a child on an overburdened planet, it is selfish to breed a child into a loveless world that quickly rips them to shreds.

In the video, *To Live Until You Die*, Elisabeth Kübler-Ross said:

> Most of us have never experienced love. We experience rewards. We learned as children that we would be 'loved' if we were polite, got good grades, smiled for grandma, or washed our hands often enough. We worked our buns off to be loved, never realizing that it was conditional, false 'love'. How can we possibly love if it takes so much approval from others? Most of us were raised by the words, 'I love you if …'

Parents have raised generations of prostitutes. Children prostitute themselves with good grades, with achievements, with honors, with degrees and they literally end up believing that you can buy love with good behavior, accomplishments, and awards. Then they become involved in a relationship with someone who says, 'I love you if you buy me a new car.' Next year, it will be a vacation home.[22]

And so it is: innocent babies become selfish children, self-loathing teenagers, entitled young adults, and arrogant, wounded adults. This is the typical coming of age within the degraded, infantile consciousness that runs our world.

Patriarchal Consciousness

Much of what children are taught is how to be compliant with an externally referenced world. Do what the teacher says, do what the white male God expects, do what your parents tell you to do, do whatever some authoritative figure commands. Be seen, but do not dare be heard.

The school system teaches children how to endure boredom. It programs into young minds how to take orders to install the dominant values, beliefs, and goals of our civilization. Education is one of the most prominent instruments of replicating mind control in our world. Depending on how and what is being taught, education can either free the mind and encourage independent, critical thought; or it can program the mind and turn students into cultural slaves who voluntarily relinquish their freedom because they know nothing else. Sadly, this is the prevailing model of education in our dominant global civilization.

Embedded within, or perhaps the driver of the Big Lie, is patriarchal consciousness. What came first is anyone's guess. In the end, it doesn't matter because patriarchal consciousness and separation are so intricately intertwined, it's difficult to differentiate one from the other.

In its simplest terms, patriarchy is a social system that values masculinity over femininity. This social system dictates that men are entitled to rule and dominate women, animals, and Earth. It implies that dominance and submission characterize our gender roles. Women, and all that represents "the feminine" (animals, nature, emotions, caring, compassion, etc.), are viewed as weak, submissive, and lesser. They exist only to be used by men. The highest standard a woman can attain within a patriarchal society is a heterosexual marriage that showcases her breeding prowess.

Patriarchal expectations of men include physical strength, emotional neutrality, virility, aggression, and domination under the guise of power.

Patriarchy infects our language and permeates all aspects of life in our world. Everyday examples of patriarchal language include *his*tory, hu*man*, and even *men*opause, the pause/cessation of the ability for a woman to breed with a man.

Culturally programmed gender roles impose the mindset of separation before conception. In a patriarchal society, human beings and their cultural functions are defined by and correspond with their genitalia. Gender roles are strictly enforced in our civilization. As soon as we are assigned gender roles in utero, we are bound by the parenting system with expectations of who and what we are meant to be in the world. If a person doesn't easily slot into their assigned gender role, they are often ostracized by society. Patriarchy is so pervasive in our dominant civilization that it is perpetrated by everyone because nobody exists outside of its societal influence.

In a patriarchal society, there is great pressure on women to have children. Women are taught at an early age that one of their primary functions is to have babies. When they don't fulfill this societal role, they may be subtly (or not so subtly) pressured by those around them to "get with the program."

Male births are generally more celebrated than female births. In some countries, females are considered worthless and are merely discarded or murdered at birth. Because of our desire for political correctness in western civilization, we tend to conceal our preference for male babies better than other cultures. The undercurrent of patriarchy remains, however.

How civilization defines male and female is a disservice to the Soul. In modern culture, the sexualization of gender comes before anything else. When a person looks at a body, the first thing they see is gender. With gender, comes sexualization. With sexualization is separation. Breeding with a mindset of inequality and separation before conception occurs, does not inspire confidence for a long-term future as a species.

Why the Obsessive Desire to Breed?

Humans have a sizeable planetary footprint. The seemingly simple acquisition of water, food, clothing, and shelter for a single human in today's fast-paced, industrialized world brings with it atrocious suffering to animals, Earth, and our species. Meeting the increasingly demanding wants and needs of 7.6 billion humans comes at significant cost to the air, water, forests, and soil. To provide for a collective who righteously demand their baubles and their babies, the destruction of a habitable, thriving planet is unavoidable. Those we share Earth with—animals, birds, insects, plants, trees, fish, and so on—are being displaced, harvested and dying en masse. Are we so filled with hubris that we believe causing the suffering of so many is our right? Do we lack the conscience to see the dreadful planetary consequences of our acquisitive needs?

No other species breeds itself beyond the carrying capacity of Earth. We are it. Hardly an endangered species, there has been no biological necessity for us to continue self-replicating for several centuries. Why then, do we persist in our mass self-replication when the evidence for planetary breakdown—by our own hands no less—is so clear?

Lingering in the conditioned human psyche is a dominant cultural expectation to breed; an expectation passed on for so many generations, it now defines us. We senselessly self-replicate to comply with unchallenged belief systems we have accepted as real.

We breed to appease our egos (to prove fertility/virility); for parental approval (parents want grandchildren); social pressure (friends are having babies, everyone else is doing it); cultural influence under the guise of "biological necessity" ("it's time", "biological clock is ticking"); self-worth issues (to feel respected, whole and "complete"); megalomania ("superior" human genes); fear of aging (someone to support parents in old age); duped by bloodline superstition (to carry on the family name); self-absorption (want to see a "mini me"); faux selflessness/delusions of grandeur ("it's selfish not to have children"); dogma (religious obligation, "god's will"); short-sightedness ("I love babies"); entitlement ("it's my right"); patriarchy (being a mother is a woman's highest calling); carelessness ("it just happened"); unresolved relationship issues (someone who will love me and not leave me); anthropocentric arrogance ("having children contributes to the survival of humanity"); unexamined cultural conditioning ("it's human nature", tradition, "always wanted to have children", "it's the 'right' thing to do"); insecurity (children add freshness to a relationship when things go stale); unfulfilled childhood ("to have the childhood I never had", "to fulfill my unrealized dreams"); and the God complex (to create a "functional" member of society, or someone to "save" the world).

Almost every parent will say their children mean the world to them, while many of their actions say otherwise. Standing idly by a dying planet as their children are culturally cannibalized while silencing their own inner voice, does not define caring and compassion. It defines madness.

If the desire for children were indeed about love for children, there would be no need for children's aid societies, adoption centers, and foster parenting organizations. Let's face it, the compulsive desire to breed is less about love for children than it is about following the invisible set of rules that determine how "normal" life is meant to appear. Generally, most women breed to conform to the groupthink mindset of, "everyone else is doing it."

In my lifetime, I've yet to meet anyone with a functional relationship with their parents based on equality, integrity, reciprocity, respect, and unconditional love. How can we possibly delude ourselves into believing that parenting and family systems are not at cause for the dysfunction in our world? If madness was meant to define our species, our prolific ability to self-replicate has successfully held it intact.

The Planetary Impact of Breeding

Any organism can conceivably become an invasive species if it finds its way into an ecosystem where it doesn't belong. Some characteristics make a species more harmful than others. If it spreads aggressively, grows and reproduces quickly, and feasts mercilessly, it will make a particularly deadly invader. Sound familiar? Homo sapien sapiens has become lord of the invasive species.

Every second there are two more people to feed on the planet, yet millions starve every year. No other species reproduce at the rate of humans, barring a virus. Considering the accelerated breakdown of our dying planet, procreation today is like renting rooms in a burning building and renting them to our children no less.

According to a 2009 study at Oregon State University, "the average long-term carbon impact of a child born in the United States—along with all of its descendants—is more than 160 times the impact of a child born in Bangladesh. An American woman who has a baby will generate nearly seven times the carbon footprint of that of a Chinese woman who has a child, the study also found."[23]

A 2012 Scientific American article takes this even further, "A child born in the United States will create thirteen times as much ecological damage over the course of his or her lifetime than a child born in Brazil," reports the Sierra Club's Dave Tilford, adding that the average American will drain as many resources as 35 natives of India and consume 53 times more goods and services than someone from China."[24]

Essentially what this means is that one can live simply in an off-grid home, ride a bicycle while growing food for their vegan household, yet as soon as a child is born, these lower impact choices are not only canceled out, they're exponentially reversed by the carbon legacy alone.

We in the western world are often quick to point the finger at others in foreign lands for their inability to control their libido. But as the saying goes, "When you point the finger at someone else, there are three more pointing back at you."

The reality is that parents don't have children (for long), they have adults. If the average lifespan of a human is 85 years, over 70 of those years are mature years. "Having babies" is not as much a problem as having adults is. The environmental impact of disposable diapers and baby items is nothing to sneeze at, but the planetary effect of adult consumption is exponentially more destructive.

Perhaps those who breed are "doing their best" with those they bring into the world, however "best" within a dysfunctional, broken civilization is not good enough for a prolonged existence on

Earth. Mass producing ourselves with antiquated belief systems steeped in anthropocentrism on a finite planet is a recipe for irreversible disaster.

The bottom line is that we have a moral obligation to Earth. Not to cultural expectations. Not to tradition. Not to self-serving wants. Not to our egos. Not to patriarchy. Not to cultural programming.

Elevating the Big Lie over a habitable planet is omnicide. It is the ultimate statement of stupidity, and of how far we've strayed from the web of life and our place on Earth.

Choosing to refrain from burdening the planet with another human being demonstrates a maturity in consciousness that connects us to a profound love for *all* life.

Too Late

All undomesticated, non-human species know their place in the web of life. Because of this innate wisdom, they operate within the laws of nature. They do not breed beyond the carrying capacity of their environment. They do not breed to the point of self-destruction. They do not breed when they cannot feed their young. They reproduce only to ensure the continuation of the species, and never at the peril of other species, or of life on Earth. The only exception occurs when humans interfere by destroying ecosystems, therefore disrupting the natural way.

Because of our prolific breeding prowess and our lack of willingness to evolve beyond antiquated belief systems, human overpopulation is choking out life on Earth. As with all problems now facing our world, we've been aware of population overshoot for decades. In typical fashion, however, we've readily chosen to ignore it.

A blog article posted in *The Oldspeak Journal* reads:

Population overshoot. Two of the most undesirable words one could ever utter in a globalized consumer culture predicated on buying ever more stuff and having ever more babies to plug into the hyperconsumption matrix and perpetually restart the cycle (closely followed by two other most undesirable words; ecological overshoot). These conditions are unsustainable and omnicidal. At some point, there's likely to be a global regime shift to a significantly less hospitable state than present conditions. That regime shift is quite possibly underway now. One need only witness the disintegration of the cryosphere, worldwide. As time passes and irreplaceable resources dwindle, these words will be harder to avoid saying. There is no infinite, exponential growth on a finite planet. In my view, the economics of 7.6 billion people on one planet point to one outcome, two more undesirable words: population dieback.[25]

We may have convinced ourselves of our moral superiority and our "right" to breed with reckless abandon, but it's also Gaea's "right" to purge herself of our "breed greed".

Louise Leakey, in her 2008 TEDx talk, *A Dig for Humanity's Origins*, said:

> From very primitive beginnings with a crude toolkit of stones, we now have a very advanced toolkit, and our tool use has reached unprecedented levels. We also have reached extraordinary numbers of ourselves all over the planet. Our global population has skyrocketed. Our technology has removed the checks and balances of our population growth. We have to control our numbers because we can't hold it together as a species. My father so appropriately put it that "we are certainly the only animal that makes conscious choices that are bad for our survival as a species.[26]

In her billions of years of existence, Gaea knows full well how to course correct to ensure her ongoing survival and evolution, despite how we've destroyed the checks and balances of our population growth. In breeding ourselves beyond the carrying capacity of Earth, and with no desire to self-regulate, we have reached the end of the line. The most significant miracle is not how we have been able to carry on with our insane civilization for so long, but how we have been able to proliferate without killing ourselves off long before now.

As Gaea continues to strengthen her immune system with her earthquakes, tsunamis, wildfires, floods, droughts, superstorms, and so on, soon there will be no habitable planet left, and we will be gone.

In her poem, *What to Tell the Children*, Rachel Kann writes:

> Tell them that everything is not ok,
>
> And knowing that is ok.
>
> Tell them that pretending that what is unacceptable is fine
>
> Is what got us to this sick and dysfunctional spot on the timeline.[27]

Extinction by childbirth. What a way to go.

The Blessed Curse of Technology

"We have created a Star Wars civilization with stone age emotions, medieval institutions, and god-like technology."

– E.O. WILSON

When I was a child, technology had little impact on everyday life. Born in the early '60's, my entrance to the world preceded bank cards, personal computers, and color tv. Neighbors kept their doors unlocked for spontaneous visits, and free time meant playing outdoors with my friends, sisters, Ozzie, the guinea pig, and Tippy, the dog. My mother's greatest concerns were scraped knees, grass stains and being able to entice me indoors before dinner got cold.

It was a simpler time where connection was personal, and people were more trusting by nature. There was no cable tv, video gaming, Netflix, computers, iPads, smartphones, social media, YouTube, or internet. There was no distraction from what mattered most: relationship. Needless to say, the sweeping paranoia of today was unsurprisingly absent.

Although technology existed in my childhood—from dishwashers to Apollo 1; to gas-guzzling cars and atomic bombs—it didn't prevent the relational nature of humanity from seeping through. In less than 60 years, however, everything has changed.

Under the guise of "progress," "convenience" and "comfort," technology has rapidly engulfed the human mind. The subsequent degradation in consciousness that I've borne witness to in my lifetime is alarming.

In our evolution from sticks and stones, to high-powered weapons, industrialized farms and slaughterhouses; Hummers, SUV's, trawl-net fishing, and nuclear weapons, we've become a force for destruction that knows no limits. Technology has altered our relationship to the body, to Earth, and to each other by elevating us above the laws of nature and the web of life that holds it all together. Our technologies may have been created with the best of intentions, but good intentions die hard when deprived of Soul.

Our technological mastery has given us revolutionary innovations in medicine that have helped us live longer, but not better. Cancer, heart disease, arthritis, mental illnesses, depression, anxiety, and a plethora of emerging new diseases are more prominent than ever. Medical technological innovations have also boosted the population explosion that now threatens life on Earth.

We have technologies to medicate, irradiate, dismember, and replace any body part in question; while an endless array of synthetic pharmaceuticals are available to numb the very ailments born from the technologies that created them in the first place.

Our technology has allowed us to build fortresses against nature with our cities and suburbs; and mobile fortresses against the natural world with our cars, trucks, SUV's, recreational vehicles, boats, and tanker-ships. Our mechanized dementia has succeeded in further separating us from the very thread of life.

Innovations in agriculture have evolved from the oppression of nature with poisons, pesticides and chemical fertilizers; to the transcendence of nature with the likes of nanotechnology, cloning, and genetic engineering.

Our mad obsession with noise drowns out the sounds of the natural world and our own hearts. Leaf blowers, lawn mowers, power washers, hedge trimmers, snowblowers, and chainsaws ruthlessly attack the senses in our neighborhoods; while the endless cacophony of cars, horns, sirens, alarms, motorcycles, transport trucks, airplanes, industrial noise, heavy equipment, machinery, and endless construction permeates our being with a low-grade state of agitation that never leaves.

The wilderness areas on our planet are shrinking, and the habitat of every wild creature is violated by those who hunt, fish, collect, and "get away from it all." They bring with them their campers, trailers, ATV's, guns, crossbows, fishing rods, snowmobiles, dirt bikes, jet ski's, powerboats, radios, plastic toys, and barbecues. They leave behind their hooks, lines, sinkers, oil slicks, shotgun casings, plastic, fast-food packaging, coffee cups, bottles, cans, and smoldering cigarette butts.

Light pollution from the urban glow of streetlights, houses, and buildings emanates a dimming haze that jeopardizes birds and wildlife and diminishes our relationship with the stars, moon, and infinite universe.

Invisible, ubiquitous electric and magnetic fields from our computers, cell phones, refrigerators, radios, televisions, microwaves, satellites, WiFi, power lines, transformers, and towers bring to us sleep disruption, headaches, anxiety, fatigue, and a profusion of unremitting issues that haunt us from the inside, out.

Technology has allowed us to travel great distances: from cars, trains, and ships; to planes, rockets, and space shuttles. From the deepest depths of the ocean to far-reaching planets, little remains unsullied by humanity. Fueling all of our methods of transportation is the black gold of industrial civilization: oil—the stuff that powers our gluttonous consumption, perpetuates war and causes exorbitant destruction to our land, water, and air.

With our race toward evermore lethal technologies, the mass destruction of life is easier than ever before. The frightening power of our nuclear weapons, chemical and bacterial agents, and war machines have brought us to a place where the simple push of a button can eliminate life on Earth. Albert Einstein understood the severity of this technological obsession many years ago when he said, "It has become appallingly obvious that our technology has exceeded our humanity. I know not with what weapons World War III will be fought, but World War IV will be fought with sticks and stones."

In the hubris of our addiction to the domination of nature, our modern industrialized/militarized technology has pushed Earth past the breaking point. In the ultimate display of arrogance, climate engineering—or geoengineering—is being employed to "remedy" the technological advances that brought us to the brink of self-annihilation in the first place. Mathematician, John von Neumann said it well, "Technological possibilities are irresistible to man. If man can go to the moon, he will. If he can control the climate, he will."

With its obsessive need for control, humanity has single-handedly rendered Earth more unpredictable and unstable. Ironically, the very creations meant to "save" us from ourselves, may well be our final curtain call.

In a last-ditch effort to escape the hell we've created on Earth, we are frantically creating technologies to colonize other planets. Fortunately, our attempts have been feeble at best, disastrous at worst.

One of the most brilliant minds in the world, the late Stephen Hawking, shared in a recent Guardian article, "We face awesome environmental challenges: climate change, food production, overpopulation, the decimation of other species, epidemic disease, acidification of the oceans. Together, they are a reminder that we are at the most dangerous moment in the development of humanity. We now have the technology to destroy the planet on which we live, but have not yet developed the ability to escape it."[28]

In the wake of our demise, will the demented creation of artificial intelligence carry on our destructive legacy, or will we leave behind a barren planet, devoid of life, burdened with the garbage and technological remains of our anthropocentric arrogance?

In his book, *The Ascent of Humanity*, Charles Eisenstein wrote:

> Futurists have been predicting the imminent rise of a technological Utopia, drawing on the premise that technology will free humankind from labor, suffering, disease, and possibly even death. Underlying this view is a defining story of our civilization: that science has brought us from a state of ignorance to an increasing understanding of the physical universe, and that technology has brought us from a state of dependency on nature's whims to an increasing mastery of the material world. Someday in the future, goes the story, our understanding and control will be complete.[29]

This begs the question: Is it naivety or stupidity that has us believe in the omnipotence of technology to conquer nature, disease, old age, and even death?

The biggest problem with our increasingly sophisticated technologies is that most of our innovations come with unintended consequences, and a worsening of the issues they were meant to solve. To "fix" these problems, we create ever more technologies to feed our insatiable addiction. Like all addictions, however, we now need higher doses of technology just to prevent the world from falling apart. We've moved from technology in service to civilization, to civilization in service to technology.

The Messiah complex that accompanies our scientific/technological mindset misleads us into believing that the benefits of our short-sighted creations outweigh the risks. We are quick to utilize unproven technologies, and slow (if ever) to critically examine their long-term implications.

On a more personal level, technologies that were meant to simplify our lives have lead us away from the real world, and into the dangerous abyss of a virtual world. In general, technology leaves us feeling alienated from, and more afraid of the very world it attempts to control.

Technological obsession infiltrates the minds of children early on. One only needs to visit any public venue to witness children who can barely talk engrossed in their own devices, or fighting over shared gaming devices, iPads and iPhones. The digital babysitter has replaced conscious parenting, setting kids up for social failure from the get-go. The seeds of technological disconnect are planted long before children know how to think critically for themselves. Before they know what's happening, kids are addicted to excessive screen time, leading to low self-esteem, relationship issues and challenges with social interaction; not to mention disconnection from their bodies from remaining idle for hours on end.

Our degraded consciousness, along with our addictive nature, ensures that we are irresponsible with our technology. What is meant to "connect" us, often ends up causing more isolation in the end. Social media has evoked more resentment, anti-social behavior, isolation, and inauthenticity in our world. We conveniently edit our lives, doctor our photos and flaunt only the happy moments; while the pain and everyday monotony of our lives remain carefully tucked away. The facade of who we pretend ourselves to be instigates envy and a "fear of missing out" (FOMO), leaving us feeling more worthless and empty in the end. Social media has disconnected us from reality at a time when the planet is begging for our unbridled attention; and our plugged in, "always on display" way of life has damaged our relationship to ourselves, Earth, and each another.

Our fanatical obsession with our "smart" phones is making us dumber by the day. Attention spans are in severe deficit as we neurotically check our devices with every buzz, beep, ding, or chime. Texting, emailing, and perpetual phone-staring have obliterated eye contact and attentive listening to one another. Few people can adequately spell anymore let alone carry on a conversation with any semblance of depth or meaning.

We are a technologically addicted civilization as evidenced by the device as an appendage. iPhones, iPads, iPods (and all their derivatives)—me, myself and i, i, I. How many consider the enslaved who assemble these frivolous items so we may have our 24/7 distraction? How many consider the mining for minerals, plastics, planned obsolescence and open-loop thinking that causes extreme planetary damage? How many consider the thousands who desperately forage through mountains of toxic e-waste in foreign lands for a few extra dollars just to survive?

Henry Miller once said:

> We clutter the earth with our inventions, never dreaming that possibly they are unnecessary—or disadvantageous. We devise astounding means of communication, but do we communicate with one another? We move our bodies to and fro and incredible speeds, but do we really leave the spot we started from? Mentally, morally, spiritually, we are fettered. What have we achieved in mowing down mountain ranges, harnessing the energy of mighty rivers, or moving whole populations about like chess pieces, if we ourselves remain the same restless, miserable, frustrated creatures we were before? To call such activity progress is utter delusion. We may succeed in altering the face of the earth until it is unrecognizable even to the Creator, but if we are unaffected wherein lies the meaning?[30]

We are so addicted to interfacing with our electronic devices that in many ways, we are more comfortable with this virtual reality than we are with a genuine connection. We now live almost wholly in a manufactured reality. As our personal and global technology increases in sophistication, we further separate ourselves from life.

Charles Eisenstein supports this statement in his book, *The Ascent of Humanity*, "Technology was created to transcend nature, therefore it is an extension of our separation from nature. It was created to improve our lives and make things easier, therefore it is an extension of our separation from our Selves."[31]

In many ways, technology has made life more comfortable, but it has come at a steep price. Our unbridled willingness to embrace the latest and greatest technology is spinning us out of control. With a collective consciousness trapped in a Big Lie, there's nowhere to go with our technologies, but oblivion. And so technology—our blessing—is also our curse.

Our technological evolution has been dizzying, while evolution in consciousness has been stagnant. To further amplify our problems, there remain many regions in the world where fundamentalism and medieval beliefs persist. Access to modern weaponry, internet, and ease of travel make for dangerous consequences, including the global uprising in violent terrorism.

As we continue to develop increasingly sophisticated and destructive technologies with an inert state of consciousness, we are losing ourselves. Our relationship with machines is now such that we need them to keep us alive, and they need us to keep them alive. This fatal codependence cannot end well.

In his essay, *Blind Spot*, Peter Russell writes:

> We are coming to the natural end of our species' journey, spinning faster and faster into the center of an evolutionary spiral. Almost every crisis facing us today has its roots in accelerating development. A system can only tolerate so much stress; then it breaks down. If a wheel is made to spin faster and faster, it will eventually break apart under the stress. In a similar way

as rates of change get ever faster, the systems involved will reach a point where they too break apart. Whether it be our own biological system, social, economic, and political systems, or the planetary ecosystem, the stress of ever-increasing change will eventually lead to breakdown. Crises will pile upon each other faster and faster, heading us into the perfect global storm.[32]

With the demented technologies we've created, we can now slaughter billions of land animals annually; billions of tonnes of fish annually; millions of our own species annually; numb our minds and senses 24/7; wipe out entire forests and ecosystems in record speed, and generate countless tonnes of garbage every day. Our rapacious contribution to the wanton decimation of the planet and its many life forms is an insult to Earth that demeans us as a species.

This is not the end of it, however.

In November 2016, a University of Leicester report declared that Earth's "technosphere" now weighs 30 trillion tons. The paper states, "The technosphere is comprised of all of the structures that humans have constructed to keep them alive on the planet—from houses, factories and farms to computer systems, smartphones, and CDs, to the waste in landfills and spoil heaps. The technosphere is a system, with its own dynamics and energy flows—and humans have to help keep it going to survive."

According to Professor Mark Williams, "The technosphere can be said to have budded off the biosphere and arguably is now at least partly parasitic on it. At its current scale the technosphere is a major new phenomenon on this planet—and one that is evolving extraordinarily rapidly."[33]

The technosphere competes with the biosphere for resources and space. However, unlike Earth's biosphere, the research team says the technosphere does not recycle much of its waste, as seen in our overflowing landfill sites and the overwhelming amount of space junk orbiting the planet.

Professor Jan Zalasiewicz (from the same report) goes on to state, "The technosphere may be geologically young, but it is evolving with furious speed, and it has already left a deep imprint on our planet,"[34]

We are so proficient in the creation of our technologies and the subsequent waste they generate that our trash has expanded well beyond Earth. In the short documentary, *Adrift*, which explores the hidden world of space junk, it is said that, "Every orbital launch generates rocket parts as debris, as do satellites. Some pieces remain orbiting forever. Some burn up. Some land unpredictably on Earth. Some, they say, are guided safely into the ocean (where they pollute the other unseen world). Space debris is a floating graveyard encircling the Earth with over 17,000 objects bigger than 10cm, 60,000 objects bigger than 5cm, 200 million objects bigger than 1mm, and a trillion objects bigger than 0.1mm."[35]

Everything from paint chips to nuts, bolts, and tools, to defunct satellites, motor casings, frozen coolant, and rocket stages the size of school buses pollute the universe, orbiting Earth at tremendous speeds of 17,000 miles per hour (27,360 kilometers per hour).

As with all attempts to clean up our mess on land, in the air, in water, and now in space, we have failed miserably. Future space exploration may very well become impossible. Never mind colonizing Mars. Because of our short-sighted arrogance, soon there will be so much debris circling the planet that we won't be able to leave Earth even if we could.

Earth is the ultimate closed-loop system. In our "out of sight, out of mind" ignorance, we've created a monster that can no longer be tamed. Our garbage is everywhere. We are now eating it, being poisoned by it, and are now imprisoned by it. Perhaps when some future evolved civilization or alien starship discovers post-apocalyptic

Earth, their first impression will be, "A bunch of ignorant slobs once lived here."

In John Weber's blog post, *A Bang and a Whimper*, he writes:

> We are slowly technologizing ourselves into extinction. Technology is seductive. Is it the power? Is it the comfort? Or is it some internal particularly human attribute that drives it? Technology surrounds us and becomes part of our story and myths. Technology tantalizes the human mind to make, combine, invent. There are always unintended consequences with technology. It affects how we experience the world in time and space. It affects how we feel the world. If all the externalities were included in the prices and cost to nature, we would be very, very wary of technology.[36]

The dream of the modern, technological world was constructed almost entirely out of assumptions that have been accepted without question for generations. Over time, these assumptions have become part of the fabric of society, profoundly embedded in all of our cultural institutions.

Of the countless assumptions that make up our modern, industrialized worldview, the primary and all-encompassing assumption is that we are separate from and superior to, the web of life. The premise of this Big Lie shapes almost all of our perceptions and actions.

Over the centuries, the story that has been accepted, and thus communicated in the modern, scientific world, is that the world operates like a massive machine made up of separate parts like a big clock. For the past 400 or so years, the scientific/technological tradition has been trying to take the clock apart and figure out how it works so that it can be mastered and used for our own purposes.

This mechanistic view has meant that instead of seeing the interconnection of things, we are only able to see the separate parts. What evolved from this story was a fragmented view of the natural world that birthed technologies with increasing dominion over the nature. We are now so hypnotized by the power of our technologies that we have lost our connection to everything sacred. The result is a way of living that allows us to decimate life with our eyes wide open. We've normalized the abnormal without batting an eye.

We can manipulate, conquer, alter, destroy, and modify nature. We can even create machines that are smarter, faster and more dangerous than ourselves. We've become both the makers and slaves of our own creations.

We may think we can "save" ourselves from ourselves by geoengineering the climate, creating artificial intelligence, designing elaborate underground bunker systems, inhabiting Mars, settling on the moon, or some other escapist notion to remedy the life-threatening errors brought on by our fragmented consciousness, but wherever we go, there we are. The band-aids will never work because the psychic wounds run too deep. Along with our immutable human consciousness, science and technology will never save us because it got us into this mess in the first place. Our scientific separation and technological destruction will only succeed in taking us further away from where we most need to go: within.

I believe that on a deep subconscious level, many of us feel a sense of loss as our cultural addiction to technology drives us further away from the natural world, and deeper into a sea of cold, impersonal circuitry. We consume an endless stream of mindless media while the world around us falls apart. We choose the faux "reality" on a computer screen while neglecting the reality of our own lives. We've lost our true humanity and are paying a hefty price for severing our connection to the web of life. This collective separation threatens our health, our vitality, our spirits, and the very Soul of who we are.

Richard Louv speaks to this nature-deficit disorder in his book,

The Nature Principle. He writes, "By its broadest interpretation, nature-deficit disorder is an atrophied awareness, a diminished ability to find meaning in the life that surrounds us, whatever form that takes. This shrinkage of our lives has a direct impact on our physical, mental, and societal health."[37]

What we are seeking in our technological addiction is nothing less than our lost wholeness, and its recovery lies in the courage to remember that we are not apart from, but a part of the natural world. It is this very courage that can lead us back home, to the Soul.

Powerless Power

"To reclaim our natural power and this birthright of real magic,
we must get naked and face ourselves."

– JACOB NORDBY

From the moment we're no more than a thought in our parents' heads, we're being groomed to search outside of ourselves for cues on how to live our lives. By the time we're birthed into flesh, we're already fragmented; domesticated by an oppressive civilization that severs our connection to the Soul. We're not taught how to think critically. We're not taught that we're worthy. We're not taught autonomy. We're not taught that our voices matter. We're not taught that the source of our most profound power lies within.

We're domesticated by systems of thought that ensure we don't think for ourselves. This results in a loss of connection to the essence of who we are: our instincts, curiosity, intuition, passion, compassion, self-trust, courage, creativity, spontaneity, and our internal moral compass. Our thoughts, choices, behaviors, and actions are thus driven by conditioning, habits, patterns, and fear, rather than the deeper truths within. We're programmed to be more concerned about what we *think* others are thinking of us, rather than standing true in who we authentically are. In this culturally conditioned smallness, we render ourselves powerless.

The culture we live in is all about repetition, monotony, compliance, conformity, sameness, and powerlessness. We are rewarded by the degree to which we can stand in line, wait our turn, await "anointment" by those deemed "authority," while others determine when we are ready for anointment; and still others dictate what our truth should be.

We are trapped in an over 3000-year-old belief system of externally referenced "power." Our entire reality is constructed around this antiquated, Soul-disabling fallacy.

In the powerlessness that ensues, we think too much and feel too little. Our heads are full, and our hearts are empty. We talk too much and say little of worth. We complain more than we care. We lie more than we love.

We have lost our wildness—our autonomy—our connection to the Soul. We've become hollow shells of monotony. We need only look at the state of our world to see the repercussions of this tedious sameness.

When we clearcut natural forests and replant monoculture, outbreaks of disease and insect infestations abound. When we "clearcut" the Soul—our natural, unconditioned Self—we create monoculture through our conformity, compliance, and sameness. When we accept sameness, we reject diversity, and diseases of the spirit abound. Infestations of violent thought—from judgment, racism, homophobia, transphobia, sexism, speciesism, and ableism; to murder, slaughter, and war—are prolific in this fertile ground. Sameness is powerlessness. By conforming to a mindset of powerlessness, we willingly sustain the Big Lie.

One of the most prominent templates for the existence of humanity is fear. We've all been well-trained by fear. Because of its pervasive nature, most people are unaware of the extent to which fear drives their lives. Identification with fear is a hideous thing. It lurks beneath conscious awareness and brings out the rigid, constricted, parochial expression of who we've been trained to be in our Big Lie world.

Our fear-based culture preys on our low self-worth and perpetuates powerlessness. We are repeatedly told by our cultural institutions and the many people in our lives, that we are less than we innately know ourselves to be. We're taught to shrink. Every time we say yes to shrinkage, a piece of the Soul "dies," and a piece of Earth dies. As long as we believe ourselves to be worthless, we will always be at war with Earth and each other.

For thousands of years, the body has been silenced so that what lives inside does not emerge. We are only permitted to select from a small range of feelings, emotions, beliefs, and experiences outside of ourselves. The root of our external referencing begins with parenting where, as little children, we learn to silence our internal cues in favor of what we are taught to believe by the authority figures who run our lives.

Every system in our civilization co-opts our power. The moment gender roles are imposed upon us by our parents and culture, we are inculcated into gender-directed modes of thought that ensure the resilience of our powerlessness.

Boys are taught that "might is right," and strength is power over another. Power comes from winning in sports, business, competition, and war. Emotional neutrality, sexual prowess, scientific intellect, reason, rational thought, and dominating and conquering animals, women, and nature are considered the epitome of masculinity.

Girls are taught that power comes from pleasing and appeasing men or adopting the competitive mindset of an "imitation man," using the words of author and women's empowerment advocate, Sierra Bender.

Gender-role messaging is so pervasive that it can be found in every culture and every system of thought in our human civilization. We are inculcated to believe that it is absolute, and we are shamed, ridiculed, and punished if we question otherwise.

In the innocence of our childhood, we don't have the knowledge, free-will or support to extract ourselves from the gender expectations, abusive situations, demeaning and unsafe experiences, and hand-me-down belief systems that ingrain our powerlessness. Every system in our civilization perpetuates this powerlessness. In our early years, one of the most influential systems (aside from the family system), is education. By teaching children *what* to think rather than *how* to think, education instills powerlessness through conformity, compliance, and sameness.

In his book, *Conversations with God*, Neale Donald Walsh wrote:

> Classes in critical thinking, problem-solving, and logic are considered by many parents to be threatening. They want such classes out of the curriculum. As well they might, if they want to protect their way of life. Because children who are allowed to develop their own critical thinking processes are very much likely to abandon their parents' morals, standards, and entire way of life.

> In order to protect (our) way of life, (we) have built an education system based upon the development in the child of memories, not abilities. Children are taught to remember facts and fictions—the fictions each society has set up about itself—rather than given the ability to discover and create their own truths.

> Programs calling for children to develop abilities and skills rather than memories are soundly ridiculed by those who imagine that they know what a child needs to learn. Yet what (we) have been teaching (our) children has led (our) world toward ignorance, not away from it.[38]

Because of the aggressive nature of our cultural programming, by the time we reach adulthood, we are lost to who and what we authentically are. We then live the story of our lives in the shadows of

our parents, teachers, authority figures, and culture—always searching outside of ourselves for what we desperately wish to express
from within.

Without the aid of our internal GPS, we fly blindly into the strategically placed webs that surreptitiously throttle our real power. For a
fly caught in a web, the spider is attracted to struggle. He captures his
prey, wraps her in silk, liquifies her insides, and leisurely sucks the life
out of her. An appropriate metaphor.

The human spider—the man-made systems created to perpetuate the Big Lie—has built around us an intricate web of greed,
self-doubt, fear, and mistrust. He wraps us in fear and authorita-
tively preys on the low self-worth that promotes unconscious consumption and a false sense of security, externally sourced through
his seductive offerings. We buy into his dominant civilization without thought, justifying the increased lunacy with phrases like,
"that's just the way it is." We blindly acquiesce as our life-force is
slowly sucked away, only to be replaced by anxiety, addiction, stress,
worry, illness, and depression. This may be "normal," but it's far
from natural.

The cultural machine conditions us to believe that we are at its
mercy. It is genius at isolating us from ourselves while mercilessly
capitalizing on our ignorance. In our uninformed stupor, we readily give our power away. We are so conditioned to tiptoe with our
two lips that we never break free from the fear that prevents us from
speaking, and living our truth. In compliant resignation, we choose
fear and sameness, over truth and evolution.

The more significant our fear, the greater our need to dominate
under the guise of power. Fear cannot tolerate complexity. Complexity is overwhelming for a human mind gripped in the chaos of fear.
When we interact with other living systems from a place of fear—
whether it be another person, animal or Earth—everything around

that complexity is filtered through the compressed, resourceless state of fear. Violence—in one form or another—is the predictable outcome.

There is a moral decrepitude that has gripped our species. In our perpetual state of fear, we've become a powerless culture of victims, perpetrators, blamers, and shamers, unable to see beyond the inauthenticity of it all.

The world is overrun by walking wounded who refuse to live as anything but victims to their choices, traumas, pains, and circumstances. In choosing this degraded consciousness, they fear what they don't understand, hate what they fear, and destroy what they fear caring about: physically, mentally, and emotionally. In refusing to take ownership for their lives, they trap themselves in perpetual denial and ignorance. Most people have denied for so long who they are, they live lost lives. There is no greater statement of powerlessness than to not know one's true Self.

Our dominant civilization offers us so many ways to maintain our disconnect from the Soul. In this disconnect, we convince ourselves that external forces define our lives and that we're trapped in a life story we cannot revise. But that's simply not true. In choosing to live the repetitive nature of what we know (and have always known), our past choices and actions will always define how we live in the present. As Mark Twain said, "If you always do what you've always done, you'll always get what you've always got." Until we make choices aligned with our inner truth, we remain trapped in the purgatory of our culturally conditioned ways.

Throughout our history as a species, many great voices have told us that the world can only change when we change; and yet we continue to wait for the world to be changed by others. Our inertia shackles us. Unless we are willing to evolve beyond the status quo, we sustain the status quo by being the status quo.

The dangers of maintaining the homeostasis of the status quo are clear: increased violence, accelerated ecocide, near-term omnicide. By not questioning the outmoded belief systems that drive our collapsing world, we create the perfect conditions for our collective demise. The gravest problem with any deeply embedded belief system is that it infiltrates the psyche and becomes part of our identity. Most people are unwilling to challenge who they believe themselves to be because they are not taught how to listen to the internal cues that tell them otherwise.

As our critical faculties develop, it can seem far more comfortable to rationalize what we have been taught to believe is true, than face the discomfort that comes from questioning it. To ask questions is to be internally referenced in an externally referenced world. We become dangerous to the status quo when we live a life of internal referencing. Few in this world are willing to allow this for themselves.

The domestication of the human spirit has devolved species homo sapien sapiens into a rather docile lot of hollow, compliant mutants. By normalizing the abnormal story of separation and not questioning the systems that hold it in place, we preserve the status quo at great expense to our own lives, and to life on Earth.

In the documentary, *Creating Freedom*, physicist Jeff Schmidt said:

> In the course of my research for my book, *Disciplined Minds*, I came across a newsletter for the Lawrence Livermore National Laboratory, which is one of the two nuclear weapons design laboratories in the United States.

> In an interview published in that newsletter, the interviewer asked some young nuclear weapons designers, 'What is the worst thing about your job?' The young guys paused to think about it, and finally, they said things like, 'The comput-

ers! They don't have enough capacity, and they're always going down.' Things like that. Very narrow answers. To me, this was a great illustration of the subordination of professionals to their beliefs. It wasn't their job, or even their interest to question the big picture: to wonder, 'maybe the worst thing about my job is that I'm making the world a more dangerous place and that I'm setting up a disaster by designing weapons of mass destruction.' They didn't comment on that at all. In general, questioning the goal of the work was not considered to be a legitimate part of their work. People are not supposed to question the morality of their roles in life.[39]

The more we comply with the Big Lie and its dominant civilization, the more likely we are to internalize its values and conform to its expectations. The version of reality we are thus presented with, serves the agendas of those who control what is offered. To shape the minds of the masses, is to shape civilization. This is what inspires good people to make mindless, cruel and destructive choices. There is no personal power in this.

Let's face it, how could we live with ourselves day in and day out working mundane jobs that bore us, endure relationships that drain us, and consume "food" that poisons us, while ignoring a planet in biosphere collapse, if we were not trapped in a mindset of powerlessness? In our powerlessness, the surface reality of society is so deceptive that familiarity blinds us to collapsing ecosystems, and the oppressive structures that shape our lives and our world.

Understanding ourselves is essential for liberation from the self-deception that mires us in the powerlessness of groupthink, denial, conflict, consumption, mindless destruction, and spiritual vacancy. But our minds are a battleground of competing forces that render us ignorant to our own ignorance. Because most people are driven by the need to fit in, they don't challenge the beliefs that cause them to make the choices they do. Without rigorously questioning our own beliefs, we cannot meaningfully question the assumptions of civilization as a whole. Because we live in a culture of hubris and blame, self-scrutiny is virtually non-existent. Without it, however, there is no possibility for the expansive consciousness required to bring peace and unity to our own lives, and to the world.

I believe that if we were to intentionally design an environment that would be most harmful to the health of the mind, body, spirit, and planet, it would look exactly like our modern civilization. We cut ourselves off from nature by spending countless hours in overpriced, toxic boxes. In those boxes, we stagnate in sofas and chairs as our bodies and minds atrophy from staring at artificial light sources for hours on end. In bizarre isolation, we chat with virtual "friends" to distract ourselves from the pain of our self-induced loneliness. We breathe polluted air, drink chemically-laden water, eat poison-filled "food" with ingredients that we can't even pronounce. We fill our bodies with the chemical signatures of fear, suffering, and violence with every mouthful of avian ovulation, bovine maternal secretion and blood-soaked flesh from brutalized animal corpses. Our pillows, mattresses, and clothing are soaked in flame retardants absorbed through the delicate membrane of our largest organ: the skin. Our modern furniture off-gasses toxic fumes as we "clean" it with pine-scented poison. We mold our hair with glues and waxes, paint our faces with petroleum-based cosmetics, and drench ourselves in hormone-disrupting colognes and perfumes to conceal everything natural about what we are. And to top it all off, nuclear isotopes are released into the water and air, as EMF radiation is blasted in every direction.

And we call this normal.

Our domesticated world has created so many factors to degrade our planetary health; our emotional, mental, and physical health; and the health of our spirits. These factors make us weak, sick, anxious, and apathetic. The deck is stacked against us for living a healthy, vital, conscious, and empowered life. Unfortunately, eating mindfully and healthfully while meditating, getting proper sleep and exercise is no longer enough. We need to go much deeper. Reclaiming our personal power is a choice. Sustaining our conditioned powerlessness, however, is also a choice.

The Big Lie preys on our deeply rooted insecurities and feeds the prevailing mindset of powerlessness. Powerlessness is a self-created prison that prevents us from claiming the comprehensive nature of what we authentically are. No amount of money, love, time, self-control, happiness, or education can release the mind from the grip of powerlessness when it believes it to be untrue. Most people are so trapped in the profound commitment to their own limitations, that they have no interest in exploring anything otherwise.

We live in a world where we readily allow the outside in, and rarely let the inside out. What has happened to us to be so fearful of our Selves that we've traded the Soul, our conscience, and our connection to the web of life, for a Lie that renders us powerless? In our powerlessness, we can only create from our separation. In creating from our separation, everything is ugly.

From judgment and blame to bullying, fear, and racism; to war, misogyny, speciesism, and ecocide; these are but a few of the manifestations of our collective powerlessness. Trillions and trillions and trillions of small, medium, and large choices to blame, judge, oppress, dominate, and hate ourselves and the "other," have brought us to where we stand today. In the quantum paradigm, the energy of thought always precedes the physical manifestation of matter. Matter, in the form of runaway biosphere decay, and the relentless, escalating violence in our world, is a direct reflection of our collective consciousness.

In Neale Donald Walsh's book, *Conversations with God*, he wrote:

At some level, you have all created that which you say you detest—and, having created it, you have chosen it.

This is an advanced level of thinking; it is one which all Masters reach sooner or later. For it is only when they can accept responsibility for all of it that they can achieve the power to change part of it.

So long as you entertain the notion that there is something or someone else out there "doing it" to you, you disempower yourself to do anything about it. Only when you say, "I did this" can you find the power to change it.[40]

Everything about our cultural narrative cultivates busyness and distraction from our Selves. Our fear of slowing down prevents us from contemplating the things that matter. The endless stream of media sensationalizing the minutia of the world's pain leaves us feeling paralyzed rather than empowered to act. Yet we live in a time that is desperate for Self-evolved visionaries with expansive ideas to commence the healing process for a world gone amiss. It makes no difference that it's too late for our species, because it's never too late for the Soul.

In a civilization that worships the frenzied pace of "doing," our imaginations are dulled into passivity. There is "no time" for evolution and the reclamation of wholeness. The disease of "busy" is destroying our overall wellbeing. It's depleting our ability to think critically, act compassionately, and express creatively. We must remember: we are human beings, not human doings. We are not the helpless automatons with endless to-do lists that we've come to believe ourselves to be.

The powerlessness we collectively feel is the basis for marketing, advertising and just about every celebrity coach in existence. There is much money to be made in selling impressive looking roadmaps to personal power. "Three easy installments of $995 and you can have all the success and meaning you've always yearned for in life!" Failing that, you can at least temporarily forfeit the longing in your Soul to *become*.

So much of what we read, watch and hear through the barrage of media in our lives, are stories of what is happening "out there." Everywhere we turn, innocent lives of all different races, genders, and species are lost, tortured and twisted beyond recognition of anything reflecting a sense of humanity. The temptation to resist the high definition images accompanying these stories is non-existent. As such, each account pulls us further and further outside of ourselves. As the increasing chaos and impending doom are described in grittier detail, each story is designed to deepen the coma of belief in our powerlessness to shape the world.

Stories of the great "out there," like the Siren's call, pull us toward the collective consciousness that holds the Big Lie intact, and away from the internal cues of the Soul. As the volume goes up and the pace accelerates, our inner truth dims and fades into some silent, forgotten place within.

Our distraction mutates us. Someone points and we seek—individually and collectively—to focus on that shiny something happening "out there"; drawing our attention away from the great within. The outcome? We are sinking faster and more deeply into a thick morass of our own powerlessness; desperately clinging to the Big Lie and becoming increasingly fearful about everything of which we seemingly have no control.

As unconditioned children, our curiosity propels us toward the expression of our unique interests. Unapologetic and impatient from the inner press to simply reach out and take what we are drawn to, we are not easily deterred from moving toward our desires.

As adults, the external pressure to conform and comply allows an external pull to drag us toward what is deemed "acceptable" and "appropriate." We thus suppress what we intuitively know is the path we should be on, and forfeit the Soul's desire to become a living expression of our essential nature.

The media images and talking heads seduce us—pull us—to consume the structures of an externally contrived reality, compromising our capacity for choice, and overtaking us with beliefs about "truths" that are far from our own.

Media and marketing masquerade as forces operating in our favor; consumption intended to make our lives "better." The requirement for us to comply is essential for ensuring the durability of the existing structures of reality, no matter how insane they may be. We are powerless in the face of our own consumption.

The things we put ourselves through not to be present, not to feel, and not to listen within, are insane.

Being plugged into the system is a choice. Although the system would like for us believe otherwise; that without it, we are not safe. Authority, through demagoguery. We give our internal power away to an illusion of external safety because we are afraid, very afraid.

We long for change, but the thought paralyzes us that it might actually happen. We are geniuses at being the biggest obstacle in our own path and trying to hide that from ourselves.

Real power is not about being better, stronger, or more dominant than anyone else. It's about claiming, owning, and expressing what we hold true for ourselves. We need not live a huge or exemplary life; it need only be a life that reflects the much deeper inner truth of who we know ourselves to be. In these rapidly imploding times, we owe that to ourselves and to Earth.

The Myth of a New Story

*"We can be blind to the obvious. And we can be blind to
our blindness".*

– Daniel Hahnemann

Every living thing has its own arc of life. A beginning, a middle, and an end. It is unavoidable. No science, technology or magical thinking can change that.

Every plant and tree has its own arc of life. Every non-human animal, insect, and bird has its own arc of life. Every human has its own arc of life. The collective human species has its own arc of life. Planet Earth has her own arc of life.

It seems that humans have rewritten the trajectory of the arc to read: beginning, middle, and "happily ever after," however. Tragically, this way of viewing the world leads to behavior that is fatal to our fellow earthlings, and to ourselves.

In times of crisis, humans are inclined to bury their heads in the sand and pretend that everything will be okay; that the illusion of social justice and the dream of collective will can be upheld if only we just believe in it hard enough. It is this same culture of wishful thinking that enables us to carry on with our industrialized ways, if only we do it more "mindfully."

Why is it that we continue to pretend everything will be ok when clearly it's not? Why do we continue to believe that everything will get better when we've steamrolled over so many ecological tipping points, that we're well past the point of no return? Why can't we just accept that it's over?

Our dominant culture is built on a foundational Lie that hates life. Rape of Earth is rewarded, peace on Earth is punished. Lies are honored, truth is vilified. Ignorance is coveted; wisdom is ridiculed. Even the so-called "awakened" remain trapped in the culturally conditioned entitlement that perpetuates the slavery, oppression, and slaughter of animals for their flesh, ovulations, and maternal secretions. Everything that represents life—particularly animals and nature—is fair game for destruction in our anthropocentric, patriarchal culture.

Sharing a similar cultural observation is author Derrick Jenson, who writes in his book, *Endgame, Volume 1*:

> The culture as a whole and most of its members are insane. The culture is driven by a death urge, an urge to destroy life. From birth on, we are individually and collectively enculturated to hate life, hate the natural world, hate the wild, hate and fear animals, hate women, hate children, hate our bodies, hate and fear our emotions, hate ourselves. If we did not hate the world, we could not allow it to be destroyed before our eyes. If we did not hate ourselves, we would not allow our homes—and our bodies—to be poisoned.[41]

With a rapidly growing critical mass in a coma, our ecocide is rendering planet Earth uninhabitable. The planet cannot regenerate itself as quickly as the Big Lie is destroying it. Even the antiquated notion of linear Newtonian science brings with it alarming predictions. What Newtonian science fails to recognize is the organic, non-linear nature of Gaea. Gaea is a living organism, and linear scientific predictions are meaningless for the accelerating breakdown we are now experiencing. We've set off so many positive self-reinforcing feedback loops, that we are officially on a runaway train to a greater hell than what already exists. When the web of life breaks down, collapse accelerates, and there is no certainty, and no predictability.

Newtonian science speaks from a linear cause and effect world-view. If "X" continues to happen, then "Y" will happen in 100 years they tell us. It always seems to be some distant event beyond our current lifetime that may or may not play out should we decide to curb our consumptive ways.

We tend to face problems with facts, figures, data, statistics, extrapolation, reason, and rationale. We believe we can master the world with a three-pound hunk of watery flab, our almighty brains. But this only serves to distance us from the place we most need to go: within, to the wisdom and truth of the Soul.

We are not only living through startling ecological, economic, system, and cultural collapse; we are living among something far more threatening: a collapsed state of consciousness—where fear, denial, and ignorance reign supreme.

Our cultural story of separation has been fundamentally contradicting truth, compassion, and life for several thousand years. It is, therefore, contrary to the essence of who we are. As such, we are confused about who and what we are as a species—especially within our modern, hubristic, mechanistic civilization. Because we are so unsure of our identity as a species, we've lost all sense of belonging in nature. It is this disconnect from the web of life has brought us to the precarious place we stand today.

While every other living being on this planet intimately knows its place in the web of life, what happened to us? Surely we were not created with the sole purpose of forgetting who we are so we could gobble up everything in our path, leaving a trail of toxic trash in our wake, while destroying the biosphere in the process. Despite everything pointing in this direction, I have a hard time believing it to be so. I confess that I am questioning myself these days, however.

For most of my life, I've felt like I've been shouting compassion for

animals, Earth, and the Soul into a hurricane, hoping for someone …
anyone to hear me. With a collective mindset ready to shred any truth
contradicting the Big Lie, however, my voice was barely a whisper in
the wind. Tragically, compassion is of little interest to the masses who
pledge allegiance to the paradigm of separation. Six-pack abs? For
sure! Sixth Great Extinction Event? Meh. Scarf down another bacon
cheeseburger, chase it with a beer and Prozac and all will be well.

On a deep visceral level, I know the world I now live in is nothing
like the world I grew up in. The degradation of human consciousness
that has accompanied the population explosion is beyond comprehension. Despite my lifelong work for a kinder, more compassionate
world, I now know it's not worth the effort anymore. I feel a bittersweet pain when I sit by the ocean with my partner and dogs admir-
ing a beautiful sunset, knowing the seas are plasticized beyond repair
and are now nearly devoid of life. Spring comes earlier every year,
flooding is more intense every year, heatwaves last longer every year,
more significant algae blooms choke the seas every year, drought de-
scends earlier every year, fire burns more aggressively every year, and
yet we still do nothing to change our ways.

If we are honest with ourselves, tipping points are well behind us,
and there is no hope for salvaging our broken world anymore. Quite
frankly, why would we want to continue with what is so blatantly cruel and destructive anyway? Because it's familiar? I don't think so.

As a relatively young species on a planet that has been around for
billions of years, it is arrogance on our part to believe that we have
the power to "save" Earth. Long before our arrival on the scene, Earth
was just fine without us, thank you very much. In her superior, Soul-
inspired wisdom, she will once again be fine once we're gone. Earth
has never needed us.

The problem with our obsession with "saving Earth" is that it is yet
another distraction from a deeper truth. Saving implies superiority

and therefore, separation. And let's get honest with ourselves, what would we be "saving" Earth for anyway? Continued plundering, pollution, decimation, consumption, and exploitation?

Our ideas for "saving Earth" essentially boil down to one thing: saving the dominant civilization we've become so familiar with because we're unwilling to let it go. Gaea has other plans, however. In his book, *The Vanishing Face of Gaia*, James Lovelock wrote, "...Gaia is no cozy mother that nurtures humans and can be propitiated by gestures such as carbon trading or sustainable development. Gaia, even though we are part of her, will always dictate the terms of peace."[42]

Many believe in the myth of a new story for humanity. From the transition movement to permaculturists, to the so-called, "green movement." There is also the New Age movement with their notion of a "feminine uprising," and the emergence of a "5th dimensional consciousness"; or the modern hippy movement with their romanticized fantasies of a revival of ancient Indigenous ways (as if us white folks can ever be authorities on anything but colonization and brutality). And of course, we can't forget the Christians with their second coming of Jesus. I'm sure there's more, but you get my point.

Despite the good intentions of these beliefs, serious problems persist:

a) They remain trapped within the anthropocentric, separation consciousness of the Big Lie.

b) Sanguine worldviews that rely on the avoidance of inconvenient truths amount to no more than delusion.

c) They are dangerous because they perpetuate inertia with the belief that something external to the Soul is coming for our salvation.

d) They are dripping with so much hopium that they inoculate their believers from truth, and do little more than sustain a rose-colored version of the Big Lie.

e) It's simply too late, even for miracles.

The myth of a new story for humanity fits into Elisabeth Kübler Ross' model of "bargaining" in her theory of the five stages of grief. Bargaining is about negotiating one's way out of painful, or fatal situations with the misconception that they can be magically remedied. Our desperate need to "look for the good" and "look on the bright side" is the kiss of death for us as a species, however.

The truth is that we're long past the feel-good "change your light bulbs, bring cloth bags, take shorter showers, ride your bicycle, and recycle," "green" mindset. Most people can't even bring themselves to do these simple actions anyway. And let's get real about the "salvation" of solar, wind, and renewable energy. What for? To fuel the same consumption consciousness that got us into this mess in the first place—only this time with a green hue? It's true that fossil fuels are expediting our ecological collapse, but we're deluding ourselves by believing that our "green ways" won't have the same outcome in the end. Let's face it, our addiction to consumption is the problem. It's not about whether our "stuff" is created with raw or recycled materials; fossil fuels or alternative energy. It's the fact that we believe we need stuff in the first place. As long as we live with a mindset that desires and promotes consumption of any kind, nothing will change. And as long as we employ "solutions" from within the box that created the problems in the first place, we go nowhere.

In our consumption-obsessed civilization, there is no incentive for awakening. Subsequently, every system running our culture has a vested interest in a human collective that remains asleep.

The sad reality is that our industrialized civilization and those who control it are hell-bent on destroying the planet, and the masses don't give a damn. Most people are too distracted by the daily minutiae of their own lives to care about the state of the world. Despite the low-grade unease that relentlessly tugs at their hearts, every day is business-as-usual. Make money, pay the bills, Facebook, text, a selfie here, a selfie there, buy stuff, eat, tweet, text, down a beer, a glass of wine, watch tv, pop a pill, try to sleep, repeat. The monotonous drone of constant distraction that silences the heart and swallows the Soul.

Even if a collective awakening were to miraculously occur and everyone on the planet chose to go vegan, live off-grid in a tiny cob home, grow their own food, walk or ride their bicycles, fall deeply in love with Earth, and never buy a single plastic item again, it still wouldn't be enough (but that doesn't mean we shouldn't still choose this simpler lifestyle). The runaway momentum from our destructive behavior is well underway. The damage is irreversible. The lag time between our past and present actions, and the subsequent repercussions of these efforts will likely play out for several millennia to come. There is no escaping the consequences of our willful ignorance, and contrary to our conditioned arrogance, we are not invincible, infallible or immortal. Let's get real here; we've screwed the planet and ourselves.

Everything we now do amounts to little more than moving the deck chairs around on the Titanic, hoping to avert the rapidly approaching iceberg strike. We've reached a point where the only way to prevent the ship from sinking, would be to have never build it in the first place.

The time for radical transformation was back in the early 1960's when Rachel Carson was persecuted for exposing the truth in her epic tome, *Silent Spring*. Even then, the madness of this civilization foreshadowed its inevitable end with its unstoppable compulsion for greed, destruction, and death. The time for collective resistance was then. The time for collective imagination was then. The time for collective awakening was then. But even then, our collective inertia prevailed. Even then, we lacked the will, desire, caring, and passion for doing anything meaningful. Our world is now filled with the spiritually atrophied shells of humanity gone awry.

For thousands, perhaps millions of years, we've allowed our separation-based mindset to rule our interaction with life. The problem has never been the human condition; it has always been the conditioned human. There is no way that a species steeped in separation sickness could ever have a glorious future. Even as a child I knew Earth would never allow it.

The collective coma of the conditioned human mind runs deep, and we've taken it too far. It's long overdue for this nightmare to end. There's no changing the antiquated patriarchal systems built on the foundation of the wounded inner child. There's no 5th-dimensional consciousness, age of Aquarius, feminine uprising, New Age awakening, second coming of Jesus, or extraterrestrial deliverance to save us. There's only the irreparable damage we've inflicted on animals, Earth, and the Soul. There's only inevitable cultural collapse and the fall of humanity.

We have had ample opportunities for transformation. So many wide open doors to walk through, and we've consistently chosen to slam the doors shut, throw on the deadbolts, toss the keys, and relocate every piece of furniture to ensure our containment. With our refusal to walk through these doors, however, we are now locked from the outside as well. In his live presentations, author, Derrick Jensen asks his audience, "Do you believe that this culture is going to undergo a voluntary transformation to a sane and sustainable way of living?" Most of us know the answer is a resounding no. With our collective indifference and denial, we've squandered all opportunities for a global revolution in consciousness.

We have had all of the knowledge, creativity, ancient wisdom, and inspiration to create a beautiful new world for several decades, if not much longer. Instead, we've chosen the familiar coma of our antiquated, separation-based worldview. The only changes we've experienced are those that clearly show how far we've strayed from the Soul. The explosion of humans on the planet—all indoctrinated into the Big Lie of separation—is the perfect recipe for biosphere collapse.

We are rigid in our worldview and refuse to look outside of our mechanistic conditioning. We persist in having the same old conversations that we did hundreds of years ago. Sexism, speciesism, racism, homophobia, transphobia, and many other 'isms and 'obia's are as prolific as ever. Climate change deny-osaurs abound. Quite honestly, I wouldn't be at all surprised if many still believed the world was flat.

The most significant crisis facing the world today is not war, terrorism, violence, or even biosphere collapse. The greatest crisis facing the world today is the crisis in consciousness that traps the human mind in the myth of separation that fuels the Big Lie. The result is a self-created, life-hating, death-phobic, planetary asylum where everything beautiful, good and real is mindlessly consumed, commoditized and destroyed by its compliant inmates.

Our civilization rewards destruction and punishes love. We've traded our humanity for profit. For anyone with a trace of critical thinking skills, it's impossible to deny that Earth is terminally ill, humans are completely insane, and a rapid acceleration of extraordinary collapse is underway. It's both confusing and disorienting as we careen our way toward an uncertain abyss.

The paradigm will not shift. There is no new story. We are now bearing witness to the splitting—the polarization—of the human race between the few who are choosing the direction of evolution without outcome; and the masses who are either denying or resisting, what is. We are enmeshed in the beginnings of a massive crisis.

Only by healing ourselves, has Earth ever stood a chance of recovering herself with humanity still in residence. The grim reality is that the masses are unwilling to even acknowledge their mental, emotional and spiritual wounds, let alone dive headfirst into their pain. If this were not so, the widespread afflictions of anxiety, depression, and addiction would no longer be rampant, and synthetic emotional suppressants (i.e. pharmaceutical anti-depressants) would no longer be a food group.

In the words of Charles Eisenstein:

> No genuine healing of society or the planet is possible without a concomitant transformation on the individual level. Even if the planetary environment were miraculously restored, in the absence of spiritual transformation we would just go about ruining it again. Our poisoned world is a reflection of our poisonous thoughts and feelings. You can't build a house on a rotten foundation, and our minds are the foundation of our common world. Yes, we must address the crisis of the earth, but at the same time, we must also address the source of that crisis in ourselves.
>
> The same goes for social change: if, say, a utopian socialist state were imposed without eliminating the roots of greed and competitiveness in each one of us, the old injustices would quickly reappear. In fact, one could argue that all such attempts have failed precisely because a social revolution cannot revolutionize the deepest reaches of the human heart; that the urge to power, to domination, to profit can only be cleansed from the inside out.[43]

It's a lovely, kumbaya-inspired thought to believe in an epidemic of spontaneous healing, but let's face it, the odds are higher that Ted Nugent would give up his arsenal of weapons, embrace compassion, and go vegan long before that ever happened. We've been broken, tainted and corrupted by centuries of the Big Lie, and there's no way out of mental illness so profoundly embedded in the collective psyche unless we allowed it to die. But we won't. Our compulsion for abdicating all personal responsibility in every aspect of our self-absorbed lives ensures our disempowered servitude.

Yet the myth of a new story carries on. Humanity, we are told by the New Age pundits, is awakening. But awakening to what?

One only needs to spend a few moments observing the behaviors in any public venue or shopping mall parking lot to see how far removed we are from anything resembling awakening.

And what about countries such as India, Iran, Iraq, China, and Afghanistan where women are worthless minions subject to oppressive patriarchal domination; where rape and misogyny are commonplace and perfectly acceptable? (Sidenote: Not that we're that much better in the west. We just hide it better.)

Of course, we cannot negate the trillions of land and sea animals brutally murdered every single year for no more than an antiquated belief system. There is no potential for higher consciousness in consuming the flesh and blood of our fellow Earthlings.

Even if we were to eliminate all slaughterhouses, animal agriculture, strip mining, clearcutting, nuclear weapons, ocean rape, garbage, corporations, shopping, pollution, fracking, and so on, nothing would change because the consciousness that created it all, remains. Wherever we go and whatever we do, we will only drag the chains of our separation sickness with us, and just do it all over again. In our separation consciousness, we are complicit in the Big Lie, and the problems of our world will not—and cannot—magically go away.

Every new generation born to this world is deemed "savior" of our past mistakes, yet every new generation plummets deeper into the culturally conditioned coma passed on by the generations who preceded them. How can they possibly be expected to fix the compounding mistakes of the past, when they are programmed by the very same separation sickness responsible for the disaster in the first place?

As a species, we do not have the courage to stop denying the obvious and the inevitable. We are hard-wired to respond to dangers in real-time—which to the perceptual senses they are—but the gravity of these dangers is not powerful enough to penetrate the impermeable wall of deeply conditioned denial.

Denial—in its many forms—insulates us from the pain of reality so we can keep on keeping on without bothering to change. When the human mind is closed, the human heart cannot be touched, and stasis is the only possible outcome. Why then, do so many still subscribe to the myth of a new story for humanity? Can they not see the writing on the wall?

Because the Big Lie has played out for so long; because there are so many simultaneous paths of converging collapse; because everything on the planet is in a state of tremendous acceleration; perhaps there is something much more significant that we are unwilling to consider: that a more expansive intelligence is at work, paving the way for the next wave of evolution for planet Earth. Unlike all previous waves of evolution, however, this wave is entirely catalyzed by one species' actions: homo sapien sapiens. Like all earlier waves of evolution, this wave will once again clear the slate for Earth to heal and prepare a new canvas for her next Creation.

Lately, I've been wondering: What if the "new" story about the evolution of consciousness that so many speak of, has never been about humanity, but in our separation-based arrogance, we made it about ourselves? What if the real story has always been about the evolution of consciousness for Earth—for Gaea? What if we were only ever meant to be participants in her evolution? What if the choices for Gaea's evolution involving humanity have been: parasite or Soul-force. The choice of Soul-force would potentially mean an evolutionary journey for Gaea that included homo sapien sapiens as we evolved with her. Parasite involved a more painful and drawn out evolution for Gaea that excluded homo sapien sapiens in the end, as we eventually brought about our self-destruction. In typical parasitic fashion, we would breed ourselves into oblivion, defecate all over the host and voraciously consume the host, at the peril of the host. Unlike parasites within the web of life, however, there is no other host to move on to, despite our magical thinking otherwise.

What if the story has always been about Gaea's evolution, and has never been about us? In either scenario, Gaea evolves. With or without us is irrelevant. It takes a powerful connection to the Soul to accept—and to trust—in this higher wisdom. It is this wisdom that few are willing, or able to consider.

In our lack of willingness to overcome our cultural conditioning; our lack of desire to overcome our allegiance to the Big Lie; and our lack of interest in realizing the Soul, we've chosen to exclude ourselves from Gaea's evolution. Let's face it, if we can't even have authentic relationships based on respect, integrity, and generosity of spirit with our own biological families, how can we possibly expect to have a functional relationship with Gaea: Mother of all living things, sustainer of life?

The hubris of our separation sickness has deluded us into believing we are somehow exempt from the repercussions of our destructive ways. We've recklessly bred ourselves beyond the carrying capacity of the planet. We've polluted every life-support system beyond repair. We've completely altered the once predictable climate of Earth. We've catalyzed the accelerated extinction of countless species. We've nurtured our inauthentic, predatory conditioning by rationalizing the destruction of every form of life. And the narcissistic selfie-culture youth of today—the "saviors of our future"—are too busy searching for the elusive Pokémon to give a damn about anything that matters.

Despite our omnicidal ways—and in the fever of our denial—we seem to believe we are absolved from our collective demise—as if the tsunami wave will magically part around us as it mercilessly hurtles toward the shore.

While the planet continues to spin around the sun in a state of increasing chaos, the masses hold steadfast in their resistance to connect the dots. Beastly wildfires, relentless droughts, superstorms, hurricanes, flash floods, atmospheric rivers, epic snowfalls, tornadoes, hailstorms, rapid Arctic ice-melt, extreme heatwaves, water crises, societal collapse, mass animal deaths, nuclear meltdown, mass shootings, xenophobia, misogyny, war, war, war, and on and on it goes. There are now so many dots that they blend together, creating an entirely new landscape. Life as we once knew it is unraveling on countless different fronts. This is our altered world folks. And our ho-hum response is to choke down a bigger dose of "blue pill" ignorance because the denial that follows ensures that business-as-usual indefinitely carries on. As the world floods, burns, blows, shakes, rattles, and collapses around us, I often wonder if there's a threshold dose of denial before we finally wake up and smell the carbon (and methane, and lies, and fear, and death rot)?

Even through the haze of our collective denial, many of us know that something is seriously wrong. If we didn't believe this to be so, we wouldn't be looking for a way out.

I confess that I used to believe I could be an influential voice for the transformation of this world. I used to believe I could make the world a better place for animals and Earth. I used to believe I was an integral player in the uprising of consciousness inspired by the "emerging feminine" (yes, even I bought into this).

I even bought into the whole caterpillar/butterfly metaphor, where humanity is said to be in the final stages of the consumptive, destructive caterpillar phase before cocooning its way into the magnificent butterfly it was always meant to be. But the truth is, caterpillars are biologically designed to become life-giving pollinators. They have no choice. We do.

I wanted so badly to believe that species homo sapien sapiens could not possibly be vacuous enough to destroy its very own life-support system. I just couldn't allow myself to believe that evil such as ignorance, denial, entitlement, apathy, and indifference could prevail. It has been painful to witness how a species with so much potential for kindness, empathy, courage, compassion, and love would choose an identity that was everything but. I was desperate to believe that we could … that we would, wake up to the Soul of *what* we are. But after decades of engaging with others through my activism and outspoken passion for Earth, I conclude that the journey toward a collective awakening is a perpetually unattainable destination. It's just not possible, and to believe it to be so, is to live in Self-delusion. I no longer choose the numbing effects of Self-delusion.

And so it is. Our alienation from animals, the natural world, each other, and the Soul has caused irreversible destruction on this planet. It's too late, and the sooner we realize this, the sooner we can let go and embrace the fullness of who and what we have always been meant to be.

These desperate times assault the conditioned human mind by hammering at the barriers created by its Self-delusion. This can either lead to increased denial and inertia, or it can inspire a hunger for accelerated evolution without outcome. This situation is the perfect cauldron for the liberation of the human race from its fantasies. Maybe this has been the "new story" all along.

It's Over

"When man interferes with the Tao,
The sky becomes filthy,
The Earth becomes depleted,
The equilibrium crumbles,
Creatures become extinct."

– LAO TZU

Like a perpetual looping track, history persists in repeating itself. Throughout the millennia, the same old story of separation continues to play out. Consciousness deteriorates. Civilizations collapse. Extinction events eradicate life. And here we stand again: collapse, extinction, and a flatlined collective consciousness. Are we some cruel cosmic joke—a 300,000-year-old failure; an outlandish biological mistake? Is it possible that we rendered all other known planets uninhabitable before being plopped on our beautiful Earth for one last ditch effort to get it right? Why do so few of us remember who and what we are, while the collective remains trapped in the mental illness of separation that disconnects them from life—from the Soul? What kind of world do we live in where the masses care more about the size of Kim Kardashian's buttocks than they do the shrinking volume of Arctic sea ice?

The tentacles of civilization have a death-grip on the psyche that has destroyed the human conscience. If we could only stop the war on the Soul, we would end the war on Earth and all life. But we've rendered ourselves incapable. In our incapacitation, there is nowhere to go but obscurity.

Collapse is not a new concept. Civilizations have risen and fallen repeatedly throughout history. The difference this time, however, is that collapse is not isolated to a particular civilization, it extends to all life on Earth. It is a mass extinction event that gets little airtime in our truth suppressed world.

The stories we tell ourselves about our existence are culturally generated. The Big Lie that defines our global civilization has led to the creation of oppressive institutions, systems of thought, and cultural memes that match the story we believe to be true. But the current narrative of oppression, commodification, violation, and the destruction of life has outlived its usefulness. If it was ever useful, that is.

The problem with our cultural institutions is that they are resistant to change. To maintain their survival, they've mastered the art of casting doubt and fear into the minds of the masses, by couching it in the language of reason and logic. This intellectual fear-mongering preys on the highly conditioned intellect and works diligently to create skepticism, if not, cynicism about efforts to live from a more life-affirming consciousness.

Despite overwhelming evidence of anthropocentric biosphere collapse occurring in real time, many are unable to integrate the multiple threads of information that are now creating a new planetary landscape. The multitude of different events happening around the globe form part of a much larger whole, and it is the larger whole that is now directing the expression of each individual event.

We were repeatedly presented with facts, and warning after dire warning, and we willfully chose to ignore them all. Instead, we grabbed onto comforting lies, unfounded suspicions and conspiracy theories, and wouldn't let go.

We arrogantly destroyed Creation with thoughtless neglect while blithely indulging our comforts, pleasures, and insatiable need for more. Now we *all* get to watch it burn. The sad part is that this was long ago predicted with incredible accuracy given the complexity of the problem, and the masses just clutched their bloated bellies in arrogant laughter. But reality has a way of creeping up on the Self-deluded, and Gaea holds the final ace for the last laugh.

Anyone who can still deny runaway biosphere decay—not just a change in the weather or climate, but something much more significant that is creating dramatic weather pattern changes—either lacks information, lacks intelligence, lacks integrity (intentional betrayal or deception perpetrated for personal gain), is delusional, or is in blatant denial of the interconnected expressions of accelerating anthropogenic change happening globally on this living organism we call, planet Earth.

Nonviolent activist, Robert Burrowes articulates our collective indifference well, "Most people are content to live in delusion: it averts the need to courageously, intelligently and conscientiously analyse what is truly happening and respond to it powerfully. In short: it makes life 'easier' (that is, less frightening) even if problems keep recurring and conflicts are suppressed, to flare up periodically, rather than be resolved."[44]

In the ocean, starfish are considered a keystone species. A keystone species is crucial for the survival of an ecosystem. Without keystone species, ecosystems are radically altered and in many cases, collapse altogether.

When the ocean environment is out of balance, starfish begin to die off. It is a grim indicator that the web of life is in a state of severe compromise. As you read these words, starfish are wasting away and dying off en masse. This is not hearsay, I speak to this from personal experience.

In the human world, intuitive, empathic and sensitive types are the keystone indicators for where we are headed as a civilization, and as a species. As one who has been tapped into Earth energies my entire life, I speak from an intimate knowing. I can unreservedly say that things are much worse than they appear to the naked eye.

For the past number of years, I've been feeling a profound sense of grief over the state of the world, especially with the dizzying breakdown of every aspect of life on Earth. I've been finding it increasingly difficult to navigate this Gaea Grief, knowing that everything I love so dearly is being mindlessly consumed, commoditized and destroyed with reckless abandon. Buddhist scholar and environmental activist, Joanna Macy calls this decimation, The Great Unraveling. An appropriate metaphor.

I'm blessed to live in a stunning geographical location that is energetically charged by rainforests, mountains, and ocean. I live in a state of perpetual awe for the beauty remaining in this part of the world. As such, I'm aware of the "thinness" of this magnificent place, where the veil between the physical and non-physical world is virtually non-existent. Unlike a city with its denuded, unnatural landscape, and the incessant noise from honking cars, blaring music, car alarms, machines, construction, techno-distraction, and the mental static of worry, busyness, fatigue, anxiety, and impatience, Earth energy is much easier to feel here, especially for the energetically sensitive like myself. I feel what is unseen and unheard by the collective, and what is subsequently ignored and denied by our civilization. For me, this is truth.

Along with explicit messages to extricate myself from civilization, have been persistent premonitions that won't let up. These warnings have a consistent ocean theme that comes with two words, "It's over."

Initially, my intellect grasped, trying to understand what "it," is over. Is it literal, the collapse of the ocean? Is it our dominant patriarchal worldview? Is it the Big Lie? Is it our consumptive civilization of infinite growth, ignorance, entitlement, distraction, and relentless destruction? Is it our biosphere? Is it humanity? Is it life on Earth? There is no doubt we are collectively committing ecocide, is it more? As my mind struggled for answers, my heart knew better. Content became irrelevant. In my heart, it made no difference if "it" was a cultural, ecological, or social collapse. Rather than allow my mind to exhaust myself with possible future scenarios, I've since chosen to be fully present with what is. In this acceptance, I've unleashed a force from within that knows that no matter how it all plays out, it's ok, because the love in my heart remains steadfast through it all.

In reaching this place of deep acceptance, the veil has lifted. It is now clear to me that we are at the end of the line for species homo sapien sapiens. It really is over.

It's over because the collective has chosen for it to be over. The collective has chosen biosphere collapse, and now all energies are aligning for the collective intent to be made manifest. Agree with me, call me "flake" or alarmist, it matters not. In over 50 years of life, my premonitions have never led me astray.

If we are brutally honest and allow ourselves to see beyond our conditioned fear, we can see how the very civilization we rely on for our survival, is killing us. We've created our own self-reinforcing feedback loop, where we are blindly destroying the life support systems of the planet, while the civilization that drives our beliefs, behaviors, and actions is in turn, killing us. In the ultimate display of powerlessness, we are also hopelessly dependent upon this mad civilization. It is a codependent relationship of a most fatal kind. If it collapses, we perish. If it persists, we perish. We are damned if we do, and damned if we don't. We are trapped by our own hand, and there is no way out.

Believing we can meditate, think positively or "love and light" our way out of this predicament; or that we have the technological prowess and mastery over our environment to avert or survive a mass extinction, is its own sort of hubris. Taking the patriarchal way out through resistance, or denial, or hope, or believing that politicians and CEO's of corporations will have a miraculous change of heart and fall to their knees in remorse; or that every living thing in the web of life can die, but somehow humanity has immunity from its own demise, is delusional.

Whether on a personal or planetary scale, the same level of conceit applies: that if we ignore it, or if we only try hard enough, we can figure everything out and live happily ever after in perpetuity. But it just doesn't work that way.

In our flippant denial, and in the refusal to evolve beyond the inertia of our adolescent consciousness, we've ignored Gaea's great wisdom, and instead, we've trashed the house. Gaea doesn't make mistakes. She's pissed, and we're getting the boot. The party is over, and it's time to grow up.

It's initiation time.

We may buy into the prevailing belief in our own superior "intelligence" over Gaea (and animals and nature). But how intelligent is a species who—at all costs—persists in destroying the biosphere crucial for its very existence, and with eyes wide open no less?

The welfare of faraway places we've never been to, and of creatures we've never connected with, is of little concern to us. In our deeply-rooted separation, we've lost compassion for other living beings, and for nature as a whole. In the dogma of this ignorance, we've betrayed the insects. We've betrayed the fish. We've betrayed the reptiles. We've betrayed the birds. We've betrayed the mammals. We've betrayed Earth.

We've betrayed the Soul.

We stand alone, isolated from life, love, and truth on our Soulless island of separation.

As a species, we seem to believe there is no evolutionary advantage to long-term thinking that is expansive and life-affirming. Long-term, narrow-minded thinking to sustain the Big Lie is an entirely different story, however. In her 2012 TEDx talk, *The Green Boat: Reviving Ourselves in our Capsized Culture*, Dr. Mary Pipher very accurately stated, "We are bombarded by too much information, too many choices and too much complexity. We have paleolithic arousal systems, neolithic brains, medieval institutions, and 21st Century technology. Our problem-solving abilities, and our communication and coping skills, have not evolved quickly enough to sustain us. The climate crisis is so enormous in its implications that it's difficult for us to grasp."[45]

With neolithic, narrow-minded brains "driving the bus," most people don't fear the unknown as much as they fear the loss of the known. Those who run the current systems fear a loss of the known more than anyone else; therefore they have a vested interest in ensuring the short-term gain of business-as-usual at the forever expense of all.

The absurdity of how these systems are kept in place with perpetual war, perpetual consumption, perpetual fear, and perpetual lies, has normalized insanity for so long that few can see the madness of it all. The omnipresence of denial ensures that what is in plain view, can never be seen. But denial cannot prevent the effects of breakdown from occurring. Cultural, economic, civilization, and biosphere collapse could care less who believes, or not. Collapse is indiscriminate in whose lives are ruined, and it will quickly impact all of us as we collectively bottom out.

In *The Ascent of Humanity*, Charles Eisenstein concurs, "As the gathering crises of the world visit themselves personally upon more and more of us, it becomes more difficult to insulate ourselves from their effects no matter how wealthy we are or how skillful we are in exercising control over the world, we are collectively "hitting bottom."[46]

Humans did not create the web of life. We are merely a strand within the web of life, and whatever we do to this web, we do to our-selves. As Earth activist Julia Butterfly Hill so wisely said, "We cannot have peace on the Earth unless we have peace with the Earth."

Perhaps the most alarming—even devastating—aspect of this unprecedented crisis is the denial, indifference, and paralysis infect-ing the vast majority of the human race. In the time of our great-est danger, we are at our most hapless, distracted, and hubristic. Journalist and activist, Chris Hedges said it well, "A society that loses the capacity for the sacred, that lacks the power of human imagination, that cannot practice empathy, ultimately ensures its own destruction."[47]

Earth is speaking loud and clear, and humanity is not listening. The writing is on the wall, and few are literate enough to read it.

There comes a point where the density of the message converts quickly into reality. When we ignore signals in the physical body, a moment eventually arrives when "poof," we have a tumor; and we foolishly believe it came out of nowhere. The truth is that it had been coalescing, aligning, shaping, and repeatedly knocking at the door of our consciousness to show us that something was wrong. In ignor-ing the messaging, however, it took manifestation in physical form to bring the message into awareness. In the physical body, we either get the message so that we don't get the tumor; or we get the tumor so that we get the message. The tumor is merely a backup of ignored information. The escalating Earth crises occurring around the globe today are also a backup of ignored information.

Runaway biosphere decay is very much like the experiments in high school chemistry class, where a drop of something is added to a clear solution, and at first, nothing happens. As more drops are add-ed, little changes until "boom," the 20th drop completely alters the color, with explosive smoke and a foul stench to boot. This metaphor demonstrates where we currently stand. Things may seem "normal" today, until tomorrow morning when we wake up with our house underwater.

We are rapidly running out of time. Not because it is claimed in ancient texts, not even because of my premonitions, but because of our decaying social structures; our imploding educational, economic, corporate, medical, and religious systems; and because the precarious state of wellbeing of our minds, bodies, and spirits tells us so. The sad joke is that most of us are remotely controlled by the old beliefs of generations gone by, and we don't even know it. Our deeply programmed minds are rendering planet Earth uninhabitable.

We are in the midst of an accelerating march toward decay; sufferers of an abstract illness that was diagnosed long before we knew we were sick. With the rabid excitement over the birth of industrial civilization several generations ago, our predecessors knew decadence and entitlement. We know destruction, death, and decay.

Reality seems to mimic a Hollywood disaster movie or a childhood cartoon, where madmen attempt to destroy the world. The reality narrative of our world is becoming more insane by the minute, as the puppet masters of the industrial machine laugh maniacally at Earth while she moans beneath their blood-soaked feet, and the masses stumble along with nary a care. Glazed eyes, deadened hearts, simple minds.

The prevailing mindset of human superiority prevents the masses from voluntarily ending their addiction to familiarity, comfort, technology, oil, meat, eggs, dairy, Hollywood, money, self-replication, and consumption. In the end, the failing systems of Earth's biosphere and the impossible equation of infinite growth on a finite planet will put a stop to this unhinged folly. Homo sapien sapiens may be a resilient species, but it is not infallible, invincible or immortal. It is also not immune from its own demise. To

believe that we are somehow exempt from our own extinction while we cause mass extinction all around us, is
moronic. As climate scientist, Paul Beckwith wrote in a recent blog
post, "Collectively, we are ignorant, brain-dead zombies, lurching
into disaster."[48] The price we pay for choosing a dystopian world
and a dead planet is the end of life on Earth.

It isn't the planet's fault this is happening. Generations of mindless
consumption, ignoring the endless warning signs, and bleeding Earth
dry has ensured that we have no future.

As my wise friend, Louise LeBrun says, "Perhaps it's time to accept that this world—in this time—is coming to a rapid completion.
Not an end, a completion. In that deep surrender lies the path to a life
of joyous creation. Living in the moment. Permanence acknowledged
and accepted for the illusion that it is. Cheering Gaea on, as She turns
into her time of hibernation, to birth yet another new world, to come."

Humans—and all species, for that matter—have always had a
finite timeline. In the direct language of, Richard Gale and
Dr. Gary Null:

> The Earth's history is a long story of numerous species
> birthing, evolving and eventually going extinct. There is no
> manifest destiny for our species. There is no divine promise
> that humanity may not in the future follow in the footsteps of
> the dinosaurs. Our lives are not transcendent to Nature nor the
> multitude of other natural forces, animals, plants, microbes
> and other life forms and molecules upon which our existence
> depends. This is a simple truth we must learn. And it must be
> learned quickly and without further delay.[49]

How can we humans possess so much ingenuity and intelligence—and sometimes compassion—yet fail on the most significant
challenge to preserve Earth, her sentient beings and ourselves? It is a
selfishly preposterous conundrum.

Death and destruction have only just begun. That is an absolute. We can no longer prevent the collapse of our global civilization. By madly continuing with business-as-usual as Earth systems collapse all around us, our final legacy will be a planet barren of life, sagging under the weight of plastic, sewage, nuclear fallout, technology, and mountains of garbage.

The world I once knew is now a distant memory—a memory that I cherish, and one that I'm deeply grateful for. The proximate future, however, brings a knot to my stomach that refuses to leave.

I confess that I'm not the least bit saddened by the end of the cruel, demented, predatory human world of separation. Good riddance! It cannot end fast enough for me. I readily admit, however, that I'm heartbroken about the destruction of the *real* world: animals, fish, birds, insects, amphibians, trees, plants, integrity, respect, compassion, truth, life, and the Soul. If only humanity confined the repercussions of its lunacy to its own species, the collapse would be easier to navigate. I never wanted to see it end this way.

We have failed the sacred. By consuming with no thought for tomorrow to fill a hunger that can never be satiated; and by gorging ourselves on a buffet of ceaseless lies, we are now bloated by a widespread ignorance that cannot be remedied. To perpetuate this relentless gluttony, we have traded the sacred for a dying biosphere. By desecrating the Soul, we have brought hell on Earth, to life.

Along with our rapidly collapsing biosphere, I believe that many of our patriarchal institutions are in their final death throes. Our schools are failing our children; our food is making us sick; our media has paralyzed us with fear; our financial institutions have enslaved us to debt; our corporations are destroying the natural world; our religions have inspired violent fundamentalism; our legal system nurtures profound corruption; our culture incites rapacious consumption; our health-care system spawns endless illness; our technology numbs our brains; and our eroded governments unflinchingly sell out to the highest corporate bidder. We are asleep at the wheel and have forgotten who we are. We don't trust the world; we don't trust each other, we don't trust ourselves. The erosion of the human spirit is destroying us all.

We are witnessing a societal breakdown in the midst of an ecological breakdown, and they are now interfacing. When countries fall apart, they often take a hard right turn to revive the "good old days." We are now living through a terrifying resurrection of white male supremacy, misogyny, fundamentalism, escalating violence, racial division, and societal breakdown; at the same time, we are living through biosphere collapse. As our world rapidly implodes, more people are beginning to notice. Some are beginning to speak out, but often in the direction of blame. As Henry David Thoreau once said, "there are a thousand hacking at the branches of evil to one who is striking at the root." The root cannot be found at the end of our pointed fingers; it can only be found in the reflection of our mirrors.

Let's face it, even if we were to own our part in this disaster, we are not a species who does anything meaningful quickly. We are addicted to the familiarity of our plodding inertia. We can't even agree with our partners, friends, and families about our collective predicament, yet to transform this world, we have to globally agree to make it happen. Because we can't agree on anything as a species, it is an impossible task. There is no miracle powerful enough to wake us up on a mass level in this 11th hour.

The sad truth is that most people could care less about the absence of fish, birds, insects, trees, forests, rivers, lakes, polar bears, rhinos, giraffes, and elephants. They are insulated in their cities; denatured and separated from the wild. They are enslaved to a life of meaningless servitude designed to sustain a sick civilization, perpetuate an artificial world, and prevent connection to a Soul-enhancing way of life.

In his online essay, *Humanity at a Crossroads*, Guy McPherson wrote:

> We're selfish creatures, after all, interested primarily in persistence. Unfortunately for our species, we're really, truly interested in the persistence of our own selfish selves, and not so much interested in our own species. Ergo, the self-induced, greed-inspired, utterly human, generally predictable (but specifically chaotic) predicaments in which we are currently marinating.
>
> As a society, we will not willingly halt the industrial economy. We would much rather reduce the planet to a lifeless pile of rubble than diminish—much less halt—economic growth. But, soon enough, we'll run out of options and the industrial economy will take its last breath. Too little, too late to provide our final, slim hope for averting extinction.[50]

Collective consciousness created the climate and global catastrophe. Runaway biosphere decay is the cohesive evidence—the manifestation—of our collective thoughts and intentions. It is not separate from what we have allowed ourselves to become. The climate is merely reflecting back to us the intensity of our demented collective mindset.

Our finite planet has never been able to accommodate infinite growth, infinite population, and endless consumption. So the story of separation has been doomed all along. No lie can live forever. The writing is on the wall for those with eyes to see it; hearts to feel it, and consciousness to accept it.

The one thing that few are willing to say is that it's too late. By not speaking this truth, we blindly carry on with business-as-usual and live in delusion, ignorance, and denial, rather than integrity, compassion, and grace.

The epic collapse upon us is pressing us to look at what we can no longer deny: the Soul. When the biosphere collapses and the planet is no longer habitable, the only place left to turn, is within. Runaway biosphere decay has made personal evolution an imperative because it is either evolve now, or die asleep.

We've chosen, and the sooner we can accept what we've done to the planet and ourselves, the sooner we can connect with our deepest core essence and be fully present for whatever comes next.

Maybe "the end" is really the beginning. As bizarre as this great paradox is, perhaps self-annihilation is the apocalyptic grand finale that will finally awaken a comatose human species to the very Soul of who they've always been meant to be.

The Fuck-it Point

"Letting go does not mean you stop caring. It means you stop trying to force others to."

– MANDY HALE

We are a collective of psychopaths.

How else can we tolerate all the insanity around us? How else can we persist in a world with endless wars, animal brutality, domestic violence, hunger, poverty, homelessness, and ecological devastation, while blindly carrying on with the mundanities of daily life? How else can we walk the aisles of grocery stores without retching at the sight of shrink-wrapped body parts on styrofoam trays, ovulations in cartons, and maternal secretions in plastic jugs; all stolen from the miserable lives of countless sentient beings, murdered for nothing more than a belief system? How else can we endure endless stagnant hours in office cubicles breathing recycled air under unnatural lighting, prostituting ourselves for paychecks that offer no sense of meaning? How else can we normalize the pharmaceutical suppressants and invasive procedures, pimped by a corporatized medical complex that commoditizes the sacred terrain of body and mind? How else can we cope with interminable corruption, violence, destruction, abuse, pollution, death, and oppression if we don't perpetually lie to ourselves?

We are a collective force so potent that we've altered the course of Earth, and are still unwilling to regulate ourselves.

We live in a world of systemic violence and cruelty, rationalized to sustain an old story. From animals and the natural world; to women, the elderly, and all those forgotten on the streets. Few are spared. Dissonance and denial are epidemic. Delusions of grandeur and megalomania abound. Insanity is the norm. We are so thoroughly entranced by the Big Lie that we are unable to consider anything else.

There is a rigid monotony to a collective human experience with an inert state of consciousness that only serves to degrade everything around it. It is a suicidal/homicidal mission wrapped in a dystopian package.

In her blog post, *Truths, Perceptions, and Choices*, Louise LeBrun writes:

> (We live in a strange world). A world where f*#k is acceptable but fuck is not. Really? Who do we think we're kidding! Is this not one of the most powerful metaphors for the hypocrisy we're willing to embrace?
>
> A world where we (the frogs) have now been in the warming water long enough to begin to notice: Uh oh, something is not right. And yet, we find ourselves paralyzed in our efforts to leap out of the roiling, boiling mess we've allowed ourselves to create.
>
> A world where it's ok/acceptable/appropriate to look away from the ravages of violence and brutality perpetrated by the few against the many (i.e., women, children, animals … those unable to defend and protect themselves) but it is not ok/acceptable/appropriate to consider the evidence of our very own eyes/ears/senses/experiences and stare into the face of increasingly extreme weather events that are wreaking havoc around the world.[51]

Most humans are so trapped in the stasis of their tedious lives that they have no clue how absolutely, completely fucked we are. They either drink from the fountain of hopium or swallow the poison of denial—whatever addiction works best to maintain the semblance of "normal" in an increasingly fucked world.

Social justice activist, Kenn Orphan digs deep into this very truth in his blog post, *The Canaries We Ignore*. He writes:

> Here is where people of conscience must be brutally truthful about our collective predicament. We must face the painful fact that our species has exceeded its limits in growth, population and the exploitation of the natural world. We must also grapple with the fact that the global north is most responsible for the decimation of the biosphere and the ruthless exploitation of the global south. And there will be no substantive actions taken by the corrupt political and business leaders who profit from this global arrangement, to halt this plunder or stem the carnage of the planet's rich biodiversity. They are both unwilling and incapable of addressing the issue with the integrity and impetus necessary. Instead, they will continue their bait and switch dance of empty placation and denialism while they stuff their coffers with coin, even as the earth rapidly transforms into another planet before our eyes.
>
> And their criminal ineptitude has never stopped at non-humans. As this century unfolds, cities will be lost to rising seas as governments will eventually find that they are too expensive to salvage. Regions will become uninhabitable from pollution and drought. The specters of famine and disease will haunt billions of people. And mass migration will put a strain on fragile social and economic systems that already suffer from vast, structurally imposed inequities.
>
> Their answer to the concomitant unrest will be more Orwellian doublespeak and insidious distraction, coupled with draconian crackdowns on dissent, protest or objection. They

will aggressively mock, smear and persecute truth tellers and peddle in jingoism, xenophobia, and nationalism. Warmongering, austerity and the scapegoating of vulnerable people will become their preferred method of deferring from their culpability. None of this is fiction. It has all happened, and not only in civilizations throughout history which have faced socio-economic or ecological collapse. It is happening today in societies which purport to be democratic.[52]

Yes folks, this really is our world.

Humans are a dominant force. A species responsible for destroying billions of years of evolution in the blink of an evolutionary eye. We were a species with so much potential, but we squandered it on an illusion that misled us into believing we were superior to—and therefore separate from—an intricate web of life. We failed the sacred—an evolutionary experiment gone terribly wrong.

A great tragedy lies in how the majority of humans are both unwilling and incapable of seeing beyond the smoke and mirrors of the Big Lie. The collective coma is just too deeply rooted. Carl Jung warned that if humans didn't evolve into a new planetary consciousness, we would—as a species—go extinct. Because of an unwavering allegiance to the Big Lie, his warning is rapidly morphing into reality.

As the global crises mount, increased suffering is the new normal, especially for those who remain attached to their stories, traumas, emotional wounds, conditioned beliefs, self-absorption, victim consciousness, powerlessness, denial, entitlement, and most importantly, to their own mortality. It's a time of great pain for those who choose ego over essence; head over heart; hope over presence; brutality over compassion; indifference over caring; denial over truth; and fear over love. As the world continues its rapid downward spiral, it's becoming increasingly difficult to cling to old beliefs and antiquated cultural programming. As we are already witnessing, this lingering attachment is leading us toward escalating hostility and violence, and significant suffering on a global scale.

Living an awakened life in an unawakened world means that we must let go. There comes a time when we not only realize, but we accept that the collective addiction to the Big Lie is impenetrable.

There comes a time when we reach the "fuck-it" point.

The fuck-it point arrives when we finally understand that there is no way to alter the course of the collective, or to mitigate the destruction and pain of the dominant reality. In this realization, we choose to live from a place that feeds the Soul instead. It is a place of authentic power that inspires the reclamation of everything stolen from us by our parents, our culture, and our civilization. The fuck-it point is a state of pure abandonment and deep love in action, detached from outcome, because that is the essence of who we are. It is the most profound sense of liberation.

The fuck-it point is not about resignation, indifference, giving up, or giving in. As Guy McPherson says, "Giving up is not giving in: accepting our fate is not synonymous with jumping into the absurdly omnicidal mainstream. Just because we're opossums on the roadway doesn't mean we should play possum."[53] In other words, it's about accepting that because of collective choices, there are things which just cannot be, and we should live with integrity, compassion, honor, and grace regardless.

The fuck-it point is about letting go. It's about knowing that our time as a species is rapidly coming to an end, and rather than falling into despair, it's about living fully now.

Be forewarned; the fuck-it point brings up deep pain. It brings up feelings of betrayal for being duped by a destructive civilization. It brings up profound grief for the ongoing decimation of the planet. It brings up righteous anger for the violation of the Soul. It reveals to us the oppression of our lives by a pervasive, painful Lie.

The fuck-it point is also a bridge to sanity that serves as a gateway to expansive awakening. It's not about hedonistic pursuits and partying until the end; it's about reuniting with the Soul and placing trust in the higher order of Gaea, knowing that it was never up to us to fix, save, or change the world anyway. Rather, it has always been up to us to reclaim the whole of who and what we are as Soul animating flesh in a physical world. This reclamation is—and has always been—the only way to live in harmony with Earth. No saving, fixing or changing required.

The fuck-it point is a profoundly spiritual place of non-attachment and deep acceptance. It's about living fully, loving hard and letting go. It's not about being uncaring; it's about caring more about what matters: life, compassion, truth, integrity, and the Soul.

In reaching the fuck-it point in my own life, I find myself increasingly dissociated from the dominant mutation of the human psyche. I do not feel superior. I do not feel inferior. I do not feel equal. I feel different—very, very different.

I also find myself quite naturally withdrawing from the external world, that is, being in the world but not of it. I rarely leave my sanctuary anymore, and when I do, I strategically plan for outings at times of the day when the foot soldiers for the industrial machine are confined in their schools and their jobs. As I withdraw from the world "out there" (the Big Lie), I expand into more of my inner world and connect more intimately with the Soul. The Soul cares not about social contact, popularity, success, or even longevity. It cares only about evolution.

After years of fighting what is, I've finally reached a stage in my life where I've let go of all resistance. I'm no longer willing to fight the machine. I've relinquished the burden of hope. I've liberated myself from all responsibility for the collective. I've released myself from the illusion, and will now bear witness to humanity's much needed dark night of the Soul.

I trust Gaea implicitly, and I know this tragic end will liberate her in ways that will finally bring peace. My love for her is so expansive that I'm willing to be sacrificed for that. I step aside and allow Gaea to do what Gaea needs to do.

Louise LeBrun recently shared with me, "I know the innate genius of the planet is to express herself as she sees fit. Gaea, in her genius, is capable of creating for her own evolution that which would quite likely destroy. I love my planet. My planet deeply moves me. And I trust that She will engage in the most powerful and meaningful way, for her. In my deep love and caring, I am willing to bear witness. To be present, and do what is most meaningful for me, as I bear witness to Gaea doing what is most meaningful for Her; knowing full well that her choices to expand her life, may well end mine. Gaea does not need my concern. What she needs is my willingness and ability to own the truth of my own experience, and to engage accordingly."

In my heart, I know that we are all so much more than what we have allowed ourselves to become as a species. It's time for all who read these words to remember this profound truth and live with intention, compassion, and integrity—fully, without restraint. This is the path of the Soul warrior.

The path of the Soul warrior is often a solo venture. It is the ultimate statement of courage. It is a path of uncertainty, discomfort, fierce love, ruthless compassion, activated presence, truth, transformation, spontaneity, evolution, and deep trust. It is not for the faint of heart, as it goes against all we've been programmed to believe ourselves to be.

Our planetary predicament is bringing us to the ultimate choice point: Do we choose to remain asleep: mutated, consumptive, destructive, indifferent, and separated from the Soul; or do we choose to awaken and expand in consciousness: alive, activated, present, lucid, and liberated from the burden of attachment to a physical world. As Peter Russell shared with me in a recent podcast, "An awakening of consciousness is important, whether it's about saving the world or dealing with a world that is falling apart. The more awake we become, the more able we are to move through these times with grace, compassion, and wisdom."[54]

The converging crises we are now living through are providing ample opportunities for us to go deep within and discover what it means to be the spiritual being—the embodied Soul—that we've always been meant to be.

And so in this tale of apparently unremitting gloom, I offer to you a wake-up call rather than a statement of despair. These volatile times can be a time of great liberation by reclaiming the undomesticated, purest nature of your core, essential being. Because "it's over" does not apply to the Soul.

PART 2: AWAKENING

Living Fully, Loving Hard and Letting Go

Planetary Hospice

"We have an eternal spiritual homeland which nobody can take away from us. With this certainty, everyone can confidently face the future, whatever fate may send them."

– LISELOTTE CARDINAL VON WIDDERN
(my maternal grandmother, in her memoir to her grandchildren)

From the accelerating demise of iconic animals; to the extinction of hundreds (perhaps thousands) of species—known and unknown—every single day; to unfathomable numbers of birds, fish and mammals slaughtered, hunted and eaten into oblivion as they simultaneously lose habitat from human encroachment; polar bear cubs poisoned by their mothers milk from ubiquitous human pollutants[55]; escalating mental illness expressed through violence toward ourselves and others; the immanent outbreak of global nuclear war; the accelerating breakdown of the ocean; the hyperactive Ring of Fire; and most troubling of all, the unprecedented meltdown of the Arctic—the now terminally ill regulator of our global climate, and the most significant existential threat to the habitability of the planet beyond all other drivers of runaway biosphere decay. A global collective of which we are all part of is shaping our reality, utterly oblivious to its impact.

Professor of Ethics, Clive Hamilton bluntly states:

> The "humans-only" orientation of the social sciences and humanities is reinforced by our total absorption in representations of reality derived from media, encouraging us to view the ecological crisis as a spectacle that takes place outside the

bubble of our existence.

It is true that grasping the scale of what is happening requires not only breaking the bubble but also making the cognitive leap to "Earth system thinking"—that is, conceiving of the Earth as a single, complex, dynamic system. It is one thing to accept that human influence has spread across the landscape, the oceans and the atmosphere, but quite another to make the jump to understanding that human activities are disrupting the functioning of the Earth as a complex, dynamic, ever-evolving totality comprised of myriad interlocking processes.[56]

In the 540 million year history of planet Earth since complex life emerged, there have been five great extinction events. According to the National Geographic Society, "We are in the midst of the Sixth Great Extinction, an event characterized by the loss of between 17,000 and 100,000 species each year."[57]

Our allegiance to ecocide has sealed our fate, and there is no planet B. When we look at our mortally wounded planet, it is far too late to create, hope, or pray for change. A deathbed heartbeat cannot be resuscitated. The collective consciousness of 7.6 billion members of a Soul-deprived species determines the final act.

As the pace of runaway biosphere decay accelerates, it appears inevitable that the Sixth Great Extinction event includes the end of life as we know it. Eco-psychologist, Zhiwa Woodbury wrote in his online essay, *Planetary Hospice*, "In effect, we as a species are now on life support, teetering on the threshold of our very own Great Dying. In short, the Great Anthropocentric Dying is upon us. Our situation is, regrettably, terminal."[58]

A terminal illness is one for which there is no cure. It is an active, progressive, irreversible affliction with a fatal prognosis.

For many, the concept of extinction in the near-term may be extreme. But let's face it, everything humans have done to Earth is extreme. We've created the perfect conditions for an extreme outcome.

At the deepest level of consciousness—whether we are aware of it or not—we are inextricably linked to Earth. Even if our consciousness is tainted by the Big Lie, by our very nature as animals, there exists within us a deeper awareness that the support system of this planet is severely compromised.

As the situation rapidly deteriorates on planet Earth, we must also be wary of the 40-year lag time between behavior and outcome; cause and effect; action and reaction. What this means is that we are only now experiencing the repercussions of our collective choices, activities, and behaviors at a time in the 1970's. Because of the lag time associated with runaway biosphere decay, the dominant mindset of human denial will not fully realize the gravity of this situation until it is much too late to avoid its grievous consequences. Scientist and futurist, James Lovelock said that we might have had a chance of turning this ship around if we acted aggressively as a global collective in the 1960's. But we didn't.

We are now living in a time of planetary hospice.

Planetary hospice is best described by eco-psychologist, Zhiwa Woodbury, in his essay, *Principles of Planetary Hospice*:

> Hospice is a subset of palliative care, and the concern of the Planetary Hospice Movement is itself palliative. To 'palliate' means 'to lessen the severity of (pain, disease, etc.) without curing... (To) alleviate; mitigate.' It doesn't mean that palliative care is incompatible with a course of treatment that may lead to a cure; rather, it is the physical, psychological, and spiritual suffering that is of concern to the palliative care team. That is the nature of the spiritual container for the Planetary Hospice

Movement as well. It is concerned neither with saving nor condemning the world during this time of great dying and grieving. Instead, it's over-riding, if not sole, concern is to alleviate the suffering attended with these most unfortunate times.[59]

In another essay titled, *Climate Catharsis*, Zhiwa Woodbury goes on to write:

> Because evolution has not really prepared us to deal with such an existential threat at this grand a scale—since we have only very recently reached and exceeded the planet's carrying capacity, and gained the kind of mastery over it that started to become apparent after WWII—there is a natural, reflexive tendency to suppress this awareness before it emerges into consciousness and to continually repress it thereafter.[60]

Repressed consciousness—denial—often provides the illusion of an easier to manage reality, but it traps us in mindless consumption that only serves to further degrade Earth. Denial is a dangerous distraction that insulates us from the pain of reality so we can keep on keeping on without bothering to change our ways. Denial is the enemy of life.

As a collective, we've been rigid about creating the future from the past. Our world has become smaller, more compressed and claustrophobic as a result. In our addiction to sameness, we've become mechanized in our compulsion to consume.

The world we live in is not sustainable. We cannot continue doing what we are doing, yet we keep teaching our children how to live the way we've always lived. How we've been living is destroying us.

For those who understand the gravity of our situation, planetary hospice is imploring us to love and let go: of Earth, of who and what we've been conditioned to believe ourselves to be, and of our own mortality.

The transformation we need in this world does not come from knowledge, content, or the coveted intellect. It comes from the courage, curiosity, and willingness to reclaim the whole of what we are beyond the limitations of our conditioned humanity.

Many of us can feel the incredible acceleration on the planet. Everything is melting faster, burning faster, flooding faster; life is moving more quickly, things are becoming more intense. If we refuse to pick up the pace of our own evolution and relax into the vibration that is naturally increasing in our own bodies, we will not be able to cope. As Holocaust survivor, Viktor Frankl once said, "When we are no longer able to change a situation, we are challenged to change ourselves."

So many people go to their graves longing for a more authentic, meaningful and interconnected life without knowing that it is available right now, simply by choosing differently.

Quoting Elisabeth Kübler-Ross from a public talk many years ago, "Are we only able to see who we authentically are at life's beginnings and endings? Do only extreme circumstances reveal ordinary truths? Are we otherwise blind to our genuine selves? Everyone carries the seeds of greatness within. 'Great' people don't have something that everyone else doesn't; they've simply removed a lot of the things that stand in the way of their best selves."

It takes exceptional courage to claim our part in the creation of this fatal crisis of consciousness. It is a painful process, but it's in this courage that we are empowered to become more whole.

In the reclamation of our wholeness, it is essential that we are brutally honest with ourselves. We must take ownership for the choices that created the smog-filled air and polluted, lifeless rivers in faraway lands because of our addiction to increasingly complex technologies. We must own our indifference to the destruction of the sacred: the countless lives, rainforests, oceans, lakes, rivers, and streams destroyed with every morsel of animal flesh consumed. We must take responsibility for the mindless consumption that pollutes the land and chokes the seas with endless streams of plastic, toxic waste, and garbage. We must become conscious of the thoughts in our heads that judge the "other" and bind us to division, hatred, and fear.

The bottom line is that we are all guilty of participating in the consciousness that removed us from the Soul and brought us to this critical place.

So the question is, what can we do about this disaster?

For starters, we must think with our hearts and leave the antiquated conditioning of our heads behind.

We must invite the shadowy parts of ourselves into conscious awareness, and become intimate with the fragmented parts of who we are. Intimacy with our wounds means walking the path of wholeness, and no longer living from the stories of what we believe ourselves to be. It means no longer choosing from a place of history, and remembering that we are not victims to our own choices, nor are we victims to the choices of the collective.

More than ever, we need to feel, heal and be real. More than ever, we need to connect. More than ever, we need to be present in every sacred moment of life.

In the wake of such outrageous lunacy, we must let go of all attachment to a possible future by living in a place of pure presence. When we are fully engaged in the present moment, the future becomes unnecessary.

Having lived through, and experienced much death in my life, I'm intimately familiar with the delay that often follows terminal diagnosis and demise. Rarely is dying a rapid process. It usually takes months and sometimes, years. The deeper awareness of imminent loss often brings with it a sacred tenderness that redefines how we live in the world. Essentially, we grow up.

The uncertainty of it all has a foreboding quality to it, and unless one lives with their head firmly planted in ignorance, there is no question that these are decisive times. As a species, this is likely to be the most significant adversity we've ever faced. It also offers us the most exceptional opportunity for spiritual evolution we have ever encountered.

These end times are inspiring us to live and choose a different way; to decide who and what we are beyond the antiquated stories that have defined our lives for so long. It's a time of growth and expansion. Living in a time of hospice with death in mind can bring us closer to our essence. It can inspire more love, kindness, caring and compassion, thus easing the burden on all those who have suffered so greatly at the hands of our species for so long.

As Elisabeth Kübler-Ross said, "When we face the worst that can happen in any situation, we grow. When circumstances are at their worst, we can find our best. In facing loss, love is all that matters. Love is the only thing that we can possess, keep with us, and take with us."

I believe that if we face the fact that we are coming to the end of our incredible evolutionary journey as a species, we can live with more love and compassion in our hearts than we have ever known. In my worldview, this is a beautiful thing.

In the wise words of Joanna Macy, "There is absolutely no excuse for making our passionate love for the world dependent on what we believe the outcome will be: whether life continues on or not. In this uncertainty, we come alive."

The Power of Grief

"The heart that breaks open can contain the whole universe."

– Joanna Macy

The cumulative effect of the collective choices we have made has taken a dramatic toll on the life support systems of the planet. The implications of these choices have perpetuated the Big Lie and subsequently degraded the biosphere. In a civilization where mass distraction is so pervasive, it's challenging to be present with pain and grief in ways that are transformed into the strength, commitment and resolve to create a different outcome on the planet.

The inability to experience our own pain as well as the pain of others, is what allows suffering to continue. Separation from everything natural—including our own feelings—breeds indifference, and a false sense of superiority. A collective consciousness existent in the realm of separation and superiority creates a loss of compassion on a massive scale. A loss of conscience follows a loss of compassion.

It is clear that humanity is in a time of great transition. The unsustainable power-based structures that drive our world are crumbling. Gaea has had enough of our conspicuous consumption, and we are being roused from the Big Lie to grieve for what we have done to the planet.

The journey we have embarked on for far too long has been a journey of separation. There have been many significant turning points along the way where we had the opportunity to address the question of what it means to be a human being on planet Earth. What is the story of Self? For far too long, the story of Self has been married to the story of separation.

The story of separation states that we are individual entities interacting with a world that is fundamentally separate from us. We are fear-filled motes of consciousness encapsulated in flesh interacting with other fear-filled motes of consciousness. We are the expression of selfish genes maximizing their reproductive desires. We are rational actors seeking to maximize our economic self-interests. There is a widespread belief that we can do anything to an "other" without consequences. It's a "dog eat dog world." Every moment that we are not doing something to get ahead is a moment lost in the competitive race to get a piece of the shrinking pie. We are running out of time. We are running out of money. We are running out of resources. We are running out of space. We must get to where we think we need to go and make the biggest impact, and it must happen now. Trapped in our beliefs of scarcity and lack, we take and take with no concern for how our culturally normalized paranoia impacts the elaborate web that sustains life. We've alienated ourselves from the Soul and the natural world in ways that have caused tremendous suffering for all.

Our war mentality—the war on terror, the war on germs, the war on cancer, the war on drugs, the war on nature, and endless wars on each another—is no longer working. The story of controlling and manipulating the "other" that is external to us, is disintegrating. Each time we implement a "fix" from within the consciousness of the Big Lie, it brings with it greater problems. Science, technology, politics, and growth-based economics—the holy grails of our industrialized world—have failed us miserably. If they were ever to save us, it would have happened long ago, and we wouldn't be in the hellacious situation we are in today. As we continue along with this same approach, the problems become increasingly challenging to overcome. Like the heroin addict frantically chasing his fix, eventually the addiction overtakes, and what follows is breakdown.

In a world that is unraveling at an unprecedented rate, it's easy to fall into helplessness and despair, but this only perpetuates the story of separation. The great paradox for remembering our connection to the world is the pain revealed through our grief. By willingly engaging our grief, we detach ourselves from the Big Lie and reclaim the deep truth of what we are as a hybrid species of flesh and spirit, connected to all.

When we remember our interdependence, we realize that the loss of one species is a loss for the collective. That violence toward other living beings, is violence toward all. That ecologies are wholly interconnected to have beautiful relationships which symbiotically support one another. By disrupting this natural interdependence, we destroy all possibilities for a long-term future for ourselves as a species. Separation has a finite existence, and the human refusal to create a more life-affirming story has finally reached its end.

The world of today is not worth saving, it is far too broken.

It's time to let it go.

Letting go is our invitation to grieve—and to grow.

Gaea Grief

Because our dominant culture pathologizes pain, we live in an unfeeling world where the labels of "good" and "bad" pervert all that is natural (i.e., feelings and emotions). As a result, grief is viewed as something to be silenced. Rather than express it, we suppress it, repress it, oppress it, stuff it, analyze it, numb it, medicate it, dismiss it, or otherwise divert our attention so that we never have to face it. In refusing to acknowledge our pain, we end up prolonging it, thus denying ourselves the opportunity for profound healing and personal evolution. Frozen by the denial of our authentic expression, we are immobilized. Whole industries profit from this immobility, and while they grow rich, we become spiritually bankrupt.

Suppressing emotion is akin to eating and quelling the need for elimination. Most of us would never do this to our bodies, yet we mindlessly do it with our feelings. By keeping our emotions in check, they become toxic. Holding toxicity, whether it is emotional, mental, or physical, is extremely detrimental to our overall well-being. When we prevent the movement of emotion, it can leak out as passive aggression, judgment, jealousy, frustration, anxiety, depression, resentment, rage, and eventually, tumors, cancers, and a host of other chronic and potentially fatal ailments. The longer we suppress emotion, the more *dis*-eased we become.

In her blog post, *The Intelligence of Pain*, Louise LeBrun writes:

> So many in so much pain. Physical pain. Emotional pain. Spiritual pain. We have been relentlessly trained to consider the experience of pain as the enemy, seeking to eliminate it and banish it from our lives. We use drugs to numb ourselves to its presence. We accept violent and invasive procedures to the body to cut it out of our lives. Perhaps what we need most is to change our perspective, making it possible for us to pause ... listen ... and hear the message our pain is seeking to deliver. Once received, the need for its presence is no longer required.[61]

Pain is an intelligent mechanism for alerting us to what needs our attention. It is not an enemy of our humanity; instead, it is a wise messenger that brings us closer to the Soul.

When the superficial layers of pain—often expressed through anger, judgment, jealousy, frustration, irritation, and so on—are exposed, repressed grief can often be found.

At this moment in time, there is overwhelming anguish enveloping planet Earth. Whether we care to recognize it or not, I believe that grief defines our current world. The relentless decimation of Earth has sickened the human spirit and numbed our capacity to feel. The cumulative sorrow of the world—both felt and suppressed—is overwhelming.

The grief we are collectively experiencing for how we once knew life on this planet to be—what we once defined as abundance in the natural world with endless bird songs, lush forests teeming with wildlife, fresh water, clean air, and healthy soil—is genuine. It is a loss on a scale that defies comprehension. By facing the Soullessness of this destruction and feeling the subsequent anguish, we can see more clearly through the eyes of the Soul. The human Soul is not separate from the Soul of Earth. It is through this bond that we acknowledge our interconnected lives.

In his essay, *Anima Mundi: Awakening the Soul of the World*, Sufi teacher, Llewellyn Vaughan-Lee writes:

> At the moment, the world is asleep, suffering the dreams of humanity, which have become a nightmare of desecration and pollution. In our hubris, we have forgotten that the world is more than our collective projections, that it is more mysterious and strange than our rational minds would like us to believe. Quantum physics has revealed a fluid and unpredictable world, in which consciousness and matter are not separate—whether a photon of light behaves as a particle or wave depends upon the consciousness of the observer. But we remain within the images of Newtonian physics: matter that is dead, definable, and solid, and consciousness that is objective, safely divorced from the physical world. Matter and spirit remain split, and we continue in the patriarchal fantasy that we can have control over our world.

He continues with, "The world is a living spiritual being. This was understood by the ancient philosophers and the alchemists who referred to the spiritual essence of the world as the anima mundi, the "Soul of the World." They regarded the World Soul as a pure ethereal spirit diffused throughout all nature, the divine essence that embraces and energizes all life in the universe."[62]

If we are at all alive to our essential being at this time, we *should* be grieving the state of the world. We *should* be grieving what has become of our species. We *should* be grieving our separation from life. Grief is one of the sanest responses to our fatal predicament. If there is no grief, there is no humanity. If one is not heartbroken beyond words, and not utterly shattered by this situation, there is no life. Without grief, there is no love or compassion. Without love or compassion, there is no Soul. In these times of ecological decay, the world is begging for our attention. The animals are begging for our attention. Earth is begging for our attention. The Soul is begging for our attention.

When pain is suppressed and glossed over by politesse, it lurks in the shadows and leaks out in ugly ways. Is it any wonder why mental illness, anxiety, and depression are so rampant? Is it any wonder why mass shootings, racism, bigotry, misogyny, cruelty, bullying, and hate are so commonplace? Is it any wonder why the masses continue to deny the reality of runaway biosphere decay, even while they wade through "unprecedented" floods, choke on drought-parched Earth, run from merciless storms, hurricanes, and typhoons; and flee in horror from wildfires that can no longer be contained?

In *The Wild Edge of Sorrow*, psychotherapist, Francis Weller writes, "How can we possibly stay open to the endless assaults on the biosphere when the urge to avert our eyes and pretend that we don't feel this pain takes over? It takes a heart of courage and conviction, one willing to look into the center of the suffering and remain present. To live a life of soul means living with sensitivity to the plight of the planet."[63]

The interweaving of personal and planetary losses has left many of us reeling with uncertainty, despair, anxiety, and ultimately, heartbreak. Perhaps the pain we feel for Earth arises from the very Earth herself.

As Joanna Macy wrote in her blog post, *Five Ways of Being that can Change the World*, "When Zen poet Thich Nhat Hanh was asked: 'What do we most need to do to save our world?' his questioners expected him to identify the best strategies to pursue for social and environmental causes. Instead, he answered: 'What we most need to do is to hear within us the sounds of the Earth crying.'"[64]

Part of the repression of the feminine within each of us is the shaming of our feelings and emotions. But our feelings show us what is true. Our feelings are the intelligent expression of energy attempting to capture our attention. Because our culturally conditioned tendency is to intellectualize and repress this energy, however, we develop rules around what is and is not acceptable. As energetic beings who have been conditioned to believe otherwise, we then block the flow of vital energy and information emerging from our most profound wisdom within.

Our grief and our pain can be the source of our greatest essential strength. If we would only just allow ourselves to slow down and breathe, we would connect to the heartbeat of Earth and feel the depth of her pain. In this profound connection, we discover that our pain for the world and our love for the world are one. In this union, our lives expand, our world expands, and we are made stronger.

In his essay, *In Praise of Manners*, Francis Weller writes:

> Grieving opens the aperture of the heart to a wider sense of identity. Rather than attending solely to the 'relentless industry of self,' grief initiates us into the more inclusive conversation between our singular lives and the extended self of the world.

We begin to understand that there is no isolated self stranded
in the cosmos, but rather an entwined and entangled net of
connections reminding us that we are in a continuous exchange
with light, air, gravity, thought, color, sound, all coalescing in
an elegant dance that is our shared life. It is holy.[65]

The question for many of us right now is how to remain engaged
and activated in a collapsing world without falling into despair, indifference or apathy. How do we stay present to it all?

The answer is simple: we must grieve. By allowing the power of
grief to break our hearts open, we are transformed. Like the phoenix
rising from the ashes of ruin, we are able to then soar to incredible
new heights.

In our pain is our compassion. In our compassion is the remembrance that we are not separate. Compassion reunites us with the
Soul. When we run away from our pain, we run away from our compassion. By stepping into our pain, it transforms. It does not remain
static. Pain is only static when we disown it. But when we bring it into
our hearts, it reveals to us its other face; the face of our absolutely
inseparable connectedness with all life.

In my own life, I cry for Earth regularly. I don't know if there is
anyone on the planet who has shed more tears for Gaea than I have—
whether in awe for her breathtaking beauty or in grief for the gut-
wrenching devastation. I'm intimately familiar with the power of this
continuous flow of tears. When I cry, I'm cleansed. When I cry, I'm
connected. When I cry, I find joy much easier. When I cry, I know
that my heart and my mind are twinned.

It's ok for our hearts to be broken. In fact, we need our hearts to
be broken to allow our grief to be transformed into an inexorable love
that cares—not because there's a sliver of hope for a happy ending—
but because love is the essence of who we are. It is the force that plugs
us into the web of life.

I believe that we all carry an overwhelming amount of grief in our hearts. For the childhood we never had, the dreams we never lived, the calling we never expressed. For the love we never shared, the people, animals and relationships we've lost along the way, and for the dire state of the planet that we know—either consciously or unconsciously—is dying.

We only grieve what we love, and contrary to the cultural shaming of our pain, grief and pain are powerful motivators for transformation. In our pain-phobic culture, however, it makes perfect sense that we stand where we do today. When we fear the immensity of our grief, we shut down and move into a state of deep denial.

In most cases, denial is the manifestation of suppressed grief—a refusal to look at the severity of what has been done to the world because the pain is too significant. Suppressed grief is unexpressed love, and I think we can all agree that we live in a world devoid of pure, essential love. Our "everything is fine" culture of denial promotes our disconnect from Earth and each other. Denial traps us in the status quo of business-as-usual, and prevents us from taking the action required to think, feel, choose, and live in alignment with the Soul.

Our ignorance, indifference, apathy, and even our despair, all stem from our fear of pain, which is rooted in our fear of expressing the immensity of our capacity to love. Our invitation to dance with despair, is an invitation to be present with our grief and our love for Earth.

Joanna Macy said in a recent interview, "The closer we get to midnight, the more we lose intellectual capacity. So not feeling the pain is extremely costly. The most radical thing any of us can do at this time is to be fully present to what is happening in the world. It brings a new way of seeing the world, as our larger living body, freeing us from the assumptions and attitudes that now threaten the continuity of life on Earth."

When we love Earth, *we are* Earth. We refuse the blinders that prevent us from feeling and seeing it all. We hold the beauty and the destruction; the love and the grief—together. When we love something or someone that is unwell, we don't turn away, because our love unites us in more profound ways. It is only when we fall deeply in love with Earth—and the Soul—that we can end our destructive ways.

When we move beyond denial and the false sense of hope that holds us captive to a complacent mindset; and when we accept the severity of our situation, only then can we open our hearts to the pain of our grief—the gateway to the Soul, and our deepest love for the world.

The Beast of Grief (A Personal Offering for Transformation)

Grief is a beast. It's a beast I know well. Despite our intimate relationship, it refuses to befriend me. I've learned to accept that this is how it is because grief is just not the "BFF" type. Rather, it is a formidable teacher meant to bring me closer to the Soul by dissolving the mental, emotional and spiritual confines of longing and attachment.

Grief is relentless in its desire to awaken. It repeatedly exposes the permanence of impermanence, and therein lies the pain. Just when I think I've mastered non-attachment, I'm flattened by my humanity once again.

Grief has a way of slowing me down and stopping me in my tracks—longing for what I once knew as reality—grasping for answers that never appear. It cripples me with its unpredictable nature, incapacitating me, and reducing me to a puddle of tears as my heart desperately aches for what was once familiar.

In grief, I feel spaced out, agitated, disoriented, ungrounded, angry, claustrophobic, broken … often a little crazy. What I once knew as "my world" is permanently altered. Who I once knew myself to be, is no more. What was once my "normal," is gone. Forever. It's a heavy burden to bear. I'm vulnerable, lost in the fog of confusion. Over time, however, I've learned that this "painful insanity" is the gateway to massive evolution.

Grief is a complicated beast deserved of the utmost respect. It cannot be controlled, comforted, or rushed. It must be honored for what it is: an intricate visceral response to the finality of loss.

Grief has a way of tearing at the very fabric of our being and casting a heavy shadow on the heart. We cannot think our way out of grief, and until we allow ourselves to feel the enormity of its power, we are bound to its debilitating pain. The only way "out of" grief, is to welcome it in.

Francis Weller says it eloquently:

> Grief is alive, wild, untamed; it cannot be domesticated. It resists the demands to remain passive and still. We move in jangled, unsettled, and riotous ways when grief takes hold of us. It is truly an emotion that rises from soul.

> What has become clear to me is the powerful role grief plays in enabling us to face what is taking place in our lives, our communities, our ecologies, families, and culture. ... Grief registers the sorrows that befall everything that matters deeply to our souls.[66]

Most of us are grieving something. We mourn the loss of loved ones, the end of relationships, or the deaths of animal companions. We lament the clearcut forests, the billions of animals killed for human consumption, the dying oceans, the innocent victims of senseless wars ... the state of the world. We grieve what we love and lose, and it hurts.

When deep in the throes of grief, I feel like I'm trapped on a leaky boat in a tumultuous ocean without compass, paddle, rudder, or sail. I have no control over direction, and even if I did, I'm clueless about which way to turn. In the fleeting moments of clarity, I'm ambushed by powerful waves of anguish that leave me clinging for dear life to the hope that one day it will end. I'm utterly lost in the prodigious sea of uncertainty.

Loss of any kind creates an abrupt identity crisis. The identity we once knew no longer applies. We are no longer somebody's daughter, son, partner, friend, or companion. We are no longer the person we once knew ourselves to be. We often lose our sense of meaning, and the question that most occupies our consciousness is, "who am I now?"

Most of us have been conditioned to source our identity from the roles we play in life. But in the midst of loss, what was once familiar, is no more. We are not only thrown into the manic sea of uncertainty; we are thrown into crisis over who we are—with no idea of who we are about to become. Uncertainty can be a frightening place when the mind resists its inevitable intrusion. When the heart takes the lead, however, uncertainty is liberation. Loss forces us to look within and discover the depths of who and what we are, independent of our conditioned persona.

When identity is ripped away, it is not uncommon to feel undefined, ungrounded, confused, and lost. When this foundational component of our being is disrupted, it forces us to search. Many remain lost as they aimlessly grasp at a false sense of hope or illusory solutions in an external world. At best, they stay trapped in low-grade unhappiness—a self-created purgatory. At worst, they succumb to life-numbing addiction—a self-created hell.

Allowing our hearts to be broken open by the pain of grief burns away all preconceived ideas of who we once believed ourselves to be, revealing more of our essential nature in the process. It is in this vulnerable "messiness" that our humanity becomes authentic.

Grief is a process with its own timeline. It takes what it takes. It can be an excuse to resign from life, or it can be used to re-design life. It is never meant to define us, however; instead, it is intended to redefine how we see the world and what is truly important to us. Grief brings us closer to the Soul by reminding us of the interconnected truth of existence.

Grief may be the price we pay for love, but it should never prevent us from loving. When we allow pain to move through us, we significantly expand our capacity for evermore love. Wherever we find sorrow authentically expressed, love is close at hand. One cannot exist without the other. Grief reveals to us the frailty of our humanity. When we surrender to its power, we are transformed. When we allow it to bring us to our knees, we emerge more whole and become solidly grounded in the core of our authentic being. This is when we no longer just feel love, we embody it. In the words of Francis Weller, "It is the broken heart, the part that knows sorrow, that is capable of genuine love."

In Kenn Orphan's blog post, *Grief and the Unbreakable Sinew*, he writes, "Love is not merely affection. It is not a drug. It is not a state of being either. Love is the unbreakable sinew that connects us to each other. And without it, we are nothing more than single cells of life drifting aimlessly in the void, meaningless, empty and featureless. Death tears apart the corporeal, but love completes us by making us one organism."[67]

So many humans fear the pain of loss that they never allow themselves to love. This avoidance of love is at the root of many of today's problems. The epidemic of chronic depression around the globe is little more than a misdirected expression of repressed grief, and unexpressed love—not the fickle, conditional, sexualized "love" that prevails in our culture—but spiritual love; the love that unites *all* beyond the limitations of physical matter.

The only possible outcome of love held back is isolation, pain, and a lifetime of regret. The pain of the "could have's," "should have's" and "would have's" is far greater than all else because it lingers in the heart as a constant reminder of who we never allowed ourselves to become. Embracing our grief and our pain is what leads us back to love. We can only love as deeply as we grieve.

Sogyal Rinpoche words say so much in *The Tibetan Book of Living and Dying*, "Whatever you do, don't shut off your pain; accept your pain and remain vulnerable. However desperate you become, accept your pain as it is, because it is in fact trying to hand you a priceless gift: the chance of discovering what lies behind sorrow. Grief can be the garden of compassion. If you keep your heart open through everything, your pain can become your greatest ally in your life's search for love and wisdom."[68]

Love and wisdom: never has Earth needed this more.

In Praise of Mortality

"Dying is nothing to fear. It can be the most wonderful experience of your life. It all depends on how you have lived."

– Elisabeth Kübler-Ross

Despite widespread denial, it doesn't take a rocket scientist to understand that a harmful way of living that devours Earth with no thought for tomorrow cannot last. If "it's over" means the end of life on Earth, there are worse things than the end of Earth's surface humanity, such as continuing in a way that systemic tyranny, omnipresent ignorance and desecrating consumption reigns; while critical thought, personal autonomy, freedom, and awakening to inclusive consciousness is forsaken.

One manifestation of our collective insanity is that we will do anything to deny our own mortality. Since our earliest years, we have all known that we are mortal beings with death ensured, yet we have adopted a death-phobic mindset in a culture that is driven by a compulsive urge to destroy life. This is madness. Facing our collective demise, however, is the critical conversation we must explore in these surreal times. Futurist, Peter Russell shared in his video titled, *Evolution's End*, "Any intelligent technological species has the potential to become a magnificent flowering of consciousness, but the side effects of its rapid evolution mean that it only has a short window of time to complete its evolutionary journey. Facing the end of our species could in itself be the wake-up call we need."[69]

Most people exist as if they are never going to die, yet they don't ever live either. The level of anxiety and depression on a global scale is profound. The world is filled with helpless, unhappy, powerless, self-loathing, self-absorbed people trapped in a victim consciousness of their own making. By avoiding all conversations about pain, grief, and death, emotional infancy is guaranteed, and the masses are unable to break free from their misery.

In his book, *Many Lives, Many Masters*, Dr. Brian Weiss writes, "How powerful the fear of death is. People go to such great lengths to avoid the fear: mid-life crises, affairs with younger people, cosmetic surgeries, exercise obsessions, accumulating material possessions, procreating to carry on a name, striving to be more and more youthful, and so on. We are frightfully concerned with our own deaths, sometimes so much so that we forget the real purpose of our lives."[70]

Humans are a hybrid species of flesh and spirit; ego and Soul; matter and energy. We are autonomous expressions of a greater whole in an interconnected world. But we've forgotten.

Embedded within the Big Lie is the mechanistic Newtonian paradigm, which quite simply states that all things living are like machines. The widespread acceptance of this dogma clearly explains the *why* behind the madness of the human species. If life is like a machine, it is unfeeling, linear, predictable, follows direction, and conforms to the same basic principles as all other machines. It can be fixed, silenced, parts can be removed, and things can be replaced. Eventually, it outlives its usefulness and is replaced by something newer, younger and more current. Sound familiar?

Life, however, is not this rigid. Nor is it this simplistic.

The Quantum paradigm is based on quantum physics which was discovered by Max Planck in the early 1900's. It was expanded by Albert Einstein shortly thereafter. At its simplest, quantum physics states that everything is energy. The quantum paradigm implies that we are both observer and participant in a holographic reality. This discovery was supported by a recent study released in 2017 by a team of international scientists titled, *From Planck Data to Planck Era: Observational Tests of Holographic Cosmology*[71]. The information in this paper is beyond the scope of this book, but suffice it to say that progressive thinkers within the scientific community are finally accepting the long-held truths of many ancient eastern philosophies.

In the groundbreaking work of cell biologist, Dr. Bruce Lipton and evolutionary catalyst, Louise LeBrun, it has been shown—through the quantum perspective—that the body is an intelligent device animated by an energetic signal that streams through it. In a recent exchange, Louise LeBrun shared with me, "I know that I am a Quantum Biological Human™. My body is a device—a brilliant, organic, amazing device—and a device, nonetheless. The vast, expansive, boundless and perpetual *I am* that I am is not the device. I am the Signal that courses through it. Over time, the device has become "crippled" in its full function from cultural conditioning, making it difficult for the *I am* that I am to flow easily through and guide expression. As we choose to live from that perspective, however, life becomes so much more fulfilling, effortless and immensely rich in its capacity for joy."

What this essentially means is that we are not our bodies. We are not our conditioned personalities. We are not machines.

We are so much more.

We are Soul inspiring creation. We are spirit activating matter. We are energy animating flesh. As Albert Einstein said, "Energy cannot be created or destroyed, it can only be changed from one form to another." In other words, we are immortal beings animating mortal matter in an infinite, holographic universe. The body is merely a conduit for the expression of the Signal—the Soul—in a physical world. It is the bridge between the realm of energy and matter. When the body dies, the energetic expression of who we are, does not.

Ironically, we know this deep truth when we are young, but it is pummeled out of us to conform to the cultural amnesia that instills compliance to the Big Lie. Essentially, we are indoctrinated into a Newtonian coma that mechanizes us to support a destructive, industrialized, consumptive machine.

In his book, *The Wild Edge of Sorrow*, Francis Weller writes:

> Modern technological society has forgotten what it feels like to be embedded in a living culture, one rich with stories and traditions, rituals and patterns of instruction that help us become true human beings. We live in a society with little regard for matters of soul. As a consequence, we need books and workshops on grief, on relationships and sexuality, on play and creativity. These are symptoms of a great loss. We have forgotten the commons of the soul—the primary satisfactions that sustained and nourished the community and the individual for tens of thousands of years. We have substituted a strange, frenzied obsession with "earning a living"—one of the most obscene phrases in our world—for the vital and fragrant life of the soul. We have sadly turned the ritual of life into the routine of existence.[72]

Many people squander the brevity of their lives with habituated patterns that entrance them into believing that tomorrow will always arrive. But the reality is that tomorrow may not arrive. Thirty minutes from now may not arrive. The next breath may not arrive. Life is not a guarantee.

There are few absolutes in the world that level the playing field for every one of us. One absolute is that we are gifted with a body. Another absolute is that we are gifted with a body that will die. Because we get to die, we also get to live. Regardless of personal circumstances, we have the choice of becoming a living expression of the Signal—the

Soul—or not. We can choose to be more than our conditioning, our stories, our history, our wounds, our fears, and our beliefs. We can choose to be so much more than who and what we have been taught to believe ourselves to be.

Ultimately, our stories can shape us, or they can enslave us.

The story of Viktor Frankl is an inspirational model for the power of choice. Although he didn't choose for his family to be brutally murdered when he was incarcerated in a Nazi concentration camp, he did choose his outlook on this merciless situation. Viktor chose to rewrite the story of his life—not as a victim to his circumstances—but as a testament to who and what he knew himself to be beyond the limitations of his horrific situation. His bestselling book, *Man's Search for Meaning* sold more than 10 million copies in 24 languages at the time of his death in 1997.

Viktor showed us the power of resilience and choice.

Rosa Parks grew up desperately poor, repeatedly bullied, abused, and the recipient of outrageous sexism and racism. She chose not to be a victim to her ugly circumstances. In an act of historical civil disobedience, she refused to comply with the demeaning racism that ordered her to relinquish her bus seat in the colored section to a white passenger when the white section was filled. Her act of defiance became a famous symbol of the modern Civil Rights Movement.

Rosa showed us the power of standing in truth, and choosing the Soul.

Malala Yousafzai refused to be silenced by speaking up for her right to an education. Born to a simple family in Pakistan—a country founded on violence, oppression, and misogyny—15-year-old Malala was shot in the head by the Taliban while returning home from school on a bus in October of 2012. She survived the trauma, which only served to strengthen her resolve to advocate for, "millions of girls around the world who are denied the right to go to school and realize their potential."

At sixteen, Malala became a global symbol of peaceful protest and the youngest nominee ever for the Nobel Peace Prize.

Malala showed us the power of perseverance and voice.

There are endless examples of everyday people who have chosen the internal voice of the Soul over the external voices of desperate lies. In facing their own mortality and not allowing circumstance to dictate the outcome of their lives, each of the afore-mentioned people were freed from a lifetime of regret and culturally conditioned Self-oppression.

When we make the invisible, visible, we remember that we always have choice about how we live our lives. Death does not belong in the shadows, it belongs in the forefront of our consciousness to inspire the full expression of life, now.

Fear: The Greatest Barrier to the Soul

When we enter the world, we are born with two innate fears: fear of falling, and fear of loud noises. All other fear is learned. The most damaging fear instilled into us is fear of the Soul. Fresh out of the womb, we are immediately being programmed to believe in our superiority over all life. It is this separation that severs our connection to the Soul/God/Buddha/Krishna/Allah/Universe/Source/Signal or whatever we choose to label this infinite energy. We are taught to believe that we are not the direct expression of a greater whole; that something more significant exists outside of us, but we are not it. We are taught that our mortality is something to be denied at all costs. We are taught to fear "death." Sadly, the result of these ridiculous beliefs is a fear of life.

This antiquated programming is the cause of the prevailing lim-ited beliefs about the true nature of our reality. It is what prevents us from understanding *what* we are, and how our multidimensional world works.

The mechanization of death and dying in the 21st century has grown out of a perverse belief system in western culture that infects our attitudes toward life. Our society as a whole denies death. Youth is worshiped, old folks are whisked off to hospitals and nursing homes, and almost everyone avoids the topic of death. Peculiarly and unnaturally, we believe it is right to suppress perfectly natural emotions, and fear entirely natural occurrences. I believe that most people not only fear death (and subsequently, life), they fear the vast expanse of their own potential. On a deeper level, I believe we all know that we are here to evolve, grow and expand into so much more than what we are taught to believe ourselves to be. But because we are so heavily programmed to serve a Big Lie rather than the Soul, we play small instead, compressing and editing our lives to map to the expectations of a dysfunctional civilization. In denying ourselves the discovery of who and what we authentically are, we fear our demise for the regret we know will emerge from living in the shadow of the Soul.

Because most people take life for granted, it quickly slips away. Benjamin Franklin said it well, "Most people die at 25 and aren't buried until they're 75." The truth is that nobody gets out alive. Upon conception, our physical death is guaranteed. Because of the conditioning that binds us to the Big Lie, however, the only two remaining aspects of our natural humanity are birth and death. Sadly, we've even managed to pervert this.

From her book, *Death: The Final Stage of Growth*, Elisabeth Kübler-Ross wrote:

> Death is a subject that is evaded, ignored, and denied by our youth-worshipping, progress-oriented society. It is almost as if we have taken on death as just another disease to be conquered. But the fact is that death is inevitable. We will all die; it is only a

matter of time. Death is as much a part of the human existence, of human growth and development, as being born. It is one of the few things in life we can count on, that we can be assured will occur. Death is not an enemy to be conquered or a prison to be escaped. It is an integral part of our lives that gives meaning to human existence. It sets a limit on our time in this life, urging us on to do something productive with that time as long as it is ours to use.[73]

In *Transcending Loss*, Ashley Davis Bush wrote, "Death puts us face to face with the most primitive and basic of existential concepts: we are born, we live, and we die. Death forces us to question the meaning of life, and leaves us with no answers."[74]

Perhaps there are no answers because the possibilities for creating meaning in our lives are endless.

At the end of life, we often don't regret what we have done and who we have been; we regret what we have not done and who we never allowed ourselves to be. Knowing one's Self is only possible when we liberate ourselves from our cultural conditioning, including the ties that bind us to appeasing and pleasing the expectations of others.

Most people simply go through the motions of their lives not knowing or questioning why they do what they do. The routine of their lives becomes "comfortable," monotonous and without risk. But what if the biggest risk we take, is not taking any risk at all?

The late actor Michael Landon, once said, "Somebody should tell us, right at the start of our lives, that we are dying. Then we might live life to the limit, every minute of every day. Do it! I say. Whatever you want to do, do it now!"

Facing our mortality can be, in many cases, a radical awakening to a more sacred connection with all life. In my own life, the most transformative and liberating experience was the untimely death of my mother. As painful as it was, it altered my perception of reality and connected me to a more profound love for life. My reverence for death now defines every moment of my life. Death is a wise and inspiring presence that has taught me more about life than anyone or anything else. It reminds me of what really matters. In its omnipresence, I feel more tender, connected and alive—particularly in the precarious times of today.

Paradoxically, in facing our mortality, we are reminded of our immortality. The closer we are to death, the closer we are to life.

Dealing with our own death in a death-denying culture can be challenging enough. But dealing with the accelerating decay of our civilization, and the widespread die-off of animals and the natural world is a heavy burden to bear.

From *The Wild Edge of Sorrow*, Francis Weller once again writes:

> We live in a grief-phobic and death-denying society. …Our refusal to acknowledge grief and death has twisted us into a culture riddled with death. Consequently, death rattles through our streets daily, in school shootings, suicides, murders, overdoses, gang violence, or through the sanctioned sacrifice of war dead. Needless to say, many of us limp through our lives, carrying the scars of our death-dealing society. Unfortunately, the fingers of death extend far beyond the streets of our cities. Hillsides are stripped of trees, leaving homeless the countless others who once dwelled within canopies, along creek beds, and in the underbrush. Mountains are destroyed for coal or copper. Oceans are mined and emptied of fish. Creatures who dwell underground in direct conversation with the living earth through their teeth, claws, and bellies are bulldozed away for malls or subdivisions. Death pervades our culture, becoming a presence we cannot contain or ultimately honor.[75]

We are living in an unprecedented epoch in the age of species homo sapien sapiens. We are being implored to choose between continuing to ignore the carnage of our collective actions; or face it with resolve and courage, reuniting with the Earth consciousness that connects us to the Soul. Given that the planet has never been in such a state of chronic crisis from so many converging places; or that humans have so starkly faced their own extinction, we must find ways to cope that evolve beyond fear, division, hope, and denial.

The notion of extinction is an extremely deep one. Buddha, Jesus, Confucius—no one in history spoke of human extinction because it was out of the realm of possibility, and beyond the extent of the human imagination. Even now, the few who grasp the severity of where we stand as a species can barely understand the immense significance of these times. While the majority of planetary destruction is taking place largely outside of our immediate consciousness, there is no doubt that we are aware on a more subtle level.

Over time, I've learned that in the midst of losing someone I love, nothing else matters. Love, compassion and presence surpass all else. I feel no differently about the dire reality of our dying planet. In knowing that this world can no longer be sustained, I've let it go. In this acceptance, I've realized a most beautiful truth: love is all there is. It is the only thing that cannot be taken from me. It is the only thing that cannot die.

There is a huge gift in these apocalyptic times that makes entirely clear the precariousness and impermanence of everything. It pummels the ego and destroys all illusion. This can lead to paralysis, horror, despair, rage, and denial; or it can lead to a hunger to connect to the Soul and act with integrity, love, and compassion, not out of personal agenda, but because that is the essence of who we are.

Paradoxically, our terminal situation is the perfect recipe for liberating the human race from its delusion of separation. In realizing our imminent demise as a species, we can awaken to the deathlessness of the Soul and live fully, with love in our hearts until the end.

Return to Essence

*"You are not your wealth, your credit rating, your resume, your
neighborhood, your grades, your mistakes, your body, role, or titles.
None of this is you because it is changeable. It is impermanent. There
is a part of you that is indefinable and changeless, that doesn't get lost
or change with age, disease, or circumstances. There is an authenticity
that you were born with, have lived with, and will die with. This is
your essence."*

– Elisabeth Kübler-Ross

At this pivotal time in our history as a species on planet Earth,
we are operating from an overwhelming state of fear. From the micro
of the fear that runs our daily lives, trapping us in meaningless jobs,
lifeless relationships and self-limiting beliefs; to the macro of the collective fear that locks us in war, slaughter, environmental decimation,
and relentless consumption.

After countless generations of fear-infused cultural programming, our resourcefulness has been thwarted, and our capacity to
trust has been profoundly inhibited. Safety within ourselves, and in
the presence of our species, has fallen by the wayside. There are so
many holes in the old story of our world that the masses are grasping for something ... anything familiar to ease their growing sense of
unease. But what once was, can no longer be because of what we have
done to the planet and the Soul.

We are experiencing an accelerating erosion of our current reality,
and there is no way back to what was once familiar and "comfortable."

The result is a desperate attempt to revive the good old days of white male supremacy that will make America—and the world—"great" once again. This pathetic attempt to revive a past that can no longer be resuscitated is the last bastion of hope binding an unconscious collective to a civilization that is over.

The decrepit state of the world is a stark manifestation of the overwhelming inertia of our collective consciousness. The endless dramas unfolding on a global scale can only be so because of what we've allowed ourselves to become in the mindlessness of our daily lives. The chaos and turmoil we see "out there", is directly sourced from the chaos and turmoil we project from within ourselves. It's a simple cause/effect relationship with deadly consequences.

As we perfect our focus on the dogma of denial, magical thinking and strange beliefs about how civilization will be "saved" by some higher authority with the solutions for our collective ills—wishing, hoping and praying for external salvation—we ignore the Soul, the very essence of who we are. And the slide into oblivion continues.

We keep waiting for the world to change "out there" so we can engage it in ways that are more meaningful. But life doesn't work that way because we live in a holographic universe. We must become it, engage it and live it before it can ever express itself in the world. The planet will always mirror back to us the individual and collective choices we make in our lives, and in the world. By holding ourselves as victims to our history, stories, decisions, upbringing, experiences, and all that has shaped us, life will always mirror back to us the outcome of these chosen identities. There is no future in that.

Because evolution and expansion are integral to creation, everything we do that doesn't sustain life will continue to intensify until we wake up. Awakening means turning our focus inward to engage the very essence of who and what we are.

In the Far East, it has been said that the innermost channel of the heart is the non-dual channel: our essential nature. Non-duality can be defined as the philosophical, spiritual, and scientific understanding of non-separation and fundamental oneness. It is what connects us to the Source of all life.

As stated in the previous chapter, we are so much more than our physical bodies. We are also so much more than our reasoning minds, our emotions, histories, stories, personalities, patterns, and life experiences.

We are essence expressed in physical matter, sourced from the purest, infinite energy. The body is not who or what we are. Without the body, however, our essential nature cannot flow into a physical universe. The body is the conduit for bringing the energetic realm of the Soul into physical reality.

Because of the way our civilization is designed, indoctrination into the Big Lie is inescapable. As a result, we are taught to dissociate from the body early on. As children, we are taught to "lock down" our emotions and the inner wisdom that can only be expressed through the body. We are taught instead to look outside of ourselves for how to think, speak, act, and live our lives accordingly. We trade our authentic nature for externally referenced conformity, prompting a perpetual stupor of who and what we are.

As we increasingly commit ourselves to the Big Lie, over time, the Signal from the Soul fades, and we experience less of our essential nature. As this happens, the messaging that governs our lives is sourced from the programming of our dominant culture, and the antiquated Newtonian worldview that holds it in place. This inauthentic messaging coagulates and sticks to the weakened psyche like an impervious tumor; morphing into our beliefs, values, strategies, choices, patterns, behaviors, and attitudes. Over time, the messaging from this internalized cultural programming becomes so dense and intense in the body, that we are barely able to hear the Signal from the Soul anymore. We may have a vague memory of having been an autonomous expression of a greater whole in an interconnected world at some time in our early years, but we have long lost our individuality. Instead, we've become homogenized. Our expression in the world is thus muted by "acceptable, and appropriate" cultural responses, never allowing the full expression of the deepest truth of who we are.

As long as we remain alive, however, the Signal from the Soul transmits through us. In fact, the Signal from the Soul—our very essence—never leaves us. We can silence it, but we cannot destroy it. It is infinite, immortal, omnipresent, and omnipotent. It is the most profound truth of our very being. It is our connection to everyone and everything.

A conversation in the film, *Powder* articulates it well:

> Inside most people, there's a feeling of being separate. Separated from everything. And they're not. They're part of absolutely everyone and everything. If they were only able to see past the blind spot in their minds, they would see that they're totally connected. They would also see how beautiful they really are. And that there is no need to hide. Or lie. And that it's possible to talk to someone without any lies. No sarcasm, no deception, no exaggeration, or any of the other things that people use to confuse the truth.[76]

Essence is the pure and authentic presence of our being. It is our true nature. It is *being* without the distortion of our personal histories and the repetitive stories that accompany our history.

Quoting transpersonal therapist, Karen Malik from a 2012 retreat, "When essence expresses itself into our lives on a personal level, it manifests as various experiential qualities that are clearly discernible, such as the warmth of compassion, the sweetness of love, the stillness of peace, the resolve of courage, the solidity of will, and the fire of strength. These qualities (and many others), in their purest form, are our potential. They are the essential qualities of our being."

These essential qualities express through our personalities as integrity, authenticity, individuality, autonomy, joy, freedom, respect, generosity, harmony, vitality, gratitude, caring, compassion, empathy, kindness, competence, and dignity.

When we source our identity from within, we untether ourselves from the cultural conditioning that separates us from the Soul, thus allowing essence to flow openly and freely through us. This flow of essence dramatically enhances the quality and meaning of our lives. It also inspires growth, expansion, evolution, and the realization that there are no limits to who and what we can become in our lives, and in the world.

Awakening to Essence

Paraphrasing the words of Louise LeBrun:

When we look up to the night sky, we see the light from long-dead stars. The notion of what we call 'our stories' shows the degree to which we attempt to live lives that are long dead—lives that don't even belong to us. They belong to our parents, teachers or other authority figures. Or they belong to another place and time.

Because we are so desperate to have some sense of certainty, stability, and predictability in our lives, we become willing to be the light of a long-dead star that has no future. It only has an emanation from the past. We do everything we can to maintain this familiarity, even—and especially—at the expense of the Soul. We do not know how to be any other way. How do we learn to live differently? How do we free ourselves from the lives we've created when they no longer hold meaning for us? How do we lift ourselves up and out of culture, history, habits, patterns, and rituals that have become so automatic that we have no awareness of them anymore? How do we wake up to our deepest core essence?[77]

When we begin to see through the cultural conditioning that holds us captive to smallness, we often become lost in the vast potential of our lives and don't know what to do with ourselves. We are so conditioned for *doing*, that we have no clue how to *be*. We are not taught how to be human beings.

By mindlessly adopting external perceptions and belief systems as our own, we end up with damaging patterns that run our lives. Most people replicate insanity from the historical patterns of intergenerational beliefs within their family systems, never bothering to discover their own truths.

The dismal fact is that we are not taught how to be ourselves and live our own truth. We are not taught that we are infinite potential in a finite physical world. We are taught instead, how to be what other people want us to be to sustain the Lie that severs our connection to the Soul. When we live our lives from the archaic, Newtonian belief systems imposed on us by others, we are disempowered. Because it is grounded into us early in our childhood, we are indefinitely crippled.

In the words of Louise LeBrun, "I think what we're teaching our kids is criminal. I think we're teaching them crap that locks them into a belief that they are a physical being; that they are not beings of light and energy when we live in a world of energy. Why do we do that? We take these massive little beings with enormous potential and quickly start hiving off their natural curiosity, their willingness to engage and so much more, and we end up with people who slot easily into the industrial model of civilization, even though we know the industrial model is not useful anymore. Despite that, we keep training our kids to slot into specific roles that perpetuate this insane civilization."

Essentially, we are programmed to become monotonous expressions of repetitive patterns with no awareness of any other way.

The truth so few ever realize is that we are so much more than what our parents and society have conditioned us to be. To fully release essence from our deeply entrenched conditioning, however, we must be willing to fall apart.

Stripped of our comforts and false assumptions about life, now faced with the vulnerability of our existence, we come to feel more intimately the emptiness in our hearts. It's only when things completely break down that we can begin the journey of reclaiming our lost wholeness.

For a seed to grow, it must turn itself entirely inside out before it can break open and evolve into what it is meant to become. The old form must be completely destroyed before it can transform into its whole being. To those unfamiliar with the cycles of growth, fertility may look like annihilation. Similarly, the cycles of spiritual growth may also look like annihilation. In effect, they are. Carl Jung said, "Only that which can destroy itself is fully alive." Reclaiming the Soul requires annihilation of the false self. It's about turning oneself inside out to break free from the cultural conditioning that holds essential expression captive.

In a world filled with suffering, I believe the pain and challenges we experience in our lives are not evidence of our smallness; rather they are persistent calls from within to embrace the limitless nature of our potential.

While essence is always available to us, we tend to abandon our essential qualities, lose awareness of their presence, and eventually forget how to access them as we mindlessly carry on with our culturally conditioned ways. We often feel an emptiness or "deficiency" as this happens. To compensate, we build structures with our programmed personalities that mimic our essential nature, and rather than expressing from our true essence, we express ourselves from a defensive avoidance of pain. The overlays of the inculcated personality, the conditioned intellect, and the unhealed emotional body occlude our essence, thus blocking it from rising into our experience.

Essence can become blocked when we get caught up in our experiences, attach to unexamined belief systems, or become trapped in the stories created by the conditioned mind. Many people are rigidly identified with the reasoning mind: the institutional education they've had, the books they've read, the experiences they've had, the beliefs, teachings, and theories they believe to be true, and the "successful" lives they've led. In our profoundly externally referenced world, it's easy to be seduced by the beliefs of others when the connection to our own internal referencing has been severed.

The prevailing Newtonian paradigm is all about external referencing. When we grow up, we learn how someone else always knows better than we do. As we move through life, our external referencing expands. We have external references labeled, parents, teachers, boss, doctors, and God for instance. We have external references for everything, and we quickly learn not to trust the truth within. We are not shown how to be the authority of our own lives. We are taught instead how to be what other people want us to be.

Internal referencing begins when we trust the internal cues—the energy—moving through our bodies, *because we are that energy.*

When we begin to drop our defenses, we soften the structures of the personality and the psyche, and our essence can reveal itself more readily. As we continue to shed our histories, stories, and conditioned personalities, we can then call upon these qualities with greater ease.

Initially, essence can be quite subtle when it emerges into our conscious experiences. To develop a higher sensitivity to the subtle levels of being, we must become present to the moment without shutting it down. We must be willing to experience the truth of what is asking for expression. Truth is dynamic, and by remaining with the truth of whatever we are experiencing in each moment, it transforms, revealing further truth. As Karen Malik says, "As we continue to stay with this dynamic unfolding, we are involved in a profound alchemical process through the body that is metabolizing and softening the structure of the conditioned persona, and healing what needs to be healed. No content or "talk therapy" is required. The natural process of the body to metabolize our pain is powerful and precise. It may be uncomfortable, yet as we stay with it and allow the body to process, eventually we come to an experience of calm, quiet openness. It is imperative to stay with the truth of this experience, for this is when essence returns and reveals itself to us once again."

As we stay with our essential experiences and allow them to fill us completely, we make space for profound healing. Little by little, the reclamation of essence reveals to us more of our true Soul nature. We become more whole.

By connecting more intimately with our essential nature, we are reminded of what we once knew as small children: that every one of us is a unique expression of the Source energy that animates *all life*. In this remembrance, we can reference our lives from within, and eliminate the dogma of a "God" (Higher Self, spirit guide, angel, Buddha, Krishna, Allah, master, guru, etc.) that is external to what we remember ourselves to be. In the internal referencing that accompanies the reclamation of our essential nature, we recognize that *we are God*. An extremely radical notion in a world that programs us to believe otherwise.

When we understand this profound truth—a truth we were born with—we remember that all life (plant, animal, human, etc.) is created

from the very same Source energy. When we realize this interconnection, we can no longer cause harm to others; through the consumption of animal flesh or secretions; the destruction of the natural world
through our choices and actions; through jealousy and judgment of
others, and so on. We remember that harm to others through our
choices, behaviors, thoughts, and actions, is harm to ourselves. We
remember that separation is a Big Lie.

Although we each have our own unique Signal, we all share the
same Source. This is why we can see ourselves in the "other." When
we liberate ourselves from the Big Lie, we expand our awareness and
see ourselves in all.

When our essential nature radiates through our being, we become
living expressions of spirit in matter; freed from the confines of culturally expected roles and identities. We can then recreate ourselves
moment by moment; breath by breath. This is when we step beyond
free will, and into free flow.

As Louise LeBrun once shared with me:

> What I've learned over time is to see/hear/know all things
> through the perceptual filter of knowing that 'I am a Being of
> Light', fully expressing through my organic device (the body) of
> matter. Rather than knowing myself as matter, seeking to be-
> come a Being of Light. Perception is critical; the lens through
> which I dare look at my existence, whatever that might turn out
> to be. To see through new eyes—to see through godforce eyes—
> changes our relationship to our Self as the Creator of it all. No
> longer passive bystander or purported innocent victim, we be-
> come the purveyors of our own potential existence—our po-
> tential reality—with the full force of clear intention, behind it.
> In that, the world reframes itself, and we live differently. Once
> we can see through these new eyes, we cannot go back. Why?
> Because there is nothing to go back to. The ultimate prize is not

to live; the ultimate prize is to be whole. When we are whole, we are at peace with who we are in the world, no matter what is going on 'out there.'

Our entire lives are metaphors for how we choose to live. They are not real. They are feedback mechanisms to help us "know our own face." Our lives reflect back to us our essence expressed. When life feels difficult, it is a clear message that the flow of essence is being constricted. By making different choices, we can increase the flow of essence into our being.

Life is a byproduct of the choices we make. A more authentic experience is as simple as making life-affirming decisions aligned with our essential nature. When we begin to remember who and what we are, our capacity to hold life-force is increased and we lose interest in the drama of the human experience, and the breakdown of our insane world.

When we begin opening to our essential nature and identifying with it rather than sourcing our identity from our conditioning or our history, we no longer do the bidding on a culture that perpetuates a destructive status quo. It is a meaningful way to live. When filled with essence, it is no longer possible to exist in the mindlessness of everyday life and blend into what the masses call "reality." That's because "reality" has expanded and grown; it is no longer confined to an externally referenced illusion. When living from our essential nature, we remember that, as Louise LeBrun said, we are the Creators of our own reality.

In the same physical space and time that is occupied by the Big Lie and the accompanying status quo, we can create a completely different world. To illustrate this, we can imagine two people sitting in the same room, at the same time. One person is thinking thoughts of scarcity, deprivation, and devastation, while the other person is thinking thoughts of abundance, possibility, and potential. In that same room, there are two very different universes occupying the same space and time. Both individuals will end up creating as a reflection of their thought form. Thought is energy, and energy structures matter. Everything that has ever been created by a human was once only a thought. The world we live in today is a direct reflection of our collective thoughts. As we can clearly see, the energies of our collective thoughts have created outcomes that are absent of our essential nature. We are not irrelevant, and we are not insignificant. We are, however, misdirected.

In our prolonged misdirection, I believe that we are here to hold space for the next chapter for Earth. I don't see this as a bad thing. Species have come and gone throughout the entire lifespan of this planet. If we look at the probability of our self-annihilation in the near-term through the lens of our essence, it is an incredible opportunity to redirect our curiosity and discovery toward something other than sustaining a destructive civilization that long ago deserved to end. It is also an incredible opportunity to explore the infinite realm of "inner space."

It may well all be a dream, as the Maori suggest, and as the dreamer, we will never know our essence when we are so distracted by the illusion of the world "out there." When we create reality from within, however, it changes in every moment as essence flows into our existence. Rather than living as victims of the circumstances in our lives and the world, we become the conscious Creators of our lives, and of *our* world.

There are many different personal "truths," but I believe there is only one truth that is absolute: that we are not separate. Separation is the grand illusion. I believe that the more our personal truths align with the absolute truth of non-separation, the closer we are to living as Soul, embodied.

When we live our lives internally referenced from the force of our essential nature, we are no longer drawn to the pack thinking that defines our civilization of separation. In the reclamation of our autonomy, we naturally move toward wholeness.

When we know ourselves to be whole, we cannot *not* be connected with—and integral to—the web of life. We cannot be in this world and hold ourselves as separate anymore. Wholeness is the ultimate awakening to the Soul.

Although it is too late to transform the world, it is not too late to transform our own world. The reclamation of our essential nature is a paradigm shift that brings peace to one's own world, at a time when peace in the external world is no more than an antiquated pipe dream.

The Paradox of Awakening

"Your own Self-Realization is the greatest service you can render the world."

– RAMANA MAHARSHI

Our collective destiny is clearly carved out on the hemorrhaging surface of the mortally wounded Earth. We have all born witness to the carnage upon the many, sourced from the greed of the few. Under the enduring spell of the Big Lie, the world is held tightly in the grip of a patriarchal consciousness gone mad. As much as madness knows no gender, the madness that has spread around the world is rooted in an arrogant sense of superiority that has severed the threads holding the very fabric of life together.

We are living in a time of accelerated falling in a culture of denial amidst the reality of demise. Paradoxically, we are also being called to awaken within this demise. We are in a hidden crisis where we can look out the window and still see "normal," but in reality, we are far from it. It's a surreal existence to be awake and see/feel with great clarity the complete breakdown of the web of life among such sweeping denial and ignorance.

Just as we have rendered Earth uninhabitable by our conditioned humanity, we have rendered our humanity uninhabitable to the Soul. The ailing outer world is a direct reflection of our sickened inner world.

Despite the now visible unraveling of our world on many different fronts, we persist in deluding ourselves into believing that everything is still okay. We live in a world that is intentionally held in a coma. When we look around at the way we live: the mindlessness of religious doctrine, the economics of gratuitous consumption, the habituation of conformity parenting, and the myth of the intact family; it is evident that we are captive to a degraded consciousness that we are incapable of evolving beyond.

The dominant "reality" that has consumed our world is unchangeable. Because it has been deemed "real" for countless generations, it has been accepted as real by the widespread collective. No questions asked. Because this belief is so firmly entrenched in the collective psyche and the masses are so hopelessly dependent on it, all energies are funneled toward sustaining, defending, preserving, and protecting this toxic reality—even at the expense of our existence.

We may believe ourselves to be powerful and independent as a species, but the truth is that we are subservient to a self-destructive civilization. We are reliant on an antiquated Newtonian pharmaceutical/medical system because we don't trust our own bodies. We are reliant on an outdated factory model of education because we don't trust our own inner wisdom. We are reliant on corporatized media because we don't trust our own critical thinking skills. We are reliant on science because we don't trust our own intuition. We are reliant on politicians because we don't trust our own power. We are reliant on the military because we don't trust the "other." We are reliant on increasingly complex technologies because we don't trust our once innate relational abilities. We are reliant on a cruel and poisonous food system because we don't trust the truth in our hearts. We are reliant on religious dogma because we don't trust our own Souls. The absurdity of it all defies comprehension.

For the keepers of the Big Lie, it is in their continued interest to ensure that the masses feel disempowered, fearful and ignorant about the plight of the planet. Spiritual lockdown guarantees compliance from the worker drones of business-as-usual who faithfully carry on despite it all.

The immensity of the problems we face and their cumulative effect has moved us far beyond our ability to resolve them, no matter how willing we may be. The sad reality is that we are unwilling anyway. By continuing to run familiar strategies, thought patterns, and habitual behaviors, we are guaranteed only to get more of what we already have. As Albert Einstein said, "We cannot solve our problems with the same level of thinking that created them."

If we are bold enough to expand our consciousness, it may well be that raising our level of thinking requires the evolution and discovery of *what* and *who* we are as human beings rather than *how* or *what* we do within the confines of what we already know.

As Gaea awakens outside in the natural world, she is stirring a sacred, primal awakening inside: an awakening to the Soul. With the planet in such a severe state of crisis—from culture to civilization, to the biosphere—the only place to turn, is within.

As a collective, we've been wounded by our Soul separation for far too long. Those who have negated the Soul will soon have nowhere to run and nowhere to hide. It's either awaken and "die," or die asleep. In her great wisdom and need to expedite her own evolution, Gaea is delivering to us exactly what we have ordered. As cartoonist Walt Kelly wrote in his 1970 Comic strip promoting environmental awareness, "We have met the enemy, and he is us."

Despite the immense suffering that will ensue, I have trust in the greater intelligence of it all, for I know this is necessary for the collective because it was chosen by the collective. After all, we live in a holographic universe, and the power of collective consciousness cannot be negated.

In a world teetering on the brink of nuclear annihilation, and ecological catastrophe, we are now being challenged to examine the most profound truth of who and what we are. We've reached a critical juncture in our evolutionary history where we are being forced to take a deep look within and ask what we have allowed ourselves to become to arrive at such a fatal impasse.

To honestly answer this question, we must turn inward. It is this inward journey that connects us to the truth of the Soul, and awakens us to the limitless potential of who and what we have always been meant to be.

The collapse that is upon us is calling out our smallness and our greatness; our ego and our essence; our conditioning and our autonomy; our domestication and our feral, untamed nature.

We are living in a crucial time in the history of the planet. We're witnessing things about Earth, about civilization, and about what it means to be human that have never been witnessed before. It is both a remarkable and frightening time to be alive.

Facing our collective demise becomes personal very quickly. It means we must finally confront ourselves: who we have chosen to be in the world, and how we have chosen to live our lives. When we face the end—individually and collectively—we can finally stop pretending. The collapsing biosphere is forcing us to let go of the notion of permanence. It can free us from the idea that tomorrow should look like today and yesterday, and it can also bring us closer to living in the moment.

In my own life, I find the poignancy of this time to be bittersweet. It's like being with a loved one in the end stages of their life. Only this time, it's me saying goodbye to everything I love, as it too is leaving. We are leaving together, while ironically I'm in perfect health: physically, emotionally, mentally, and spiritually. Quite frankly, I feel more awake, alive, activated, lucid, and energized than I have my entire life. And so I live for moments, connected to the presence of the sacred.

Biosphere collapse does not speak to our physicality. It speaks to a more expansive aspect of *what* we are. It speaks to our emergence beyond the confines of physical matter. There is no way we can "get through this" relying on our physicality. We will have to discover something else, and that something else must emerge and transform our addiction to physical matter so that we are not trapped in the collective nightmare of biosphere collapse.

The things we hold onto: the "comfortable", repetitious nature of our lives, our tedious jobs, our cd, stamp or coin collections, long-dead relationships, wayward children, favorite books, bank accounts; these are the things we use as an evidential trail to validate our existence because we feel so lost to ourselves. To fill this void, we compulsively consume as the world crumbles around us; trying to find outside of ourselves what can only be discovered within. We are never present; always distracted by the past, whether it is memories from days gone by, or past projections labeled, "future". Imagine if we eliminated everything that triggered memories of the past and learned instead, how to live in the now. It would be a very different world. It would be a world of Soul.

For most of my life, I have known myself to be a human being having spiritual experiences. There was little freedom in this, however. The pains of the world still gnawed at me from the inside, out. The limitations of my conditioned humanity prevented me from knowing that I was so much more.

Since awakening to the Soul, I no longer "think" about being a spiritual being having a human experience, I am the spiritual being having a human experience—aware of my human awakening. I am both participant and observer to what I call, "my life." It is a profound paradigm shift that is difficult to articulate because it's so deeply personal. Suffice it to say, it has freed me from the confines of my conditioned humanity. Paradoxically, this liberation has inspired from within me, a more profound love for life.

Awakening to the Soul is akin to rebirth. It's about seeing through new eyes and a bright, expansive heart. New perspectives emerge. Wisdom replaces intellect. Critical thinking skills are radically enhanced. Internal referencing is the driver of life. The capacity to feel expands exponentially. Embodiment, for the sake of the Soul, becomes empowerment.

The veil is lifted.

Awakening is about living the limitlessness of our energetic immortality, through the finite aspect of our physical mortality. It's about living fully, loving hard and letting go. The Soul doesn't care about longevity or attachment to a physical world; it cares only about evolution.

When we awaken to the Soul, we no longer want more; we want less. Less stuff, less distraction, less talk, less stress, less effort, less conformity, consumption, judgment, fear, and indifference—less of everything that comprises the shaky foundation of the Big Lie.

Instead, we want more tranquility, more ease, more inspiration—more connection. As we expand into our true Self, life simplifies. As life simplifies, we naturally grow into more of what we have always been meant to be. We become more authentic, giving, compassionate, creative, and loving. We become discerning over judgmental. We choose faith over fear. We become engaged over indifferent. We care. We act. We love. Paradoxically, our caring detaches us from the world because the love we express is essential and liberating. It is warm and real, yet detached and universal. It is blissful; not smothering, emotional or binding. It is not attached to results or outcomes. It is the ultimate expression of the Soul in a finite physical world.

In her book, *New Paradigm—New World!*, Louise LeBrun writes:

> I invite you to rename the meaning of the journey of your life, moving away from the struggle that we are nothing and

must spend our lives seeking to become; to recognizing that we arrive as, and already are Spiritual Beings having a human experience, and remember that which sources every breath we take. Choose to live from that fundamental truth and act accordingly. The simplest of an individual waking up to this birthright is a shift, in the nano-second of its expression. Waking up is the way we get out of the nightmare. There is no struggle once we rediscover and reclaim the truth, not of who we are, but of what we are. We are so much more than what we have been taught to believe![78]

How ironic that these times of accelerating demise are imploring us to live as we have always been meant to live: fully, authentically, expansively, with presence—now. Perhaps this is the simple consciousness shift we have needed all along.

The truth is that consciousness is already—and has always been—present in its full expression. Where we have been challenged as a species, is with freeing its emergence from thousands of years of separation. To whatever degree we are willing, however, we can reclaim the Soul and remember who and what we are at any given moment. No circumstance, life situation or other human beings can take this choice away from us because it is entirely sourced from within. Personal evolution is the gateway to expanded consciousness.

My own life revolves around this simple mission statement: "Evolve as if you will live forever, live as if you will die tomorrow, and act as though a future still matters." These words activate me. In this statement, the truth of my experience is more important than anything else: more important than the approval of others, the applause of others, the opinions of others, the judgment of others, the thoughts of others, the rejection of others, or the punishment of others. My ongoing evolution lives in the truth of every moment of every experience. If I don't own this, I become frozen, small, and fade into the background of the status quo. I will not allow for this because of my hunger for evolving into, and becoming a living expression of essence, rises above all else.

Along the path of my evolution, I have discovered that it's not what we know that makes the difference; it's our willingness to be in the "space between knowing" that allows the discovery of other than what we know. In untethering from the confines of the known, we make space for further evolution and a greater expression of our essential nature as we move through life. When we allow our truth and our "reality" to be as fluid as our curiosity, we become living expressions of the Soul in physical matter. It's that simple … and that challenging.

One of the many profound things I've learned over time is that genius often lies in the quiet spaces between breaths. When I'm able to step back from the routine of human life; when I'm willing to be without guidance, roadmaps, signposts, or the GPS of predetermined outcomes and conclusions, I'm called into the unknown of my potential. A life of the Soul is far removed from the beaten path. It's an exploration of the thicker, more dense territory that remains feral, unrefined, endlessly fecund, and rich in its potency to inspire endless potential. It's a moment-by-moment, breath-by-breath existence. It's about living in the perpetual now in the unknown of my own boundlessness.

The thought that captures my interest as I know more of my essence is: how does the Soul live in a world of matter, when matter, no longer matters? I confess that I'm still in the process of discovery.

From the moment of our conception we're trained into a world of humandroids (metaphorically, like androids). We're taught to know ourselves as matter in service to an external "God" to which we are tethered. This external binding then transfers to all of its surrogates:

parents, teachers, boss, doctors, politicians, priests, ministers, science, technology, media, culture, and so on.

We know well how to know ourselves as humandroids, and we have no awareness that any other state of perception or being is possible. Humandroids are adept at mindless, habituated repetition, external referencing, and creating the future from the past. They're terrified of evolution, transformation, uncertainty, and knowing the vastness of their own potential.

In our dominant, humandroid civilization, life revolves around addiction: food, alcohol, technology, work, shopping, drugs, pharmaceuticals, sex, exercise, and so on. These addictions are incessantly reinforced in our culture, making it difficult for the conditioned mind to break free from it all. Distraction and numbing of the body is so normalized in our world that our chances of ever knowing ourselves as Soul animating flesh are slim. The plethora of addictions that rule the humandroid psyche are also reinforced as acceptable and "normal," which means our internal sensing is denied. External referencing—that is, looking outside of ourselves to provide sensory gratification within ourselves—is the ultimate "God." This flies in the face of our internal cues, specifically our instincts, intuition, impulses, and the unconditioned nature of what we authentically are. Because we are profoundly conditioned to deny our inner world, we become increasingly empty as we stray further from the Soul. The tragedy is that we really are lost to ourselves. The paradox is that we are already whole and complete. We've been taught to be infinitesimal in the discovery of ourselves, and so we spin our wheels in a perpetual search outside of ourselves for who and what we already know ourselves to be, within. This is lunacy.

I believe that we are born into the material world to find our way home to the Soul, and when we do, live from that in our mortal lifetime. The few on this planet who do live from the Soul are powerful, and profoundly threatening to a civilization based on separation and an externally worshipped God because they shape a more life-affirming reality. This is why awakening is so vital in these dire times.

The most significant challenge for me has been not to follow the path long taken; the one that presumes that now that I know something different, I should apply it to the "reality" at hand. In truth, now that I know something different, I can create whatever reality I choose. This is a radically different place to stand. Do I choose to continue in a world of matter? If I don't, what does that mean? That I "die"? That my body dies? Can I choose not matter and still have a living body? I don't yet know. Do I prefer to create a different world of matter—a different timeline? One that is more appealing to the Soul?

What happens if I surrender all "realities" except that which says I am Soul embodied? What happens then?

Underlying all of these lines of inquiry is a presupposition that I must know something; that before I can engage in whatever meaningful way might present, I need to know "what else" beyond that which already is. This means defaulting to something that traps me in matter as a "real" reality. The truth is, I no longer believe this to be so.

As I continue to expand and evolve, I find myself increasingly dissociated from the prevailing (and normalized) mutation of the human psyche. I have always felt like I'm not of this world. Perhaps I'm finally realizing the truth of this.

I've reached a place in my evolution where I know that I'm here to let go of my identification with the human species because I am so much more than that. I'm learning to live this way, day-by-day, breath-by-breath. Initially, it was disorienting. Now, however, it comes with greater ease.

When we are committed to our own evolution and we live the truth of that, the world around us changes. It is a path few are willing to take. Most choose instead to live the aftermath of a lifetime of disconnected choices that perpetuate the negation of their emotions, their bodies, their truth, their essence, and the Soul. Empowerment through evolution is a choice, but the underlying presupposition is that if empowerment is a choice, disempowerment is equally a choice.

While few are committed to their own evolution, there are many others who are deeply committed to "the search." But heaven forbid should they find anything—particularly "the thing" that will profoundly transform their lives. They claim to be open to it, yet they will step right over "the thing" that will transform their lives so they can keep searching—and continue to feel soothed by the fact that they are still in the search. Searching is not enough, however. We must be willing to find. And when we find, we must be willing to claim. And when we claim, we must be willing to own—and this means everything— what comes easily, and what doesn't; what we are applauded for, and we are condemned for; what feels good, and what hurts. When we claim and own all of who we are, we allow what lives inside to move us forward. We free ourselves from external referencing and no longer reinforce the status quo. When we begin living this way, the mindless, habituated, unconsidered expressions of our being begin to break up and fall away.

Accelerated evolution is the path of the warrior. It's about saying yes to the Soul, from the Soul, for the Soul: without stories, excuses, content, details, or intellectual drudgery to slow the process down. Evolution of Self never ends. From a Newtonian perspective, it often feels exhausting. From a quantum perspective, however, it is exhilarating and enlivening because potential continually expands, allowing the emergence of an ever-increasing flow of essence through physical matter.

Those who trust the spontaneous nature of their Selves and the altruistic nature of their impulses, have merged with the wholeness of their being: flesh and spirit. Ego and Soul.

The paradox of awakening is knowing that there is nothing we need to do but express our pure, unconditioned nature. To make a difference in our own world, is to make a difference in the world. To make this happen, there is nobody we have to be but more of who and what we authentically are.

The Paradox of "God"

We are all unique expressions of a greater whole in an interconnected world. Without exception, however, we are inculcated to believe otherwise.

We are taught that there is a "God." We are also taught that this God lives outside of us. By accepting this myth, we sever our connection to the Soul.

External personifications of God have been created to perpetuate our collective separation and ensure our allegiance to this Lie. The quintessential personification of God is the big "eye in the sky," inaccessible, judgmental white man with a profusion of different names such as Lord, Almighty, Maker, Creator, Father, Buddha, Krishna, Allah, Higher Self, Guides, Angels, Spirit, Source, and so on.

With the plethora of labels we employ to identify a God that is not us, comes dogma. Dogma requires external referencing to sustain separation from the body and the Soul. Dogma is the most effective tool for controlling a collective. It is through dogma that compliance, conformity, and disempowerment are sustained on a mass level.

Because we live in a world that is separate from the body, those who present themselves as spiritual or "God-loving," (relative to the external referencing of their particular dogma) are often rigid, inflexible, and without compassion for themselves; and therefore without essential compassion for other living beings. Rigid adherence to the rules of any particular spiritual belief system elicits fundamentalism that taints one's humanity, and feeds a generalized cognitive dissonance toward those deemed, "other."

In his book, *Many Lives, Many Masters*, Brian Weiss succinctly shared, "Most people recite prayers in their churches, synagogues, mosques, or temples, prayers that proclaim the immortality of the soul. Yet after worship is over, they go back into their competitive ruts, practicing greed and manipulation and self-centeredness. These traits retard the progress of the soul."[79]

The cultural programming that entrances us to believe that the *I am* that each of us is, is merely the body, permeates every aspect of human life. From birth on, we are taught never to question that *I am*, is not physical matter. The body is the living, breathing, sensing, organic, intelligent, and mortal conduit that allows the immortal *I am* to stream through physical matter as the unique expression of who we authentically are. As miraculous as our bodies are, however, we are so much more.

From every possible direction in our culture, we are profoundly conditioned to believe that the body and *I am* are one thing. But they're not. When we decouple *I am* from the physical body, we become aware of so much more beyond the confines of our physicality. The moment we decouple the body from *I am*, internal referencing becomes possible. When we believe that who and what we are is the body, however, the only way to move through the world is by externally referencing a "God" of some sort (including the prevailing cultural devotion to science and technology). If we believe ourselves to be the body, and "God" lives outside of us, then *I am* cannot possibly be God. This is where our collective separation begins.

There have been countless documented accounts of near-death

experiences where the body appears to be dead, yet *I am*—the Soul—is still very much alive and aware of everything going on. When the body is reanimated, a conduit is once again available for *I am* to stream into a physical world and recount the conversations and details that occurred during "death." Near-death experiences are now so numerous, that to negate the proof—or to rationalize the evidence as something otherwise—is little more than Newtonian denial spawned from a rigid allegiance to the Big Lie.

If we were to collectively remember that there is no external God—that we are it—the Big Lie would immediately collapse. If there was no God to reward us; no God to punish us; no God to enforce compliance; and no God to impose the dogma that frames culture, industrial civilization would rapidly break down. The paradox of awakening to the Soul is that peace on Earth would finally become more than just a few meaningless words on a token Christmas card. It would become real. There could be no other way because we would remember our connection to the web of life, and each other. If the world were to wake up tomorrow and remember the godforce of who they authentically are, everyone—without exception—would lay down their guns, bombs, and weapons. No negotiation required. The tragedy is that it's so simple, and once again, so hard.

In every culture around the world, God is an external reference. As a collective, there is little dispute that some form of God exists, yet we are certain that we are not it. This deeply entrenched belief system paralyzes us in many ways, and diminishes the Soul by forcing the immensity of who we are into the dogma of whatever external God we subscribe to. The result is a bloody history of violence and war—all in the name of God.

The fundamental requirement of an externally referenced God is that we silence our inner truth. In doing this, we end up judging ourselves as being evil, wrong or sinful. An externally referenced God can be hugely loving, but only if we follow his rules. An externally referenced God can also be enormously punitive if we don't adhere to his dogma. This madness serves to distance us from the Soul and reinforce flawed beliefs about our internal cues, wisdom, instinct, impulses, and intuition as irrelevant at best, and deficient at worst. Either way, we end up denying who and what we authentically are.

In my own search for the Soul (God), I've done it all. I've chanted, "ohm'ed," affirmed, prayed, meditated, done the workshops, retreats, rituals, trainings, programs, certifications, learned the techniques, done the practices, run the routines, and so much more.

I've "Buddha'ed," "yoga'ed," "shaman'ed," "goddess'ed," counted mala beads, burned sage, rubbed gemstones, done breath work, listened to countless hypnosis and meditation cd's, and read more books than anyone I know.

As the saying goes, "Been there, done that, bought the t-shirt."

When I think of the time invested, the miles covered and the dollars spent on "finding my Self," I feel exhausted.

In the end, I learned that no ritual, practice, prayer, meditation, affirmation, workshop, retreat, cd, or book could bring to me what I desperately searched for. By not believing that I already was the very thing I was looking for, my search remained perpetually elusive. What I was looking for could never to be sourced outside of myself. I finally realized that the paradox of God is that there is no external God. *I'm it.*

Every one of us is a unique Signal of Source energy expressing in a physical universe. We are Soul animating tissue. There is nothing else outside of this. There is no wizard, or "Greater Than," holy puppet master. We are not reflections of God. *We are God.* We are godforce energy embodied. We are the Creator of our lives and our world. Nobody else is. This goes against everything we are taught to believe in a world that teaches us otherwise. I now know differently.

Reclamation of the Soul is the moment of our rebirth. It is the moment of birthing our deepest, most authentic, essential Self. It cannot happen in our heads because we've read countless books, obtained new knowledge, learned different techniques or philosophies, tried various spiritual practices, or completed the workshops, retreats, and certifications. Rebirth happens because we allow what lives inside of ourselves to come alive. From there, we emerge. We become the living expression of essence and Soul embodied.

We are meant to be expressions of wholeness in a physical world, not aspects of expressions of wholeness. *We are designed for wholeness.* The body is the miraculous device designed to take us there. It isn't that the body drives the sacred; the sacred is meant to drive the body. In a civilization where the prevailing worldview is one of separation from both body and Soul, a life of expanded consciousness is one of remembrance. This means engaging the body to continually open and make room for the sacred to lead us through a physical world. In this reunion, there is ease.

Our lives are not meant to be about tolerating the intolerable. They are intended to be about remembering who and what we are and moving through the world *from this knowing.* In this profound remembrance, we are home. Whatever happens "out there," no longer has the same impact because we can now see through the illusion of it all.

If we were to think of ourselves in terms of the metaphor of a television, the signal for each tv channel comes from a source energy (a tv station). The television is then able to pluck the signal for each channel out of an endless ether of radio waves, microwaves, cell phone signals, etc. at our command. It then processes the signal for each channel and converts that signal into something the rational mind can manage, that is, pictures and sounds.

The same process is occurring with the Soul as a means of expression in a physical universe. In our case, the Signal for the unique expression of who we are as an individual is transmitting from the ether of a greater Source energy. Like the television, the body is the processor of that Source Signal. It plucks the Signal from the vast field of Signals for every living being and brings the unique Signal that each of us is, to life. Without the body, the Signal cannot express in a physical universe. The body converts the Signal into something meaningful that our rational mind can comprehend. Each expression is unique, so the Signal of who I am does not express through the body of someone else. What this means is that to discover our connection to the Soul, it can only come from—and through—the body.

It is a quantum shift in identity when we remember that the "I" that each of us is, is not a mortal, fleshy water bag with an overactive, easily distracted, profoundly conditioned intellect. The *pure* "I" that each of us is, is the infinite, immortal, non-physical, energetic Signal. This Signal then animates an organic, mortal, miraculous, fleshy water bag that makes expression in a physical world possible. This is not what we are taught to believe in our antiquated worldview of Newtonian, "matter as God." When one thinks about it, identifying with something temporary, conditioned and mortal is absurd when we are so much more than that.

With this profound realization, I finally understand that I am not the personification of anything. I am *not* the corporeal expression. I am the force itself. There is not one other living being on the planet—human and non-human alike—that is not also the force itself. When we remember this, we awaken to a unified consciousness that frees us from the Big Lie once and for all. This is a radical notion for the masses who, in their culturally conditioned state, will fight to the death to preserve the dogma that binds them to an unwavering belief in the Big Lie.

In the spoken words of Louse LeBrun:

You and I are godforces. We are the living manifestation of the force of Creation. We are Creators. That is what we are here for. We are not here to hang out comatose on the fringes of reality. We are here to create reality. That is pretty immense. None of us had parents who taught us that. Because they didn't have parents who taught them that. The story we've been living as 'the norm' is an aberration. There is much more occurring that is far more compelling than the story of what we've been told about who we are and what we are—not our personality or our character—*what we are*; that our bodies are quantum biological devices, and that the *I am* that I am is the Signal that streams through the device, and emanates. And in that emanation, reality forms itself. We are manifesting all the time. When we manifest from a coma, we are still manifesting. The question is, do you like what you're manifesting? When you look around at your reality, do you like what you're creating? Because you are creating it, and as you created it, you can change that creation in a nanosecond, if you own that you created it. But if you think somebody else did it to you, you have no power in that creation.

To fully understand the immensity of this paradigm shift, we must redefine what we believe a human being to be; not who, but what. The exploration of 'who' has always been tied to personality, which hugely limits us. It's not enough to redefine who we are anymore. We must redefine what we believe ourselves to be in order for transformation to be accessible. We are not what we've been taught to believe we are. We are godforces expressing in a physical universe through the conduit of a physical body. Contrary to what we've been taught to believe, we are so much more than human; we are godforce energy expressing through the physical matter of human. The *I am* that every one of us is, is a godforce. What's so threatening about this is that it's all about internal referencing in a profoundly externally referenced world. The ultimate internal reference is the remembrance that, 'I am godforce— I am God.'[80]

When we own the godforce that we are, personal evolution requires no purpose or outcome. Instead, evolution of consciousness becomes self-perpetuating for its own sake.

Most people are taught to shut down the body to adhere to the status quo. A body in lockdown is a mind in lockdown … is a Soul imprisoned. For many, the awareness of potential is paralyzing. They consider, ponder, explore, talk about, and long for potential, but they refuse to engage it. This causes paralysis and keeps them stuck where they are. Potential unengaged is the thread that binds us to puny, unfulfilling lives of repetition, monotony, inertia, and fear. It's a world of "should have," "could have," "would have," and "maybe someday" excuses that render evolution impossible. Because of the relentless pursuit of approval, many squeeze their lives into tiny little boxes to measure up to the low-grade standards of our oppressive civilization.

Reclamation of the Soul is the willingness and ability to stand unfazed in uncharted territory. It is a highly personal journey with no set path. It is a path that cannot be carved out by anyone else, for anyone else. It is a turn in the kaleidoscope of our being which puts us in a radically different place. When we stand in this new personal paradigm, we can now filter all of our historical references and constructs of reality through this new filter, and it tears at the very fabric of our existence.

When we awaken to the Soul, we become profoundly internally referenced. Those who are internally referenced are non-compliant. Behavior can no longer be leveraged through humiliation, shame, or judgment because the internally referenced don't care. Those who are internally referenced care much more about honoring the Soul than they do about "fitting in" and conforming to the status quo.

When we free ourselves from our history so that our history is no longer the reference point for our present and future, we liberate ourselves to become the immense spiritual being that we have always been meant to be.

The Paradox of "Community"

There is much talk these days about seeking "like-minded community" in these troubled times. But what is community? As no more than a semantic nominalization, community is whatever we make of it. In my life, the very essence of community is about feeling safe in a nurturing, non-judgmental, interconnected relationship. It is not human-centered.

As the dominant paradigm becomes increasingly foreign to me, my community consists of the forests, lakes, rivers, streams, trees, mountains, stars, sky, sun, wind, moon, deer, birds, chickens, pigs, bobcats, bears, cows, sheep, turkeys, dogs, cats, and all things natural in this world. I understand them. They don't judge me. They never impose their beliefs, advice or opinions on me. They don't try to change or "fix" me. They don't live in entitlement, hope or denial. *They don't lie.* They are pure presence. They are exactly who and what they are, in all of who and what they have always been meant to be. I feel connected and safe in their presence, and I never, ever feel alone. In their presence, I'm plugged into my essence. My "community" helps me cultivate my inner sanctuary in ways that are deeply connected to the Soul. The most significant gift in these apocalyptic times is the sacred tenderness that inspires me to love more deeply, intensely, and intimately than ever before. My community inspires this within me.

The prevailing anthropocentric paradigm tends to pressure us into like-minded human collectives so that we don't feel isolated and alone. I've discovered the opposite in my own life, however. I feel more isolated and alone in "like-minded" collectives because they compromise the full expression of my essential nature. The *I am* that I am has no desire to think or be like anyone else. When external referencing is no longer the driver of life, "community" becomes redundant.

Personally, I don't believe we are better off in collectives. As a species, we have lost the art of relationship. In our mechanized madness, we tend to relate better to our technological devices and "social" media than we do with each another. There is no safety in that.

In the presence of collectives, we can only become as evolved as the most evolved person in the group. Rarely are collectives willing to push the boundaries of evolution, so compliance often wins out while groupthink engulfs the mind. This stifles the Soul and creates the very feelings of isolation and aloneness that community is meant to alleviate.

Collectives also tend to reinforce the inappropriateness of our individuality. If we don't map to the groupthink of a community or collective, we are often shunned. As long as we believe that we must be part of a community, our autonomy is compromised by the undercurrent of compliance required to meet the unwritten rules of the collective. Standards, expectations, and frameworks are often reinforced within collectives. The question then is: How do we stand autonomous and distinct inside a collective, when the safest place for ourselves to be independent and distinct, is outside the collective?

Many people search for collectives, looking for "the place" where they can finally feel appropriate to themselves. If they can only just find the right community or group, they can finally relax into knowing the truth of who they are. But it doesn't work that way. We will never find what we are looking for. *We must be willing to be what we are looking for.*

We are conditioned to believe that safety lies in the collective. This is not my experience. Safety is an inside job. When I live from the essence of *what* I am, I'm safe.

When we live from the inside out (Soul expressing in matter), there is no longer any need for like-minded community. The power and connection come from within.

From the outside looking in, a life of Soul expressing in physical matter may appear small because there is no need for others. In fact, it is quite the opposite. The expansion that accompanies the expression of Soul in matter is limitless. There is nothing small about being the living expression of Soul in a physical world.

Reclamation of the Soul is a journey of one. In the words of Louise LeBrun, "We are not pack animals. Slaves are pack animals. Godforces are not. This doesn't mean that godforces can't interact, but I don't believe godforces make good choices based on what another godforce is doing."

The ultimate paradox of awakening is that in reclaiming the Soul we become willing to stand "alone," knowing that we are far less alone than we have been our entire life.

Being is More than Enough

"To know yourself as the Being underneath the thinker, the stillness underneath the mental noise, the love and joy underneath the pain, is freedom, salvation, enlightenment."

– ECKHART TOLLE

There was a time in my life when I truly believed I could make a difference on Earth by being a voice for the voiceless, restoring justice, easing suffering, "rescuing" others, and "saving the world." After countless years of exhausting effort, I now know that I have only ever been able to share what I've discovered, experienced, and learned along my own journey of life. Attempting to save others is disempowering for all involved. Sharing my own journey, awareness, and experiences with those who choose to engage, on the other hand, is empowering for all because the power lies in the choice, not in my efforts.

What Self-evolution demands of us, is that we discover how to live with intelligence and resourcefulness while knowing that in many ways, we are powerless. We are not powerless in the creation of our own lives, but we are powerless in the lives of anyone else. What this means for me is that I'm able to manifest what is meaningful and aligned with the Soul in my own life, and I'm not able to manifest what is meaningful and aligned with the Soul for anyone else. How I live my life as an embodied expression of essence; how I choose to move through the world, engage the challenges that come up, express my truth, and allow myself to feel (including my own powerlessness);

in this vulnerability, others bear witness to how I live, and they can then choose to move through their own experiences in similar ways. I become a model of what is possible for others regarding how they live. So many others are models too, however, so I don't deceive myself by believing I can make anyone be or do anything, no matter how much effort I put into it. All I can do is continue my path of Self-evolution while merging my essence with the material expression of what I call, "my life." I then become an invitation for others to shape their lives in meaningful ways for themselves. At some point though, I must let go and allow the path of others to unfold as it will. As a species that is programmed for control, Self-evolution is not for the faint of heart.

In a global civilization driven by consumption, there is no value to society in becoming Self-evolved because we make lousy consumers. People who are Self-evolved are non-compliant. They tend to think more critically by questioning the status quo, and choosing that which aligns with their internal truths rather than the dominant external reality. They do not look outside of themselves to external references that tell them other than what they know internally to be true. Self-evolution defies everything we are conditioned to become as a consumptive species in compliant service to a Big Lie. It is a path of awakening that few are willing to embark upon. The overwhelming majority choose instead to zealously defend the Big Lie and their embroiled affair with it, just as they will defend the oppressive culture of their country, or their dysfunctional family systems despite visible signs of discord. It is a complex entanglement filled with dogma and fanaticism that leads to a profusion of unnecessary suffering.

One of the most challenging things we must come face-to-face with in these times of rapid ecological and societal breakdown is that we must be willing to love and let go. We must accept that many people—along with countless other beings—will die. No matter how much we attempt to prevent death, with collective choices creating conditions that do not support life, death is guaranteed, regardless of what we do or do not do.

Where most humans are terrified of pain and death, I personally don't see the avoidance of pain or the desire for longevity as worthy aspirations. I also know that when it's time for the body to cease functioning, the Soul does not. My body may have fear associated with its termination, but the *I am* that I am has no fear of the body being terminated because I know that I'm not that. The *I am* that I am that is sustainable, is not the body. It is the energetic whole of the Soul within which my body is suspended. This realization brings me great peace and a profound state of acceptance. In reaching this state, I had to be ruthlessly honest with myself by going deep within and asking: at what point do I stop sacrificing myself with the hope that others will wake up and choose life?

Self-sacrifice is a strategy that many are familiar with—particularly those engaged in any form of activism. It is a strategy that amounts to little more than a thinly veiled expression of patriarchy. Patriarchy has "effort, "sacrifice" (under the guise of "service"), and "work" built into it; along with resistance, competition, judgment, "otherizing," domination, oppression, and separation. It makes no difference if self-sacrifice is expressed through activism or war. Both are about struggle, exposure to violence, more losses than victories; and both are extremely ineffective at producing the outcome they aspire to create: peace. By resisting and fighting what is deemed undesirable, we only end up feeding the very thing we wish to resolve. If selflessness and self-sacrifice were truly effective, the world would be a very different place, and history would not be littered with examples of people who were assassinated, ostracized, marginalized, hunted down, and humiliated for their self-sacrifice and service to "a better world."

When I finally allowed myself to see through this more expansive lens—free from the fog of delusion or denial—I was genuinely discouraged. I now understand that "solutions" (effort, struggle, resistance, self-sacrifice, service … patriarchy) from within the box that created the problems in the first place can never amount to anything. Unless we expand our consciousness into the creation of an entirely new paradigm, we remain trapped in the current one; a paradigm where we only know how to do, what we know how to do. We cannot stay in the present paradigm and expect anything to change because of what we already know. In the present paradigm, our collective identity will always be one of separation. We can shift strategies as much as we want, but those approaches will not make a difference. Now that I understand this, I see that the greatest gift I can offer as an invitation to choose life, is for me to live as an expression of essence so that others can see what is possible. There is no sacrifice, effort or struggle in this. There is only endless opportunity for evolution and expansion.

As a species, we are designed for evolution and expansion. That is what we are here for. The more authentically we become living expressions of the Soul, the better our lives become; the better the world becomes. We begin to touch the lives of everyone around us just by being our Selves, not from the effort of trying to affect their lives, or by rescuing, serving, saving, or inspiring them. In the words of Maharaj, "It is neither necessary nor possible to change others. But if you can change yourself, you will find that no other change is needed."

The power of living a life of the Soul is the remembrance that we are the Creators of our reality. The moment we discover how to free ourselves from all things external and all things historical, we create an entirely new paradigm for ourselves where life is now experienced in the internal, eternal now. Our willingness and ability to be in the internal, eternal now makes it possible to see, hear, feel, know, and experience things that cannot be so in an externally referenced, "not now" world. The things that once mattered in the current "reality" no longer have relevance in the new paradigm, and there is an ease in life accompanied by a more expansive sense of meaning. I say this from personal experience.

Allow me to share my journey of discovery.

The past several years have been dedicated to a profound inward journey to satiate a hunger to know myself as Soul embodied. It's been a journey of ruthless Self-evolution that revealed to me all of who I once thought I was—and all of who I now know as someone from the past. No crevice, crack, or corner of my life remained unturned. All layers of past identity were stripped away, leaving me naked, disoriented, and with no sense of the "I am" that I have always known myself to be.

I was nothing … or so I thought.

As I continued to shed the illusion of who I once believed myself to be, what remained was more potent than anything I've known: *I am*.

For the past few years, I've been feeling increasingly in the world, but not of it. I was able to disengage from civilization to a significant degree, but I was still trapped in the confines of conditioned beliefs about what it meant to be a human being. I knew myself to be a human being having spiritual experiences, but I didn't know—viscerally—that I was so much more.

As mentioned in previous chapters, I now know—intimately, viscerally, the Signal, the Soul, the Force—the *I am* that I truly am.

I am not "my" body. I am essence embodied. I am an expression of infinite life-force sourced from a greater whole animating a mortal, fleshy, water bag—with an amazing intelligence of its own, granted—and a finite water bag, nonetheless. Without the body, there is no expression of essence in a physical world. Without the Soul, however, there is no life.

The *I am* that I am *is the Soul*. "Deb Ozarko" is a mortal expression of Soul in physical matter. *I am* is not. This is a massive paradigm shift that has liberated me from all worries about a future, as well as any attachment to the trappings of being a culturally conditioned human: possessions, status, beauty, success, careers, degrees, relationships, money, technology, consumption, civilization, identity, mortality, and longevity.

This is not what we are taught in our patriarchal, Newtonian world of "physical matter as God"; doing, doing, doing, and Soul-separation.

With the reclamation of the more profound truth of *I am*, I'm no longer of this world anymore. I'm completely detached, and yet still able to move through the world as an observer to my life without attachment to my physicality. From competitive athlete and devoted activist, to *I am*; the personal paradigm shift has been—and continues to be—profound. Quite frankly, it defies words.

My days are now all about being. From there, doing flows with ease. Effort and struggle are now things of the past.

I am is who and what I am, and *I am* can change, moment by moment. *I am* the Creator of my experiences, my perceptions, my life, and my world. *I am* a blank slate with every breath I take. Living as *I am*, the possibilities are endless. So the question I now ask myself is, "How can I be the greatest expression of essence embodied: breath by breath, moment by moment"?

In the past, my life was defined by squeezing my essence through an identity that mapped to a physical world—a strategy—a distraction. I now live in a void, with no identity to confine me to physical matter, and no interest in seeking to replace it with another. I can now fully relax into being the immortal energy that *I am* with complete trust in the unfolding of … everything. This defies everything I've been taught about living in this world as a human. There is immense freedom in this.

My life is now about living in the internal, eternal now, allowing *I am* to present moment by moment with no need for a "what else."

Quite honestly, I'm not interested in a "what else" anymore anyway. Without the need for a "what else," I'm also finding myself increasingly detached from the material world.

As Louise LeBrun recently shared with me,

> For myself, it became evident that the more my physical/matter/identity self was overtaken by my Self (the Soul), I lost interest in all things connected to consumption. Consumption at all logical levels. Consumption of "stuff". Consumption of the ideas and thoughts of others. Consumption of the attainment of some externally driven destination of some kind. It all just left me. The moment became the Life in flow. And then this moment. And then this one. Letting go of all striving and attaining—and all things external to my own inner cues. Stillness. Silence. The inner dialogue stopped.

Living this way—in the internal, eternal now—means that all objectives, outcomes, goals, and external referencing disappear because it is attached to identity, and to a future. In the internal, eternal now, there is no identity. The layers of identity that define physical existence disappear, and what remains is the Soul.

The simplicity of it all is astounding. The complexity of what our species has normalized is absurd. The cultural training to separate us from the power and simplicity of the Soul, is insane.

With this profound transformation, I now find civilization—and the entire human world for that matter—bland. I've lost all interest in the world "out there." I'm indifferent to the drama, stories, and minutia of the content that drives our increasingly insane world. The only voice I give credence to is that which lives inside of me: the voice of the Soul.

It is an enormous paradigm shift when, as an expression of a being through matter, we lose interest in matter. I wish to highlight that we are not beings *of matter*, we are beings *in matter*. So here I am, the expression of Self as a being expressing through matter, and I no long-er find relevance, meaning or joy in anything that is matter driven. All that defines "happiness" in a consumption-driven, material-obsessed world, holds no meaning for me anymore. And yet, I find myself still expressing through matter. Because I haven't yet figured out how to evolve beyond matter, and because there is intelligence in everything, I know there must be brilliance in still being in matter, while no long-er having interest in a material world.

I'm not suggesting that the material world is not without impact or effect; I'm suggesting that meaning is no longer about the material world itself. Instead, it's about the much higher order of thinking that emerges from my experiences within a material world. It is these ex-periences that leave me with insight and discovery.

So now what? Because this is uncharted territory, I remain open to whatever presents. This opening is the next layer of my journey in being an observer to myself while still tethered to a meaningless world of matter. What I've discovered so far is that if there is no "what else" in life, then meaning—along with "identity"— is defined in each new moment. Because I have no future orientation anymore, every new moment becomes a blank canvas.

Despite my increasing disinterest in "what else" and "what is," my life is filled with the simple joy of being. I go to bed each night with a sense of peace. I wake up in the morning, grateful for another mo-ment of existence to create and discover more of I am. I feel attached to, obligated to and propelled by, nothing. Initially disorienting (as a former, perpetual "doer"), it is now what I know as a profound truth that has lived within all along.

I'm also mindful that I have no longing. I have no sense of being pulled into tomorrow or drawn away from the moment I'm in. Every day feels more peaceful. I notice. This is truly a life of the Soul: a spir-itual being living a human experience. I know that my world is the only place I want to be. I no longer have a sense of impending doom, even in the recognition that collectively we are well past the point of no return. I know the Arctic is terminally ill. I know the Great Barrier Reef will soon be gone. I know the ocean contains more plastic than life. I know global nuclear war is more than an imminent possibility. I know that collective consciousness has chosen extinction for all.

Most humans don't think of themselves at the level of a species. They think of themselves at the level of their bank accounts; what they have, what they don't have, what they want, investments, savings, possessions, and so on. They don't think in the greater scheme of creation and interconnectivity. This is where they fall. The collective human influence is devastating when it need not be so. In my own life, I can look at many individuals and see great good. When I look at humanity as a collective however, I see great evil. I cannot change a force so powerful; a force that only increases in density and intensity as the Big Lie rapidly devours itself. All I can do is live my life and continue to know my Self as Soul embodied. And so I choose my life in each new moment that presents. Does this mean that I no longer care? Not at all. In fact, my caring has deepened. The difference now is that I have no attachment. It's a sacred place to stand.

My life is exceedingly simple. Other than the basics: food, shelter and water, I'm uninterested in consumption. This includes the consumption of technology, travel, "stuff," videos, news, social media, audio, books, ideas, beliefs, opinions, advice, thoughts, etc. I own no tv, smartphone, stereo or any other technological distraction other than my old laptop to support my writing. I've lost all interest in "out there." My life now is all about whatever moves me in the moment.

There is no future orientation to seduce me or pull me away from the internal, eternal now anymore. I couldn't live this way if I was still trapped in the scarcity consciousness that accompanies belief in a long-term future; or if I held myself hostage to the dominant reality in ways that exceed my basic needs. I've chosen mindfully to create a world that is no longer connected to either.

When living a life with no future orientation and a remembrance of the *I am* that I am, all ties to the Big Lie vanish, and I clearly see the illusion that it is.

As I let go of my identification with species homo sapien sapiens and fully claim the *I am* that I am, I remember what I knew as a child: that I'm here to live through, and witness the end … and a new beginning. In this, I know that Earth will finally heal.

Despite the destructive manner in which humans are terminating life, endings are a part of existence. If we think about this from a Soul perspective, it becomes an incredible opportunity to redirect curiosity and discovery toward something other than sustaining a civilization that was always meant to fail. When we resist what is, or we try to fix, change, or make things better, paradoxically, we are still defending the Big Lie. We can reform our strategies, such as moving from fossil fuels to wind or electric, consuming less plastic, converting to permaculture, or altering our consumptive behaviors; but in the end, we're merely sustaining what we know—albeit this time, swathed in a delusional hue of green. Elisabeth Kübler Ross called this "bargaining" in her model of the stages of grief. Bargaining will not transform the world.

Reclamation of the Soul will transform *our world*.

One of the most significant challenges during my recent deep dive exploration/revelation of Self, was letting go of the "hero" strategy that has influenced my life. My value and contributions to society and the world were all connected to being a "hero" for animals and Earth. Anything less was not enough.

Part of letting go of the pull of the "inner activist" was the release of all aspects of identity that fed off the hero persona, including the competitive athlete so deeply enmeshed in my being. It was a painful transformation. Everything I've ever known about contributing and "making a difference" in the world meant effort: reforming, resisting, fixing, saving, teaching, coaching, training, guiding, changing, defending, protecting, serving, inspiring ... doing, doing, doing—patriarchy cloaked in "selflessness." Like so many others on this planet, I was taught to believe that *being* was not enough; that *doing*—and the more, the better—was the only recipe for change.

The hero/activist strategy/identity was so deeply interwoven into my being that my sense of worth, value, and meaning were all sourced from how much I "served the world."

In my activist identity, I was entranced by my role as a "hero" to "change the world" and make it a kinder, more compassionate place. The effort I expended to create the more beautiful world I believed was possible was exhausting, and ultimately, demoralizing. I now know that it is impossible to shift collective consciousness, particularly against the will of a collective trapped in an immovable inertia of their own making.

I'm also aware of how little my actions affected the global picture, and how much my actions affect—and continue to affect—the interpersonal picture. By divesting myself from perceived responsibility for the wellbeing of things outside my control, I've discovered greater personal happiness and inner peace.

I now know that both my activism and athleticism were always meant to be personal. It was about creating the beautiful world *for myself* with choices and actions that aligned with the Soul. It meant unplugging from everything I was conditioned to believe, and delving deep into my essence to become a living expression of just that.

I've never been able to change others. I've always been able to evolve and transform myself, however. When I show up fully for my Self, I show up for the world.

In reclaiming the fullness of my essence, I now know this to be more than enough because I choose who I am in every new moment.

In this ever-changing choice, I create an expanding reality. My reality is based on the foundation of peace, integrity, and compassion. I choose essence over all else. I choose to not live as a victim to this world. I choose to stay true to the Soul, knowing that the *I am* that I am, *is the Soul.* My body is merely the conduit for expression in a world of matter, and the *I am* that I authentically am, is so much more. This is no longer just an intellectual concept, it is how I express in the world. It is who I am. It is who we *all* are.

We are all so much more than what we have been conditioned to believe ourselves to be.

We were not born into this world to breed ourselves into oblivion while working meaningless jobs as the biosphere collapses from our distracted indifference. We didn't choose to leave the bliss of "the void" to become a tiny, irrelevant piece of dust in an infinite universe for nothing. We are here for impact. We are here to shape the world in some way. We live in a beautiful world when we know that we are here to create it from the essence of who we are rather than just tolerate it, save it, change it, or fix it from the illusion of what we were conditioned to become. We are all a piece of the grand universal puzzle, and the piece of the puzzle that each of us is, in some way defines the puzzle.

We are all aspects of one another. When I live from my deepest authentic Self, I'm a mirror for others to remember that within their own selves. I'm learning—beyond the conditioning that tells me otherwise—that this is enough.

As I shed the story I've been taught about what it means to be human, I see how my "worth" is in my being. It is not in my doing. My worth is in my willingness to *be more*: to grow, expand, evolve, and become more whole. It's not about saving, fixing, rescuing, and inspiring; it's in *being* and expressing all of what I am. Nothing else required. We are not taught this in our culture. Instead, we are taught that we are not worthy unless we are in service to others, and often at the expense of our Selves. Unless we are the savior or the hero, we are nothing. This is total rubbish.

Living closer to my essence, I'm no longer interested in what most others have to say; nor am I interested in the drama of the human experience. I know my continually evolving truth, and that is all that matters. I know that I'm powerless to change the outcome of anything in the world "out there." I'm not powerless to continue evolving myself as Soul embodied, however. My passion now lies in becoming a more expansive expression of essence in a physical world. I'm no longer concerned about the fate of humanity, or of the planet for that matter because *I trust in the higher intelligence of it all.* This has been a pivotal shift for me—a profound letting go. I know this only to be a concern if I lose faith in Gaea, or if I believe that I'm my body. But I'm not. *I am* the Soul animating a body, a truth for all things living.

Does this mean that I've given up on the world? Absolutely! I say this with remorseless conviction. I hold no belief in, or connection to the illusion of separation. Other than create and choose in my own life, I'm unable to do anything about the world "out there." In owning my powerlessness, I've claimed my most profound power: the Soul.

My life is a reflection of the level of commitment to my own evolution. The accelerating breakdown of the habitability of the planet is offering me a deeper level of commitment to my own evolution. Because I'm not separate from Earth, we evolve together. This applies to everyone with the courage and willingness to choose evolution in these strange times.

Personal evolution is a choice that appeals to few. As far as the overwhelming majority of humans are concerned, the choice is clear: business-as-usual at all costs. The "in plain view" destruction of Earth and Soul will not stop until it destroys itself. Mindless, habituated choices, and insatiable consumption will continue to escalate.

As humans continue to recklessly self-replicate with no thought for tomorrow, the problems on this planet will only worsen. Just as I'm powerless to stop the tsunami wave as it hurtles toward the shore, I'm powerless to stop the wave of ignorance as it swallows the planet whole. I've let go of the world, and in this, despair is no longer a dominant factor in my life. Seeing the world through the eyes of the Soul detaches me from the illusion the masses believe to be real. It's not my story. It's not my choice. It's not my reality.

In my reality, I choose life.

I choose connection, compassion and living meaningfully for my Self. Not because it will make a difference "out there," but because that is who I am.

When we live our lives as embodied expressions of essence, we no longer need to rescue, save, or serve. We just need to live—and be. Choosing life is more than enough because it aligns with the Soul, and connects us to the web of life.

Let me be clear about living a life of being: it is not about spiritual bypassing or New Age magical thinking. It is not about chanting, meditating, or affirming for a better world. It is also not about denying or ignoring the terrible reality created by a collective hell-bent on self-destruction. Being is not a passive state. It is activation in presence. It's about painful self-revelation and transformative personal evolution to free the Soul from the shackles of cultural conditioning. It's about allowing—not guilting, shaming or forcing—*doing* to emerge from there, organically.

Confession: There are occasions where I still struggle with being as more than enough ... where I ask myself, "why am I still here when it all feels complete?" And then I realize, it is complete. There is nothing for me to do, be, say, or create within an antiquated reality anymore. Now that I see it for what it is, no sense of meaning or purpose can ever be found within a version of reality to which I no longer subscribe. In my journey of letting go, I know that I am here to witness the end as an essential presence, holding space into which the collapse will fall. My greatest challenge in these times is finding within myself the sustained ease to no longer feel compelled to do anything about it. In Gaea I trust. In that, there is nothing left to be done.

In evolving beyond the illusion, my sole purpose now is evolution for its own sake. After all, I either know myself as a spiritual being or not. When I forget, I suffer in grief and despair over the brutality of this world. When I remember *what* I am, I see the illusion of mortality. I'm then able to live more connected to each new moment, as the madness of the dominant civilization fades into the background of my consciousness.

The "end" may be near, but it only applies to this incarnation. Infinity—as Soul—remains.

In his book, *Life After Death*, Deepak Chopra wrote:

> The wise know that "death" can be turned away with two words: I am. There is no permanence in life. Possessions come and go, as do other people and beings. By clinging to the notion that we are permanent and that the world is forever, we bring great suffering to ourselves.
>
> In I am, there is nothing that can be destroyed. I am has no possessions, no expectations, and everything you will ever need, in this world or the one to come.[81]

In my quest to master impermanence, all that I continue to let go of liberates me further from the Big Lie. I'm now officially retired: from civilization, from worry, from fear, and from all strategies and identities that once bound me to a physical world. There is no more, "now what?" in my life. My creation now is about mastering how to live in the face of the internal, eternal now with no future orientation, because it's not about the world "out there" anymore. It's about me.

Ironically, it has been all along. Only now, I remember.

Perhaps living this way—in the now as a "being" rather than a "doing"—is what ancient cultures knew before being decimated by white man. In other words, living for life's sake. Non-human animals who have not been domesticated or mutated by humans know well how to live this way.

Maybe the purpose of life has always been to simply live for life's sake. Perhaps our "purpose" is to remember what we are and from there, evolution and growth are natural byproducts that follow with ease.

Perhaps being a living expression of the Soul is doing far more than I've been conditioned to believe in a patriarchal world of, "no rest." Perhaps this is the Great Secret that has been under my nose all along.

If we no longer buy into the stories we've been taught, and if we eliminate the strategies we've employed throughout our lives, the need for purpose vanishes. We remember that we are here to experience the fullness of our mortality, through the immortal energy animating our temporary physical existence. Perhaps the greatest purpose in a human incarnation is to experience life through the eyes of the Soul.

When we let it all go, we are left with just living and creating, moment by moment by moment.

Could it be that the meaning of life has always been this simple?

Beyond Hope

"When you give up on hope, you turn away from fear."

– DERRICK JENSEN

Hope. The quintessential human delusion, and one of our greatest weaknesses.

By its very nature, hope is a passive state trapping us in the mundane. When lulled by hope, we are wishing for some semblance of a future that is comfortable and familiar. Familiarity can only be sustained by creating a future from a past that is already known, thus perpetuating what we already have. There is no power in hope to produce anything else. Hope transforms nothing.

Hope soothes the docile psyche into believing we can indefinitely sustain the commonplace. It is a dominant force for securing passivity, particularly on a mass level. Because of its ubiquitous nature, the most significant contribution to a "better world" is hoping it will magically appear. Given our individual and collective commitment to hope, it makes perfect sense that things are getting worse. Hope is not—and has never has been—a creative force for change.

In the words of author and environmentalist, Derrick Jensen, "Hope is a longing for a future condition over which you have no agency; it means you are essentially powerless. When we realize the degree of agency we actually do have, we no longer have to "hope" at all. We simply do the work. Frankly, I don't have much hope. But I think that's a good thing. Hope is what keeps us chained to the system, the conglomerate of people and ideas and ideals that are causing the destruction of the Earth."[82]

In my life, hope was a tenuous thread that bound me to magical thinking and wishes for a kinder world. In my heart, I knew better, but I just couldn't go there. If I didn't know hope, what else was there? How else could I navigate my way through the darkness of a world built on a foundational Big Lie? How else could I cope without the "beacon of light" I'd come to know as hope? I was desperate to believe that compassion would cleanse the human psyche of the blight of separation, and set free the forces of the essential Soul. I wanted to do more than just imagine the world that John Lennon sang about, the world that still makes me cry every time I hear that song.

I convinced myself that my tireless activism, conscious choices and mindful living would influence the creation of a new story for humanity. I hoped for a happy ending for all.

I deceived myself.

I tried on so many different versions of hope that I could almost convince myself they were true had it not been for the persistent ache in my heart telling me otherwise.

I now see how the real story of our world was never about a human awakening. It has always been about the trillions of fish, birds, mammals, trees, plants, fungi, insects, reptiles, amphibians, coral reefs, and phytoplankton needlessly dying because of human arrogance, ignorance, greed, entitlement, bloodlust, appetite, indifference, and inaction.

The new story of our world is being written by the escalating wildfires, droughts, floods, cyclones, tsunamis, earthquakes, hurricanes, heatwaves, desertification, melting Arctic, and ocean dead zones.

Earth is bleeding, and we are doing nothing to tend to her wounds. Until the blood soaks our front yard, it's just not our problem. Even then, however, we are hell-bent on finding others to blame.

With runaway biosphere decay already engulfing us, and with a cultural narrative collapsing at an accelerating rate, I no longer believe we have it in us to evolve to the consciousness required to create what Charles Eisenstein calls, "the more beautiful world our hearts know is possible". Our hubristic sense of entitlement has fragmented our consciousness and severed our ties to everything good and real, and our anthropocentric mindset ensures that we remain fatally trapped within a Big Lie.

A stroke of midnight miracle would require a massive upgrade in our collective consciousness. It would mean taking ownership of everything in our lives, and making choices aligned with the Soul rather than our patterns, history, wounds, fears, victim consciousness, and conditioning. But this is not a new message. Jesus, Buddha, Lao Tzu, and so many others had first dibs on it centuries ago, and we still haven't caught on. In fact, we are so far removed from catching on, it's pitiful to believe otherwise.

Most humans have no idea that anything else exists other than for their own sense of entitlement, entertainment, and gratification. No matter what happens on the planet, they have no capacity for anything other than indifference or hope. As long as they get what they want, they're good. Most use everything—animals, nature, things, other people—to their full benefit, regardless of how destructive these choices are to existence. Humans are a species with no ability to see the bigger picture.

There have been many times in my life where I pondered the "why" behind the collective choice of culturally conditioned coma over all else. I've felt like a dunce for believing that *homo sapien inertia* could possibly evolve into *homo sapien awakening*. I've wondered if collective inertia was so impenetrable because we refuse to talk about it. And I've wondered if we refuse to talk about it because we are too busy hoping—pretending everything will be ok.

But hope—in its bland passivity—is little more than a desperate wish for a future that looks better than the past or the present.

As Derrick Jensen wrote in his book, *Endgame, Volume 1,* "We've all been taught that hope in some better future condition—like hope in some better future heaven—is and must be our refuge in current sorrow. Hope serves the needs of those in power as surely as a belief in a distant heaven; that hope is really nothing more than a secular version of the same old heaven/nirvana mindfuck."[83]

Filmmaker, Paul Schrader supports Jensen's view and takes it even further. In a 2017 interview at the Toronto Film Festival, he said, "Anyone who is hopeful is simply not paying attention. There may have been a reason to be hopeful ten or 15 years ago, but we've played our hand now. We've indicated what our priorities are. Our priorities are our immediate comforts and not the existence of future generations. I don't think intelligent life will end with humans. There may even be moral life after humans. But we have more or less soiled our nest. The universe will be well rid of us."[84]

Our entire species has become so toxic that we affect the quality of existence by our very presence. If we were capable of seeing ourselves through a bigger perceptual filter, what would other species be saying about us? Is there a single species that would even miss us when we're gone? Would we waste our time hoping anymore, or would we finally get on with living as the essential beings we are meant to be? Would we choose to go down on the ship of enlightenment, or continue our spin down the filthy sewage drain that has become so familiar?

At this time in our collective history, I believe that letting go of our right to exist, as well as our perceived "essential role" in the unfolding of the network of life, is the enlightened conversation we must have as a species.

For those who still cling to the hope of some epic awakening, spontaneous consciousness shift or utopian new world (been there, done that, drank the Kool-Aid), or for those still living in denial that it can't possibly be that bad, my question is this: What is it that you're really hanging on to?

Let's be realistic, how many people do you know (yourself included) who endure unbearable relationships, jobs, or situations because of the hope that things will change?

How many people know deep down how screwed we are but refuse to talk about it because they hope things will miraculously improve? Hope binds us to intolerable situations that blind us from truth. Hope has us believe that things are getting better, but they're not. They're getting much, much worse.

Hope comes from a place of fear. It blurs our vision and tethers us to delusion thinking that sustains business-as-usual. It unloads the burden of personal responsibility in the present moment, by soothing the human mind with the illusion of a better future.

Hope allows us to drag our feet with baby steps that feed the fantasy of "a better world" (i.e., free-range, grass-fed, cage-free, all natural, green, humane, eco-friendly, non-toxic, biodegradable, sustainable, etc.), but feel good labels warp the mind and distort truth; they do nothing to heal Earth.

Hope traps us in an arrogant sense of entitlement. We may hope all will be well with Earth, but dammit, don't take away our iPhones, SUV's, air conditioning, bacon, burers, fish, chicken, turkey, cheese, or we get mean and ugly.

Let's face it, any species that domesticates, commoditizes, tortures, and slaughters sentient beings by the billions every year—from the micro backyard farm to the macro factory farm—is delusional to believe it has the ability to save itself from its own demise; is delusional to believe it can infinitely operate outside of the web of life and remain unscathed; is delusional to believe it has the capacity to pull off a miracle well past the 11th hour.

As long as we hope our way to a better world and still feel entitled to take life—directly or indirectly—we will always be trapped in the Big Lie.

What we need right now is a quantum leap in consciousness that evolves us far beyond our conditioned humanity. Hope will never get us there.

Quoting Derrick Jensen once again, "Hope is partly what keeps us chained to the system. Firstly there is the false hope that suddenly somehow the system may inexplicably change. Or technology will save us. Or the Great Mother. Or beings from Alpha Centauri. Or the second coming of Jesus Christ. Or Santa Claus. All of these false hopes—all of this rendering of our power—leads to inaction, or at least to ineffectiveness."[85]

When I look back at hope in my own life, I see how it held me captive to denial. Yes folks, *hope is denial in drag.*

Hope trapped me in a low-grade state of inertia that I was unaware of until I let it go. It kept me just out of reach of the present moment so that I didn't feel the severity of it all. Yes, it motivated my actions and impassioned activism (or so I thought), but would my actions and activism have been more effective if I were present rather than hoping for an illusory future?

An amazing thing happens when we let go of hope, which is that we realize we never needed it in the first place. We recognize the burden it has been all along.

When we finally stop hoping for external assistance, or that the catastrophic situation we're in will somehow rectify itself, or that things will be better in the future, or that things will not get worse; that's when we liberate ourselves to start doing something about it— not to change the world—but to live as we have always been meant to live: as awakened expressions of the Soul, connected to a miraculous web of life.

When we let go of hope—along with the dreams for a future that often accompany it—we move into the "internal now," and the carrot disappears. There is no longer anything to chase, and the whole idea of "other" becomes insignificant. In a world where we've been taught to focus on others as being the crucial metric for our value in the world, we realize our inherent importance for the first time in our lives. We realize that our *being is more than enough.*

When we release ourselves from hope, we are able to see the present moment with honesty and clarity. When we hope, we are pretending that everything is ok. When we stop wishing, pretending and hoping, we empower ourselves with presence. When hope dies, presence springs to life and real, meaningful action finally begins.

By freeing myself from hope, I stopped lying to myself and allowed space to accept what is.

You may be asking, "What if everything she writes about is wrong?" To which I respond, "What if everything I write about is right? What if humanity does have a finite number of days left on Earth? What does that mean for you as an individual? How does that influence how you live your life? Are you happy as a corporate or government drone in an office surrounded by computers, artificial lighting, and recycled air while pushing around empty words and meaningless digits? Is that your version of a meaningful way to live?"

What if we stopped living in hope and instead, lived from acceptance of what is, despite how gloomy it may seem to be?

Climate scientist, Kate Marvel shares a supportive perspective in her blog post, *We Need Courage, Not Hope, to Face Climate Change*:

> Our laws are changeable and shifting; the laws of physics are fixed. Change is already underway; individual worries and sacrifices have not slowed it. Hope is a creature of privilege: we

know that things will be lost, but it is comforting to believe that others will bear the brunt of it.

We are the lucky ones who suffer little tragedies unmoored from the brutality of history. Our loved ones are taken from us one by one through accident or illness, not wholesale by war or natural disaster. But the scale of climate change engulfs even the most fortunate. There is now no weather we haven't touched, no wilderness immune from our encroaching pressure. The world we once knew is never coming back.

I have no hope that these changes can be reversed. We are inevitably sending our children to live on an unfamiliar planet. But the opposite of hope is not despair. It is grief. Even while resolving to limit the damage, we can mourn. And here, the sheer scale of the problem provides a perverse comfort: we are in this together. The swiftness of the change, its scale and inevitability, binds us into one, broken hearts trapped together under a warming atmosphere.

We need courage, not hope. Grief, after all, is the cost of being alive. We are all fated to live lives shot through with sadness, and are not worth less for it. *Courage, however is the resolve to do well without the assurance of a happy ending.* (Italics, mine).[86]

Despite our seemingly gloom-ridden fate, I confess that I remain open to quantum leaps, spontaneous awakenings, consciousness shifts, tipping points, the 100th monkey effect, the second coming of Jesus, miracles, and anything beyond my limited realm of awareness. But I no longer hope, wish, dream or otherwise attach myself to these long-shot outcomes. I choose instead to courageously embrace the truth of what is. When courage replaces hope, presence prevails, and happy endings are no longer required.

The truth is, the present moment is all we've ever had. The more present we can be with what is transpiring right now, the more authentic, courageous and activated we are. If we hope for a different future, we're living a fantasy. Hope feeds inertia. Presence inspires action.

You may be asking, "Why bother with action in a world that is going to hell in a hand basket anyway?" Like Guy McPherson says, "If you're damned if you do and damned if you don't, then do. Do something. Action is always the antidote to despair, even if it's too late, especially if it's too late. Let's act as if moments matter, not in a hedonistic fashion, but in a meaningful way that connects us deeply to the planet."

I can hear it now, "But Deb, if there's no hope, what is there to live for?" To which I reply, "Presence. Live fully in the present moment." This is when we come fully alive!

It's ok not to be brimming with hope. It's ok not to be optimistic. Many ancient teachings tell us that the ongoing maintenance of hope will cause burnout. When we hope, it's not enough. But when we're present, it's more than enough. In our presence, we're organic, flowing, and activated. We show up in ways that allow us to discover ever more capacity to love this world. The greatest gift we can offer the world right now is our full-on, activated presence.

Beyond hope lies acceptance. In acceptance is peace. In peace, is liberation.

Redefining Meaning

"If you let go a little, you will have a little peace. If you let go a lot, you will have a lot of peace. If you let go completely, you will discover complete peace."

– AJAHN CHAH

Throughout human history, linear time has been the age-old buffer to postpone our lives. Our entire global civilization has been engineered to inoculate us from being present in each unfolding moment. So we live our lives perpetually looking ahead, but never at what really matters. We are obsessively short-sighted in our future orientation, trading time for money to fund dreams for a future we think we control. Sadly, the joke is on us.

The accelerating Earth changes catalyzed by our short-sighted ways, means that Gaea is now robbing us of the buffer of time that has conditioned into us such passive complacency.

When the rug of the buffer of time is pulled from beneath the feet of humanity, most people become hostile and angry. Life without a future orientation in a civilization that knows no presence is profoundly intimidating and disorienting. But the compression of time is also great motivation to live as we've always been meant to live: fully, now.

Whether we care to admit it or not, there are things we know intuitively on many different fronts. The undercurrent of accelerating change is to some degree, being felt by all. Because a lag exists between thought and its coalescence into matter, it's easy for many to negate what they intuitively know and feel. Thought is a much more etheric construct than physical matter. It moves much faster, so we tend not to believe it if we don't already see the real-time outcome.

With the intuitive knowing I've held my entire life, along with the ocean premonitions that have haunted me the past few years, I've long ago known a profound truth about this pivotal time. In the structure of my reality, and in the timeline that occupies my advanced knowing, the ocean (and therefore, Earth) is already devoid of life. In the collective "reality" currently underway, my advanced knowing is presently coalescing into matter, and it is becoming increasingly clear that the habitability of Earth is in rapid decay.

At this very moment, Earth is preparing for its next phase. Over several billion years, it has flourished and withered several times. For much of the 300,000 plus years of human existence, we have been living through a planetary inhalation phase. Since the dawn of industrial civilization, however, overpopulation, excessive consumption, and human hubris have hastened the deterioration of a once thriving planet. The result is that we are now living through the long exhalation phase of the planet. There will once again be a long inhalation phase when Earth has had several million, perhaps billions of years to heal from our destruction. I trust that rhythm. I don't have to like it, but it is what keeps Gaea's heart beating in the end.

When we look at everything going on with Earth, especially with the removal of the buffer of time, it's a curious thought to consider the genius of it all. Where is the great intelligence in what we are experiencing as biosphere collapse? It's as if we are being pressed into the recognition of something about ourselves, and we're losing all our emergency exits. Time has been our greatest emergency exit, and we are quickly running out.

With the acceleration of my advancing timeline and personal evolution, I no longer live for a future. Truth be known, I can barely think beyond a few months anymore.

The question this prompts is, "What happens to purpose and meaning when I no longer live for a future?" What I've discovered is that meaning is—and has always been—to become an evolving expression of embodied Soul. In this, everything I do right now is an expression of essence, and the need for a future completely falls away.

What this exploration highlights for me is how our "civilized" world has been designed to prevent the *internal now*, to steer our minds in a future direction. When it comes to the direction of a life-sustaining future, however, we've failed miserably. Our future orientation is not about an evolving future; *it's about sustaining sameness into the future.* We are taught from early on to think about "saving for the future," "education for a future career," "finding a future partner," "having future children," "working for future retirement," and so on. It's no wonder things never change. We have no vision for a future that includes life in the long-term because we're incapable of living in the now. There is no meaning in this.

The challenge for us now is to redefine meaning as it presents in the *internal now*. It's not about tomorrow, and it's not about yesterday; it's about right here, right now. As individuals and as a collective, we have no concept of what that is, or where the value lies in creating meaning without a future. But true meaning connects what lives inside with how we express ourselves outside. This can only happen in the *internal now*.

Derek Rydall shared his version of this thought in an Unplug podcast interview, "The sad fact of the human experience is that most people lead lives of quiet desperation, never saying yes to the yes within them, waiting for some perfect or safe condition to finally act upon their deepest desires—a condition that never comes. It can't because it won't come to them; rather, it must come through them."[87]

Saying yes to the yes within connects us to the *internal now*. The more we say yes, the more we evolve, and the more we can become. The more we become, the more we can still be.

Our lives are not a process of discovery; they are a process of ongoing creation. Life is not about finding ourselves; it's about deciding who we wish to be—over and over, and over again. *There is no finish line.* We are not here to create ourselves from the experiences of others. We are here to design our lives as we choose so that we live life on our terms. We are here to shape our world, not to be shaped by it; and every time we expand beyond our perceived limits, there is endless room for further growth to discover who we have the potential to still become. True meaning lies in our own evolution; moment-by-moment, breath-by-breath.

Reclaiming The Now (A Personal Offering)

So much of my life has been tied to bringing meaning to the "now" through intentions for a future: hopes, dreams, goals, desires, visions, and outcomes. Without a greater purpose with a future outcome/hope/dream/vision, I found myself feeling lost, useless, frustrated, and hopelessly sad. This revealed to me how much of my identity was tied to an illusory future. It also showed to me the degree to which we have collectively been trained to focus on tomorrow, only to become lost when faced with the prospect of only the "now."

In accepting the collapsing biosphere that is upon us, and in facing my own mortality (and that of everything I hold dear), I've stripped away the layers of conditioning that taught me that who I am is what I do, how I serve, and how I am recognized in my service to, and for others. I now see how this was only ever a partial expression of who I am because it hinged on the illusion of a future of which I had no control. It is also impossible to live entirely from my essence when I'm hoping for a better future or living from a nostalgic past. In other words, living within the confines of what is already known.

In Guy McPherson's blog post, *The Absurdity of Authenticity*, he writes:

> There is no meaning beyond the meaning(s) we create. In attempting to create meaning, which often involves attempts to outrun our mortality, we generate distractions. We occasionally call them objectives, goals, or acts of service to others. And the result is our legacy.
>
> Yet it's too late to leave a better world for future generations of humans. The concept of leaving a legacy becomes moot when staring into the abyss of near-term human extinction. What, then, is the point?[88]

I've since realized that the point was never about what I do, how I serve or how others recognize me. The point has always been about my evolution and the expanded consciousness that connects me to my essence. I need no future for this because I can evolve in each unfolding moment.

In honoring my core purpose to evolve and to be, what I do and how I serve is expressed effortlessly, with organic, flowing, ever-changing ease—not to save a world I no longer relate to, but because that is who I am. How others recognize me is unimportant because it is—and always has been—about me being 100%, authentically me. What others think becomes insignificant when I'm standing in the power of the internal now and my ever-expanding essence.

With this pivotal realization, my only intention now is to let go of all that doesn't feed my Self in the moment. In this, I'm accessing a fire within that motivates me in the present, without the need for a future to move me through the now. I've let go of my need for an outcome and instead, I naturally move through life at a pace of my own design, with meaning found in that pace rather than any outcome or byproduct of it. By letting go of a need for an outcome, I can no longer be bought or controlled. I am no longer compelled or motivated by anything outside the Soul. This is not what my parents knew, not what theirs before them knew, and certainly not what the collective knows.

Meaning is now defined by moments: spreading feed for, and watching the birds savor life; relishing the glisten of the sun on the ocean; enjoying the taste of homemade, vegan chocolate cake; conversing with the homeless just because I care; belly laughing at the silly antics of my animal family; learning to play the ukulele because it brings me joy; being awestruck by the mountainous beauty in which I live; impulsive bouts of dancing just because it feels good; loving hard now because that is who I am. I've freed myself from the addiction of strategically creating for tomorrow, rather than living fully today and allowing tomorrow to emerge from that. It's both disorienting in its "newness" and liberating in its profound truth.

The reality is that Earth is going to do what Earth will do. Can I prevent the collapse of the biosphere? Not likely, because collective intent is for biosphere collapse, and collective intent outweighs all. Our reality is a byproduct of collective consciousness, and the mechanism, motivation, inspiration, and willingness for anything other than what is, is absent. Despite this dreadful truth, what I can do is shape a new collective—even if it's a collective of one. Holding to the formation of a radically different truth is often a solitary path.

When we live with a consciousness that includes recognition and acceptance of biosphere collapse, few others have the capacity to be present in that consciousness. It is the ultimate assault on the mortal, heavily conditioned, anthropocentric ego. It is, therefore, a solo venture. It takes a profound connection to the Soul to process and hold this information with peace in one's heart. It means redefining meaning and cultivating a robust inner sanctuary that masters activated presence.

As sacred activist, Andrew Harvey says, "If we are going to face near-term extinction with the kind of savage stupidity that we have faced almost everything else, then this time in our lives will be unimaginably violent, horrible and disgusting. And yet, if we face it with grace, we will seize the opportunity that the Divine is offering us to become truly adult, truly open, truly surrendered, truly loving, and we will confidently enter this crisis with trust."

Trust. In Gaea, and the Soul. These are deeply spiritual times.

For the few who choose to consider their own evolution in these surreal times, it is often exhausting to always be thinking outside the box, especially when the masses are fixed in their choices to speak, choose, behave, think, and act from within a deleterious box they've come to know so well. Such density of thought, behavior, and intention creates an experience in physical matter that demands acquiescence to itself, just by virtue of the extent and longevity of its existence.

To intuitively know that something else has at least equal, if not more legitimate "truth" without the benefit of the density of coalescence with "others," can lead to a sense of overwhelm and discouragement. Pursuing this truth seldom producers sufficient "evidence" to legitimize the search. It becomes not only easier, but from time to time, essential to give up the pursuit of this alternative truth— not necessarily within one's Self, but most certainly, with anyone else outside the Self.

As I turn my attention more and more to the intentional path of the *internal now*, the illusion of my "reality" becomes more evident. Like being on the edge of awake and dreaming; knowing that the dream is so real, and yet the nagging and pulling to awaken begins to cause the dream/reality to crumble at the edges. With that crumbling comes a sense of isolation, like waking up alone, in a space that once accommodated the dream and no longer does. What then?

What I notice most is that the structures associated with maintaining the dream are impediments to being activated in presence. The structures of good and bad; right and wrong. The structures of history. The structures of an essential tribe or community. The structures of the status quo. The structures of collective consciousness. The structures of mortality.

When we let go of the stories that run our lives, we're free to live in the *internal now* to realize the spiritual beings that we are.

In the book *Conversations With God*, Neale Donald Walsch writes, "There comes a time in the evolution of every Soul when the chief concern is no longer survival of the physical body, but the growth of spirit; no longer the attainment of worldly success, but the realization of Self."[89]

There is something immensely potent about living in the *internal now*, and letting go of the need to have an intended future be what shapes the unique and consecutive moments of our current lives. In truth, an intended future locks us into a reality constructed long ago, with continued use as a template for our "meaningful" existence.

I'm now gaining capacity for ease with the weightlessness of living in the *internal now*, and allowing an emerging reality to present itself from that. This ensures an increasing disinterest in consuming the offerings of the cultural master that holds the Big Lie in check. I'm sometimes amazed at how little I'm drawn to purchase/obtain/collect, and how effortless it has become to let go. In truth, my interest in consumption has pretty much disappeared.

In the dominant reality, marketing is a dedicated process that creates a pull for consumption. A life without a pull is unfamiliar because it is not what we are taught. We are taught to believe that there is something wrong with us if we are not pulled toward something in the future: a bigger house, a bigger car, a bigger pay cheque, a bigger following or audience, a bigger purpose; we are pulled to live only for the future. A life that no longer has a pull is unfamiliar as a valid way of living.

The experience of how we have been taught to live "successfully" is predicated on consumption: material goods, food, relationships, ideas, opinions, beliefs, technology, processes, jobs, religion, advice, etc. We have endless strategies for multiple layers of consumption to shape our reality.

If we no longer consume, the structures of our reality open up and become more spacious, and we no longer need to fill this vast, open space. Rather, we are content to be present and fill each moment with whatever feels right *in that moment*. Without consumption, reality is radically altered. At multiple levels of thinking (environment, behavior, strategy, identity, etc.), consumption becomes obsolete in our lives. When the world we live in spins on consumption, and when we can no longer relate to or participate, how do we then define what reality is?

In my life, reality has become living for life's sake. No goals. No ambition. No desire to serve or contribute. No fixing, saving or rescuing. It means reclaiming the *being* aspect of what I authentically am.

Paradoxically, freedom came to me when I let go of everything I worked so hard to create. The irony was that as soon as I let it all go, the "empty" space was filled with a sense of ease. In having no pull anymore, I'm more present and able to see the beauty of the world, even as it falls apart. I'm now able to hold it all. When I'm pulled toward a future, however, I more clearly see the ugliness, violence, destruction, denial, and collapse. This doesn't serve me, and it offers no meaning; it only sends me into a tailspin of anger and despair. I do not delude myself about the reality of our crumbling world; I do, however, choose to no longer consume what pulls me away from the *internal now.*

Consumption directs our focus in ways that ensure continued blindness to our own potential. Perhaps now, as the press into fear is frantically provoked by those who stand so much to lose in our collapsing world, we might simply choose to step aside and listen for a higher-order expression of what is possible. I know without a doubt that the only voice I choose to attend to, is the one that emerges from within. It never leads me astray.

As we begin to evolve beyond consumption, we no longer fit into the designated intent of what defines the value and purpose of a human in our world. When we choose a path of discovery that leads to evolution and the reclamation of Self as the driver of our lives, everything civilization is intent on perpetuating and perpetrating disappears from our lives. When we remember that we are living expressions of Soul in physical matter, we dare to test it, and create our reality from that.

When we reclaim the essence of what we are, we are more able to see the illusion of our world and how quickly things can fall apart. We discover that what once seemed so real and stable, is all just smoke and mirrors. The journey of the reclamation of the Soul deconstructs our conditioned reality. As this happens, we must have sufficient capacity to be able to experience disorientation and confusion, while trusting the unfolding of it all. We must trust the unfamiliar and not doubt ourselves because we have no new content to replace what was once familiar. Personally, I believe the fact we think content is required for living our lives, is the ultimate illusion. As we seek to replace content with content, we only end up shooting ourselves in the foot by negating the power of the *internal now.*

As I let go of my conditioned humanity, I increasingly find myself letting go of the material world. At the same time, I'm becoming more present to what matters most to me: animals, the natural world, simplicity, and moments connected to the sacred. I feel more connected to the pulse of Earth than ever before, and this is bringing to me profound moments with all things alive: breathtaking sunrises and sunsets, animals, ferns, trees, and the handful of people in my life who are deeply committed to their own evolution in a world that is falling fast and hard. I feel disconnected from the Big Lie, and quite frankly, indifference toward the human-created material world. I spend a lot of time in the presence of my Self, my partner, and my animal companions. I never feel deprived or alone. I live in the moment, trusting entirely that this is where the *I am* that I am, is intended to be.

It is challenging to be surrounded by a story of separation without the propelling force of "the next": the next moment, the next accomplishment, the next outcome, the next provocation, the next win, the next whatever. In my life, I've finally reached a point where there is no more "the next." This leaves me with a lightness of being: wondering and wandering in the current moment, knowing that the fullness of meaning I seek is found there, and nowhere else.

Activated Presence

"Acceptance looks like a passive state, but in reality, it brings something entirely new into this world. That peace, a subtle energy vibration, is consciousness."

– ECKHART TOLLE

This book has taken me almost two years to write. As I've been writing, I've been evolving while I embody and live my words. I've moved through the lingering inertia of my own denial, grief, sadness, anger, and despair; and evolved into the serenity of acceptance. Although serenity is not always the dominant feeling in my life, acceptance is the foundational energy that now moves me through the physical world.

As I've been evolving, my love for Earth has deepened. At the same time, I'm increasingly detached from the physical world. I've let go of humanity, and I've let my humanity go. What remains is the essence of *I am* experiencing a material world without attachment. Acceptance of what is, comes with more ease because I trust the greater Earth wisdom at work.

In reaching acceptance, I've released myself from the emotional pain that once bound me to the ongoing horrors of our sacrificial reality. The brutality and injustices of our industrialized civilization; a planet decimated by our addiction to dead flesh, dead forests, dead mountains, dead air, dead soil, and dead oceans; and the forces of entropy closing in all around us.

The state of detachment that now defines my life brings with it a sense of calm, reminiscent of times in my life when faced with the looming transition of a loved one. It is a sacred time that reminds me of the beauty and frailty of life: heartbreaking and awe-inspiring; sad and tender. It's about letting go, while simultaneously feeling a more profound sense of connection.

In processing the somber truth of near-term extinction over the last few years, I've reached such deep acceptance that I have no fear of dying tomorrow because I'm living fully today. Truth be known, I'd rather die awake, present and activated, than live asleep, distracted and numb. I'm grateful for the spiritual awareness of these final times so I can live my life accordingly. It is a most sacred gift in facing this terminal predicament.

When we free ourselves from all things external, all things historical, and all things future-oriented, we liberate the Soul to live presently with acceptance. What follows is a release of attachment to our own mortality, and to any specific outcome. It means love for love's sake alone. It means compassion for compassion's sake alone. It means living fully now because that is the only way.

When we no longer deny what is self-evident, we can face the truth of our inner experience and engage the essential power that flows through us. The infinite love of Gaea herself will reward those who live in these final times with the spirit of love and compassion in their hearts. I know this because I feel it every day.

Perhaps accepting that this world, at this time is coming to a rapid completion—not an end—is our absolution. In that deep surrender lies the path to a life of joyous creation and living fully in the moment; with permanence acknowledged and accepted for the illusion it is, while cheering Gaea on as she turns into her time of hibernation to birth yet another new world, to come.

This depth of acceptance means bearing witness to the masses as they carry on with their frenzied pace of business-as-usual while the world crumbles around them. Go to school, get a job, self-replicate, buy a house, consume, accrue debt, save for the illusion of a predictable future, distract oneself from the pain of an inauthentic life, negate death, resist death, and then die. To this, we bear witness—and we let go. It is not nihilism; it is the essential strength of compassionate detachment.

Personally, I believe that our "salvation" lies in accepting and embracing our transience. In this, great freedom will come—possibility like we have never before known.

The illusion of permanence, including the belief that tomorrow will predictably follow today, has been our undoing. We've been deceived by our conditioning to believe that if we trade today for tomorrow, we will have a better future. The result is a moribund world in decay. There can be no other way unless we, as autonomous individuals, are willing to choose otherwise.

To stay in the now effectively, we must be connected to the Soul. Our entire global civilization has been shaped to prevent us from ever being in the now, however. So we are only capable of living in the past and the future, while being profoundly disconnected from the Soul.

Imagine the possibility of creating our lives so that we live only in the perpetual now—in this very moment and nothing else. When we live only in the moment, there is no judgment and no pejoratives because the unfolding of each new moment is all there is. Each moment is experienced detached from the one before it, and the one that follows it. There is no fear of illness, tragedy or death when we live entirely in the perpetual now. It is precisely the anxiety produced by modern life that prevents us from living in the perpetual now, however. In this frenzied state, we convince ourselves that we cannot afford to engage in "being here now" because *being* demands a powerful connection to spirit in tissue; where the essence of our being creates, and the tissue converts the intention of creation in each unfolding moment. When living in the perpetual now, however, we are finally able to understand that there is nothing to fix, nothing to save and nothing is broken.

This has been a pivotal realization for me, and I now see that what must die, is our refusal to die. We must also release our resistance for this world to come to an end.

The absurd reality is that the masses are okay with the grief and anxiety of some distant future generation experiencing the collapse of humanity, just not this one. This mindset tells us everything we need to know about ourselves: that we possess precisely the same procrastination, ignorance, selfishness, and denial of the generations who preceded us—the very generations who established the foundational beliefs for the Big Lie in the first place. By blindly committing ourselves to an epic Lie, and mass reproducing a global population who are asleep to the Soul, we are responsible for perpetuating, accelerating and exasperating an ugly mess, turned terminal disaster.

Until humanity is eradicated, there is no room for Earth to heal and birth the possibility of a more consciously evolved species. While every past extinction event paved the way for more complex species to emerge, humans have regrettably proven that complex species do not necessarily operate from an evolved state of consciousness.

As we continue to compulsively eat our own tail, soon there will be nothing left. While everything in our world continues to accelerate, it is becoming increasingly clear that all evidence of our species will soon be eliminated to prepare the fertile ground for the next wave of Gaea's evolution. My hope is that Gaea's rebirth will include evolved species with a unity consciousness that matches her own.

I don't know, and cannot predict the timeframe for a lifeless Earth. I do know that my premonitions and internal knowing are great motivation to live fully, love hard and let go, right now. Perhaps the desperate timeframe that haunts my consciousness will awaken some readers from the trance of living for tomorrow, to notice today—this moment—and choose mindfully.

The accelerating collapse of industrial civilization and the web of life that sustains existence, is showing us the absolute frailty of life. It is a profoundly spiritual time that can ignite the fundamental courage to uncover—in the face of impossible odds—a profound connection to the Soul. It can inspire outward expression from our deepest core essence: with acceptance, compassion, and presence; giving up the fruits of all action, come what may. It is this form of activated living that finally frees us from the oppressive confines of the Big Lie.

Our current desperate situation is a perfect recipe for the liberation of the Soul from the destructive realm of separation, once and for all. Essentially what this means is that we are born in our death. In facing the deathlessness of the Soul, we connect to our essence on a deeper level and emerge as a new kind of human. This is a profound evolutionary shift. Many mystical traditions have stated that one who is liberated from identifying with the physical world, acts out of love and compassion for the sake of love and compassion alone. Not out of a personal agenda tainted by the burden of hope, or attached to the illusion of a utopian future. It is a compelling place of connection and pure presence.

The passage of time is pivotal to our existence as human beings. But the notion of the passage of time makes it difficult for us to live in the now. Because we are so preoccupied with having the moment of the now be the platform for looking back and looking forward, we negate the moment we are in. In a consumptive world, living in the now is not useful because the whole idea of a consumer-driven economy is that we use today as the platform to create for tomorrow. Our lives are all about bouncing in and out of today. In other words, we don't live in our house right now, we live in what our house will be like in five years when the renovations are complete. What this means in Earth terms is that we don't live on Earth as it is right now, we live on the Earth of our future-oriented programming—an Earth that can be interminably raped, polluted, pillaged, and populated to support the model of infinite growth that has poisoned the human species.

But the rapidly accelerating Earth changes and accompanying cultural collapse are forcing us into the moment. This is an unfamiliar place to stand because the undercurrent of the passage of time, is what shapes the reality of the collective. This is why living in the now remains elusive for all but a few of the human species.

In my own life, I realized the elusive nature of the present moment when I finally faced the depths of my own grief and despair. Hope was my way of bargaining. The energies of anger, sadness, frustration, joy, awe, and peace moved through me like breezes, gusts, tornadoes … and then stillness. I knew nothing of my own denial until I stopped hoping. In releasing myself from hope, I was no longer bound to this world, and acceptance came with ease. With acceptance, I allowed space for the reclamation of my Self. In this profound union of flesh and spirit, my grief morphed into what I now call, "activated presence."

Many important questions have since emerged, such as: "Who do I choose to be in the face of collapse?", "How do I choose to live in a dying world?", "What does it look like to live fully in a world in collapse?", "How do I choose to live my life in the face of uncertainty?", "How do I find beauty and joy in a dying world?"

With repeated consistency, one word arises: love. Love is the answer—the salve for every wound—the force that inspires courage, creativity, compassion, being, trust, joy, acceptance, and activated presence.

Activated presence is a radical paradigm shift in a distracted and indifferent world. It's about engagement, tenderness, passion, meaning, being, doing, laughter, tears, and noticing the absolute sacredness in the smallest moments.

It's about unapologetically feeling the depths of grief and despair, and emerging with salty tears, snot, and grace. It's about being comfortable in the uncertainty of collapse without collapsing in it. It's about doing what I love and being the change in the face of devastation, detached from all outcome. It's about loving harder than ever before. It's about being detached from the collective while trusting the genius of it all. It's about living on the razor's edge of knowing how dire our planetary situation is while remembering intimately, viscerally, deeply, the profound sacredness of life. It's about allowing the Soul of who I am to live fully in the perpetual now.

Activated presence is an embodied awakening to my most profound essential nature—my primal, unconditioned, deeply connected, Soul-Self.

It's one thing to fight for the rights of animals and Earth to be free from the blight of humanity's separation. It's something entirely different to feel inextricably connected to *all life* within every cell of my being. This shift has helped me realize that I'm not being called upon to save Earth. Rather, I'm being called upon to activate my love, and as Ram Dass says, "Be love now." For me, this means being love in action. Being love in action frees me from the burden of hope, and the pain of attachment to any outcome.

Activated presence does not imply inaction; it inspires a spontaneity in action that encourages living in the present moment, for the present moment. If an awakened future was ever to be had, spontaneous action in the present moment, for the present moment is the only way it could be. In activated presence, we free ourselves of our addiction to the strategy of creating for tomorrow in the present moment. Instead, we live fully today and allow tomorrow to emerge from that.

In activated presence, we discover a fire within that sparks us without the need for a future to motivate us to move through the now. We let go of our need to "chase the carrot" and simply move through life at a pace of our own design, with meaning found in that pace rather than any outcome or byproduct of it. Once we lay down our need for the carrot, we can no longer be compelled or motivated by anything outside the Soul.

It takes great courage and a sincere desire to carve out a meaningful life to override our commitment to the past and future. In this courage, we discover a new place to stand. Far too often, we lose ourselves in the habits and patterns of the past or to the uncertainty of the future; forgetting that our point of power is always in the now of our existence.

What better judge of our character than how we think, choose, behave, and act in the face of the impossible odds of our present reality? Even if we still had thousands of years left (we don't), should we not still act as if life mattered? Should we not still care about animals, Earth and each other? We are being implored in these end times to live the way we've always been meant to live: fully, authentically, compassionately, presently.

In the expanse of our deepest humanity, we unite with our core spiritual essence, and reunite ourselves with the web of life.

In her book, *Coming Back to Life*, Joanna Macy writes:

> The deteriorating conditions of our world and the plight of other beings impinge on us all. We are in this together. Never before have our destinies been so intertwined. The fact that our fate is a common fate has tremendous implications. It means that in facing it together openly and humbly, we rediscover our interconnectedness in the web of life. From that rediscovery springs courage, a deeper sense of community, and insights into our power and creativity.[90]

This is activated presence.

The grave state of the world and its subsequent uncertainty is calling us out on all of who we are: our greatness and our smallness. Crisis can bring out the expansive truth of *what* we authentically are as Soul, embodied. This shift alone would heal *our own world* in the blink of an eye, and allow space for us to leave with dignity and grace.

For the longest time, I wanted to be sure about how it would all end. I was afraid to be unsure. I was fearful of what could or would play out in the uncertainty. I wanted to be able to say with conviction, "It's going to be ok." But I've since realized that this helps nobody. First of all, nobody knows. More importantly, even if we can be convinced that everything will be ok, would that evoke from within us our deepest love, compassion, and courage? Would it inspire the potency of our activated presence?

By teetering on the precipice of uncertainty, we come alive to our most genuine power. This is when we step into our deepest love for the world and experience life from a place of activated presence. With this profound internal connection, it no longer matters that there are no guarantees for a happy ending. Let's face it, there are no guarantees for happy endings in any aspect of life. There are no guarantees when we fall in love that the relationship will last. There are no guarantees when we take on a job that it will provide happiness and security. There are no guarantees for health, despite how clean our lives may be. There are no guarantees for ample sun and rain to bring us a bumper garden crop. Other than death, there are no guarantees for anyone or anything. Uncertainty is the nature of life, and by stepping into it, we step into the radical nature of activated presence.

In a recent meditation, I asked Earth what she needed most from me. The answer was immediate, "Be yourSelf." I sobbed. So loving. So simple.

In evolving to a place of activated presence, I now know that I was never meant to "save the world." I've always been meant to *save myself from the world* by remembering who and what I authentically am, and expressing that in a world of matter. I now know no other way.

Every night before I go to bed, I sit under the stars with my canine Soulmate, Francis. I breathe deeply into my heart, taking in the immensity of the sky, listening carefully to what she has to say; remembering the stardust that I'm made of. I close my eyes and see Earth. She weeps. I weep. I wrap my arms around her, offering the only solace I know. I give myself wholly to her—the only gift I know. It rarely feels like enough, yet she makes it entirely clear to me that in standing in the truth of the Soul, I'm more than enough.

Gaea may bat last, but when she does, we realize who has been in charge all along. With or without us, she will prevail. I choose to give myself fully to her—in faith and in trust.

As Joanna Macy shared in the documentary, *Planetary*, "What instantly touches the heart-mind— and it's sudden, and you can count on it—is the kiss of the universe when you glimpse its beauty. It strips you of all your explanations and all your notions of who and what you want to be as an achieving individual. And you're struck with such a gladness at that beauty and the originality of life that you don't have time to think about 'how is it going to turn out?' All you know is that you will serve it to the last breath."

I couldn't have said it better myself.

I end with this offering: The fate of the world cannot be changed. Stop fighting, resisting, bargaining, and denying otherwise. Let it go. Accept the greater intelligence of Earth and the infinite universe by remembering the immortal Soul of what you authentically are. Activate your presence by living for moments, in the moment; not for wishes, dreams, faraway thoughts, or future outcomes. Savor the tender times that lift you, bring joy to your heart and fill your life with meaning. Let go of hope and embrace the tears that may come. These very tears will liberate you with a love for life like you've never before known. Choose to be extraordinary in ordinary moments and do what feeds the Soul. Not for recognition, riches or fame, but because that is the essence of who you are. Even if it seems pointless in a sea of disconnect, never, ever stop loving Earth. And for the love of the Soul, be fiercely committed to your deepest Self by choosing gratitude for every sacred breath of life. I guarantee that no matter how it all plays out in the end, you will not regret it.

Endnotes

The Big Lie

1. https://en.wikipedia.org/wiki/The_Big_Lie
2. https://en.wikipedia.org/wiki/The_Big_Lie
3. http://necrometrics.com/all20c.htm
4. http://www.animalequality.net/food
5. https://www.ted.com/talks/louise_leakey_digs_for_humanity_s_origins/transcript?language=en
6. https://www.theguardian.com/environment/2017/may/05/the-great-climate-silence-we-are-on-the-edge-of-the-abyss-but-we-ignore-it
7. https://www.globalresearch.ca/climate-change-saving-the-planet-saving-ourselves/5624919

The American Dream

8. James Truslow Adams, *The Epic of America* (New Brunswick, USA: Transaction Publishers, 1931), p. 214
9. https://www.rogerebert.com/reviews/waking-life-2001-1
10. https://www.theguardian.com/books/2017/may/17/generation-sociopaths-review-trump-baby-boomers-ruined-world
11. *Racing Extinction* directed by Louie Psihoyos, Discovery Channel, 2015

The Culture of Addiction

12. Soygal Rinpoche, *The Tibetan Book of Living and Dying* (New York, New York: HarperCollins, 2002), p. 20-21
13. Soygal Rinpoche, *The Tibetan Book of Living and Dying* (New York, New York: HarperCollins, 2002), p. 60
14. Soygal Rinpoche, *The Tibetan Book of Living and Dying* (New York, New York: HarperCollins, 2002), p. 17-18
15. http://www.rense.com/general43/eating.htm

Breeding Ourselves Into Oblivion

16. https://www.globalresearch.ca/killing-the-biosphere-to-fast-track-human-extinction/5620827
17. https://louiselebrun.ca/book/decloaking-and-living-authentically/
18. http://www.wel-systems.com/programs/engaging.htm#.WWhScIqQyEI
19. https://louiselebrun.ca/memory-lane-children-and-potential/
20. Neale Donald Walsch, *Conversations with God* (Charlottesville, VA: Hampton Roads Publishing Company, 2005), p. 440
21. Neale Donald Walsch, *Conversations with God* (Charlottesville, VA: Hampton Roads Publishing Company, 2005), p. 445
22. https://www.youtube.com/watch?v=jTxOiq3V7Bw
23. http://www.sciencedirect.com/science/article/pii/S0959378008001003
24. https://www.scientificamerican.com/article/american-consumption-habits/
25. https://theoldspeakjournal.wordpress.com/2017/05/19/the-absurd-economics-of-7-5-billion-people-on-one-planet/
26. https://www.ted.com/talks/louise_leakey_digs_for_humanity_s_origins
27. http://hevria.com/rachel/what-to-tell-the-children/

The Blessed Curse of Technology

28. https://www.theguardian.com/commentisfree/2016/dec/01/stephen-hawking-dangerous-time-planet-inequality
29. Charles Eisenstein, *The Ascent of Humanity* (Berkeley, California: Evolver Editions, 2013), p. 1 (Kindle)
30. http://www.goodreads.com/quotes/256682-we-clutter-the-earth-with-our-inventions-never-dreaming-that
31. Charles Eisenstein, *The Ascent of Humanity* (Berkeley, California: Evolver Editions, 2013), p. 17 (Kindle)
32. http://www.peterrussell.com/blindspot/blindspot.pdf
33. http://journals.sagepub.com/doi/pdf/10.1177/2053019616677743
34. http://journals.sagepub.com/doi/pdf/10.1177/2053019616677743

35. https://vimeo.com/186141191

36. http://sunweber.blogspot.ca/2015/06/a-bang-and-whimper.html

37. Richard Louv, *The Nature Principle* (Chapel Hill, North Carolina: Algonquin Books of Chapel Hill, 2011), p. 11

Powerless Power

38. Neale Donald Walsch, *Conversations with God* (Charlottesville, VA: Hampton Roads Publishing Company, 2005), p. 289

39. http://www.creatingfreedom.info/film.html

40. Neale Donald Walsch, *Conversations with God* (Charlottesville, VA: Hampton Roads Publishing Company, 2005), p. 39

The Myth of a New Story

41. Derrick Jensen, *Endgame*, Volume 1 (New York, NY, Seven Stories Press, 2003), p. 283

42. James Lovelock, *Vanishing Face of Gaia* (Philadelphia, PA, Basic Books, 2009), p. 3

43. Charles Eisenstein, *The Yoga of Eating* (Washington, DC, NewTrends Publishing Inc., 2003), location 1378 Kindle

It's Over

44. https://www.globalresearch.ca/killing-the-biosphere-to-fast-track-human-extinction/5620827

45. https://www.youtube.com/watch?v=iozxLbuPiX4

46. Charles Eisenstein, *The Ascent of Humanity* (Berkeley, California: Evolver Editions, 2013), p. 107 (Kindle)

47. https://www.commondreams.org/views/2012/04/30/welcome-asylum

48. https://paulbeckwith.net/2017/01/21/methane-burps-and-farts/

49. https://www.globalresearch.ca/climate-change-saving-the-planet-saving-ourselves/5624919

50. http://weeklyhubris.com/humanity-at-a-crossroads/

The Fuck-it Point

51. https://louiselebrun.ca/truths-perceptions-and-choices/
52. https://kennorphan.com/2017/12/09/the-canaries-we-ignore/
53. http://weeklyhubris.com/no-surrender/
54. http://www.debozarko.com/120/

Planetary Hospice

55. https://www.sciencedaily.com/releases/2017/01/170105082806.htm
56. https://www.theguardian.com/environment/2017/may/05/the-great-climate-silence-we-are-on-the-edge-of-the-abyss-but-we-ignore-it
57. http://bit.ly/2n200Ar
58. http://www.planetary-hospice.com/wp-content/uploads/2014/07/Planetary-Hospice.pdf
59. http://www.planetary-hospice.com/wp-content/uploads/2014/10/Principles-of-Planetary-Hospice.pdf
60. http://www.planetary-hospice.com/wp-content/uploads/2014/10/Climate-Catharsis.pdf

The Power of Grief

61. https://louiselebrun.ca/memory-lane-the-intelligence-of-pain/
62. https://www.goldensufi.org/a_animamundi.html
63. Frances Weller, *The Wild Edge of Sorrow* (Berkeley, California: North Atlantic Books, 2015), p. 48
64. http://www.filmsforaction.org/takeaction/five-ways-of-being-that-can-change-the-world/
65. https://carolynbaker.net/2014/03/03/in-praise-of-manners-by-francis-weller/
66. Frances Weller, *The Wild Edge of Sorrow* (Berkeley, California: North Atlantic Books, 2015), p. 10
67. https://kennorphan.com/2016/12/27/grief-and-the-unbreakable-sinew/
68. Soygal Rinpoche, *The Tibetan Book of Living and Dying* (New York, New York: HarperCollins, 2002), p. 320

In Praise of Mortality

69. https://www.youtube.com/watch?v=Ouxj5ZFg_BM

70. Brian Weiss, *Many Lives, Many Masters* (New York, NY, Touchstone Books, 1988), p. 31

71. http://journals.aps.org/prl/abstract/10.1103/PhysRevLett.118.041301

72. Frances Weller, *The Wild Edge of Sorrow* (Berkeley, California: North Atlantic Books, 2015), p. xx

73. Elisabeth Kübler-Ross, *Death: The Final Stage of Growth* (New York, NY: Simon and Schuster, 1975), p X

74. Ashley Davis Bush, *Transcending Loss* (New York, New York: Penguin Group, 1997), p. 106

75. Frances Weller, *The Wild Edge of Sorrow* (Berkeley, California: North Atlantic Books, 2015), p. xvii

Return to Essence

76. http://www.imdb.com/title/tt0114168/

77. From the cd series for *Engaging and Awakening Others* http://www.wel-systems.com/programs/engaging.htm#.WnNwmoJG2EI

The Paradox of Awakening

78. Louise LeBrun, *New Paradigm—New World!* Ottawa, Ontario: WEL-Systems Institute, 2014, p. 14

79. Brian Weiss, *Many Lives, Many Masters*. New York, NY, Touchstone Books, 1988, p. 123

80. https://louiselebrun.ca/life-called-i-answered/

Being is More than Enough

81. Deepak Chopra, *Life After Death* (New York, NY, Harmony Books, 2006), p. 120

Beyond Hope

82. Derrick Jensen, *Endgame, Volume 1* (New York, NY, Seven Stories Press, 2006), p. 329

83. Derrick Jensen, *Endgame, Volume 1* (New York, NY, Seven Stories Press, 2006), p. 329

84. http://variety.com/2017/film/news/paul-schrader-first-reformed-toronto-film-festival-1202560593/

85. Derrick Jensen, *Endgame, Volume 1* (New York, NY, Seven Stories Press, 2006), p. 325

86. https://onbeing.org/blog/kate-marvel-we-need-courage-not-hope-to-face-climate-change

Redefining Meaning

87. http://www.debozarko.com/derekrydall/
88. https://guymcpherson.com/2013/09/the-absurdity-of-authenticity/
89. Neale Donald Walsch, *Conversations With God* (New York, NY, Hampton Roads Publishing Company, 2005), p. 157

Activated Presence

90. Joanna Macy and Molly Young Brown, *Coming Back to Life* (Gabriola Island, BC, New Society Publishers, 1988), p. 63

Where to Go from Here

I feel it would be negligent for me to not mention the catalyzing force that brought me to where I now stand in my life: solid in the Soul and liberated from the burden of a broken civilization.

Because the world is breaking down in so many ways at an accelerated pace, it's easy to fall into overwhelm, despair, apathy, numbness, and even nihilism. This does nothing but magnify our problems, however.

To move forward with grace, we must acknowledge the natural intelligence in the rhythm of our own personal and planetary mortality by remembering *what* we authentically are. In that, overwhelm, despair, apathy, numbness, and nihilism have no fertile ground to take root.

It's one thing to understand *what* we are on a cognitive level; it's an entirely different thing to embody it, engage it and live it. After years of elusively searching, I finally "found" my Self when I discovered the profound work of Louise LeBrun. My life has never been the same. For that, I'm eternally grateful.

My journey with Louise commenced with an audio series titled, *Decloaking and Living Authentically*. Rather than attempt to describe the indescribable, I share the words of Louise herself:

> The *Decloaking and Living Authentically* audio files are a Self-directed experience of a deeply personal journey of mind. They were created with an eye to the future and the escalating challenges we would face. With intention, they offer up an exploration of the process of mind that recognizes and respects that only you can affect the change you desire in your life, and

thus, in the world. This audio program can show you how to go about doing just that. It will not define you, but it will help you discover how to redefine yourSelf.

All is first filtered through and expressed from mind. Agility of mind to shape and reshape perceptions and attending choices is essential to living fully and living well. In today's world—given the immensity, intensity and speed at which undeniable Earth changes are touching our lives—we *will* reveal to ourselves the truth of who we are choosing to be. Will we surrender to fear? Or will we awaken to the deep well of courage, integrity, and grace that is our birthright? We cannot teach our children what we ourselves are unable to live.

Every moment, of every day, we are invited/compelled/driven to be distracted by all that surrounds us—from the likes of climate collapse, all the way through to reality tv and Game of Thrones—ensuring that inside ourselves is the last place we will ever be called to direct our attention. Busy lives tear at us to focus on everything outside of us that competes for our limited attention. In the meantime, the one thing—*the only thing*—where power will ever be reclaimed becomes more and more an increasingly distant memory of our own existence; of the intimacy of our unique personage and the deep awakening that, if sparked, can and will transform reality.

Louise LeBrun's work breaks down the barriers of cultural conditioning that hold us hostage to this profound separation from Earth and Soul. By making the invisible, visible, we are offered a choice to break free from the spell of our own captivity of mind and embrace the truth of what we authentically are. This is the only way to navigate these increasingly dire times.

If it calls to you, the *Decloaking and Living Authentically* audio program can be purchased at this link: https://louiselebrun.ca/book/

decloaking-and-living-authentically/. I cannot recommend this invitation for exponential evolution enough. As life on this planet degrades at dizzying speed, connection to Self/Soul is the only grounding force that ensures sanity and ultimately, peace.

I share this information with no personal gain other than knowing there is potentially one less member of the human species who has chosen the fear and suffering of separation, over the grace and compassion of the Soul.

Gratitude

Eternal gratitude to my life partner, Deb Gleason for not only supporting my work and my message, but for choosing to become a living expression of the words in this book. We walk together on the infinite path of evolution. I can't imagine anything better!

To Louise LeBrun who continually challenges what I believe myself to be, inspiring the endless realization that I am so much more. You, my friend, have helped me become ... and become ... and become ...

Many thanks to my dear friend, Gigi Hoeller for offering the sacred space to bring this book to life. Your beautiful home provided the sanctuary I needed to bring this project to completion.

To Hauk: Although we've never met, your energetic presence continually inspires me. Thank you for your support and humor. It means more than you can imagine.

Thank you Gaea for your endless patience with a species gone awry. I give myself to you in trust.

About the Author

To understand Deb Ozarko is to understand the Soul. In letting go of the physical world, she has paradoxically embraced the tender sacredness of life. To be in the presence of Deb is to be in the presence of wisdom, joy, humor, passion, compassion, and raw authenticity. Despite the weight of our collapsing world, she lives with a sense of levity that is profoundly contagious. Her liberation is palpable.

Deb's heartfelt love for animals and the natural world is unequivocal. Her commitment to the Soul defies words. Not only does she walk her talk, she lives it with grace and ease. If there was ever an embodied expression of essence to be modeled, Deb Ozarko is it.

Deb is the creator and former host of the Unplug podcast and the author of *Unplug: 26 People Share How they Recharge and Reconnect to Passion, Presence and Purpose.*

As a former Ironman triathlete with a love for movement, she can often be found in the pool, on her bike, paddling, or hiking in stunning natural settings with her partner and dogs in beautiful Ontario, Canada.

You can discover more of Deb's work at debozarko.com.

If this book was meaningful for you, please consider leaving a review on Amazon.

Printed by Amazon Italia Logistica S.r.l.
Torrazza Piemonte (TO), Italy

10854306R00162